MW01006079

This book belongs to:

Tish Holt

Cover Photo by Skip Moen – Door panel of the baptistry
Duomo Santa Maria del Fiore, Florence, Italy

Spiritual Restoration

Reclaiming The Foundations of God's World

Volume 1 Revised

By Skip Moen, Ph.D.

Copyright 2008

Unless otherwise indicated, all Scripture references are from the
NASB.

Scripture quotations taken from the New American Standard Bible®,
Copyright © 1960, 1962, 1963, 1968, 1971, 1972, 1973, 1975, 1977,
1995 by The Lockman Foundation. Used by permission."
(www.Lockman.org)

Scripture taken from the HOLY BIBLE, NEW INTERNATIONAL
VERSION®. Copyright © 1973, 1978, 1984 by International Bible
Society. Used by permission of Zondervan. All rights reserved.

Revised Standard Version of the Bible, copyright 1952 [2nd edition,
1971] by the Division of Christian Education of the National Council
of the Churches of Christ in the United States of America. Used by
permission. All rights reserved.

Reclaiming God's World

$\mathcal{R}$eading this book will be an unusual spiritual adventure. You're about to discover incredible truths that have been buried from view in our modern Bible translations. For millions of Evangelical Christians in the western, post-modern world, this book contains Biblical treasures that will absolutely change your life! You will uncover ancient truths that have been hidden under centuries of the sands of Greek thinking.

If you are up to the challenge, there are untold riches waiting. But proceed with caution. You are likely to encounter challenges to your usual understanding of spiritual life!

As we get started, there are a few things you need to know in order to claim your treasure and live a blessed life. You must know that you have been deceived. This deception has gone on for thousands of years largely undetected. It now operates in our lives almost unconsciously. It has so completely affected our way of living that we merely accept the implications as perfectly normal. In order to see this deception for what it is, we will need to arrive at the work site with clean hands, a pure heart, and a contrite spirit. Ask God to direct your paths and bless the work of your hands. That way you will show yourself approved by rightly dividing the His Word. So, bring your Bible. Open your mind. And get ready to restore the foundations of your faith.

HOW TO READ THIS BOOK

I suppose you're wondering why anyone would bother to tell you how to read a book. Most of us just plow right in, starting at page one and proceeding through the material. But this book is a bit different. First, it's made up of bite-sized vignettes taken from Scripture. Each page is a tiny look at a much larger theme – the shift from the contemporary Greek post-modern worldview to the ancient Hebraic worldview. This is intentional. This shift affects nearly everything about the way we think and live, so we will examine it very slowly. Read a page or two. Meditate on what you read. See if it rings true. Then imagine what will happen to your life as you make the shift from Greek to Hebrew.

In addition, this book is designed to push you to change. In the Greek world, life is about information. We've heard it a hundred times: "Knowledge is power." But the Hebrews had a different point of view. Just knowing something does not transform behavior, and for the Hebrews, a life without transformation isn't worth living. So, the purpose of these little vignettes is to get you to question what you believe, re-evaluate your mental architecture, be renewed in your mind *and do something about it*. Without this last step you'll be just as lost as you were when we started and this will be just one more information transfer manual. That's not what we want. If what you find here is true, then it calls you to action. Without the action, you might as well not read these pages. If you're not willing to consider changing, then just close the book now and give it to someone else with your blessing.

Finally, this book is small enough to whet your appetite. It's not the end of the story. It's just a teaser; the preview of another way of life. If you decide that it has something for you, then you will need to jump into a bigger pond. Join the daily interaction with thousands of others who are swimming in cleaner water by receiving *Today's Word* in a daily e mail. To join, just log on to: skipmoen.com

Then, **give this book to someone who needs it.**

TABLE OF CONTENTS

(Does anyone actually *read* a table of contents?)

*I*n this book, we will examine just a few of the many elements that make up the shift from a Greek worldview to a Hebrew worldview. We don't have the time or space to look at all the complexities that are involved in more than two millennia of cultural change. But some of these elements seem to have greater priority right now and these are the ones we will look at first. Before we get started, however, it is a good idea to take a look at the big picture; to get a kind of global view of where all of this is going. So, the first thing we need is a big picture comparison. Then we can jump into the deep end of the pool.

Introduction

$\mathcal{F}$or twenty-five hundred years, the Western world has been building its civilization on sand. The castles we erect look wonderful. People are amazed at the design and complexity of the architecture. In fact, these magnificent structures have become the envy of the global village. But when the tide comes in, all that work will be washed away; gone as though it never existed. At the end of the day, civilizations built on sand simply disappear. The only thing left will be the empty beach. Fortunately, there is a something buried beneath this sand. That's what we are here to find.

We've seen it before. The Egyptians, the Assyrians, the Babylonians, the great empires of India and the Far East and the Holy Roman Empire have all come and gone. We find vestiges of their existence in ancient ruins, artifacts that should remind us about the treacherous sand under those magnificent structures. Of course, we never imagine that we might be building on the same beach. We think that our foundations are strong, enduring and tested. Unfortunately, we're wrong. The truth is that our contemporary society rests on the same shifting sand as those great empires of the past. Unless we confront this fact, and face the inevitable consequences, we are also doomed to be washed away with the tide of time.

This book will not examine the sweeping panorama of the rise and fall of human civilizations. That's a subject far too great to tackle here. This book concerns itself with one tiny element of the global picture. Nevertheless, the element we will investigate is *crucial* to the structures built on these shores. We will look at the cornerstone of our civilization, the foundation that holds up the rest of the architecture. We will do that by examining the difference between the Greek and Hebrew views of the world, Man and God.

In one sense, our contemporary civilization is like a cake. The icing on this cake is the overlay of Judeo-Christian morality, but the cake itself is thoroughly Greek. Our approach to justice, economics, community, politics, education, success and meaning are derived from Greek philosophy, tempered by Judeo-Christian influence.

Once the icing on the cake is eaten (and it has been fairly much consumed in the last 500 years), what's left is the Greek cake itself. Our task is to scrape away what little is left of that Judeo-Christian icing so that we can clearly see and taste the real Greek cake underneath. We need to do this because we must understand the inevitable consequences of sustaining ourselves by eating Greek cake. The effort in this book is to simply demonstrate how different the real substance of the Greek-based worldview is when it is compared to the biblical, Hebraic worldview. The God of the Bible is not Greek. The men and women of the Bible are not Greek. Even the books of the New Testament are not Greek. Of course, they are written in Greek, but the men who wrote them, and the thought patterns they employ are thoroughly Hebrew.

The Hebrew worldview is radically different from our contemporary, Greek-based worldview. Once we begin to see just how different it is, we will discover a new hope for our physical and spiritual existence. In fact, this discovery is really not *new* at all. It is as old as the sands of the seashore on the day God said to Abraham, "Indeed I will greatly bless you, and I will greatly multiply your seed as the stars of the heavens and as the sand which is on the seashore" (Genesis 22:17).

This book is the direct result of prodding by readers of my daily e-mail meditation called *Today's Word*. Now in its fifth year, the thousands who read it every day have asked over and over for something in hard copy. Here it is. To each of you I give thanks. Special praise belongs to my wife, Rosanne, who has put up with my hours at the keyboard, my passion for reading theological dictionaries and my own spiritual journey into unfamiliar places. She has been my *'ezer* (a Hebrew word that you will come to love).

AN OVERVIEW

The Man of Athens – The Man of Jerusalem

*O*ne of the reasons that we have such a hard time putting our faith into practice in the everyday life is that we have never taken time to understand our own roots. We are part of a heritage that reaches back to ancient Greece; hundreds of years before Christ walked the Palestine pathways. We are also part of a society that was reshaped by Judeo-Christian influences from two millennia before we were born. As a result, we are the product of a cultural clash.

The world of the Greeks was not at all like the world of the Hebrews. The Greeks are the fathers of western thought. The Hebrews are from eastern backgrounds. The Greeks were a culture of city-states, a government of the rule of Law, a population of diverse ethnic groups and an intellectual history of scientific measure and theory. The Hebrews were a pure genealogy of tribal descent, a government by God's revealed character, a culture of nomadic wanderings and an intellectual history of wisdom and cultic ritual.

We are the product of both of these streams. Our problem is that we haven't taken time to see what these two great streams mean for us. We haven't listened to the difference between the Greek and Hebrew answers to the biggest questions of life. And since we have not realized that there is a very big difference, we have all sorts of problems when we try to practice a belief in God based on the Hebrew culture within a framework of the world based on the Greek culture.

These two cultural streams answer our fundamental questions of life very differently:

What is Man?

What is the nature of the universe?

Who is God?

Any significant differences in answers to just one of these fundamental questions will cause problems, but when you put all three together at once, confusion and chaos follow.

The Greeks would answer our questions like this:

1. Man is unique in the world because he is the only creature who can exercise reason. It is reason that makes Man who is truly is.
2. Man has a spark of the divine within him.
3. Man can know the universe through his reason.
4. Knowledge is power.
5. Societal institutions are extensions of Man's knowledge and abilities.
6. Man is capable of solving the world's problems.
7. Man has no cognitive limits.
8. Self-sufficiency is the only attitude needed to accomplish whatever can be imagined.
9. The destiny of Man is to control his world.
10. The world can be fully understood through scientific investigation.
11. Belief in God is unjustified because it is not capable of scientific proof. It might be useful fiction, but ultimately this added baggage must be discarded by the truly educated man.

How would the Hebrews answer these questions?

They might say something like this: (pardon me if we use a Greek technique to do this).

1. All creation begins and ends with God.
2. Man's only uniqueness is a result of God's choice to gift him with authority.
3. Man shares fundamental aspects with all of creation.
4. Man is completely dependent on God even if he does not acknowledge this dependence.

5. Every aspect of Man's life is under God's sovereignty and control.
6. Man is essentially and fundamentally a being who chooses to rebel against His creator.
7. Man is not a spark of the divine. He has "fallen' from the original design and is now a wicked and disobedient violator of God's perfect harmony.
8. Man cannot solve his most fundamental problem on his own.
9. God is responsible for human societal institutions.
10. God will judge Man's deeds on the basis of absolute holiness.
11. God is the central focus of all creation, not Man.
12. Knowledge, self-reliance and self-sufficiency are vanity and folly with regard to Man's real problems.
13. God's Truth is power.
14. Wisdom is the application of God's Truth.

This helps us see how completely different these two views of Man really are. Fundamentally, the Hebrew view is that God is the principal player in this universe. Everything revolves around Him, His purposes, His will and His control. The Greek view is that Man is the central player on the world's stage. Man's goals, creations, abilities and decisions are the most important elements in this world. These two approaches are simply *not compatible*. Their differences are so far apart that no compromise can even be imagined.

We can picture some of these thematic differences with the following word pairs:

Greek		**Hebrew**
Believe correctly	vs.	Behave correctly
Education	vs.	Submission
Knowledge	vs.	Wisdom
Reason	vs.	Revelation

Mind	vs.	Heart
Material	vs.	Spiritual
Outer recognition	vs.	Inner/Outer Harmony
Fulfilled	vs.	Fruitful
Psyche	vs.	Person (*nephesh*)
Enlightenment	vs.	Repentance
Destiny	vs.	Purpose

Of course, there are overlaps in concepts. Whenever entire cultures are reduced to a dozen words, many of the nuances are lost. But in general, we can see the striking differences between these two views. And the differences are not just about the nature of Man. They are different in their outlook regarding history, purpose, epistemology (how you know what's true), ethics and religion.

How many times have we been frustrated in our spiritual growth or the application of Christian beliefs in our everyday circumstances because we have been trying to fit a Hebrew peg into a Greek hole? Look over the lists above. How much of your own belief system is really Greek? Ask yourself these questions to see if you aren't making Greek assumptions about the world.

1. Do you place a higher value on gaining knowledge than you do on submitting to God's wisdom?

Perhaps you will say, "Oh, no. I don't do that. I want to serve God's purposes". But the truth is usually found in our actions, not our words. How often have you shortened your time studying God's word so that you could get to a training class for work? Do you tell your children that the way to success is by getting a college degree? How much emphasis do you and your family put on understanding God's precise purpose for your daily life or do you "assume" it while you rush to get to work or school?

2. Do you think that hard work and understanding will solve all your problems?

Here's another example. The last time you made a job change or took a promotion, did you pray asking God to show you what was best for you, or did you go with the status and money? When you face financial difficulties, do you put in overtime or do you spend more time on your knees? When you are in conflict with your spouse, do you ask to pray together *before* you begin arguing, debating or justifying?

3. Do you measure achievements according to the standards of your career instead of according to God's revelation?

I have many college degrees. They are displayed on my wall. Do you think that they make me a better person? When you meet people, do you judge them by their accomplishments before you know if they have submitted their lives to God? If someone asks you what you do, is God's purpose part of your answer?

4. Do you listen more to your mind than to your heart?

When you face a really stressful problem, where do you turn first, to your own mental resources (trying to figure out how to make things work) or to God (asking Him for His guidance)? When bad things happen to you, whom do you blame? Why do you blame anyone at all? Do you believe that God is using these things in your life for His purposes?

5. Are you shaped more by your outward circumstances than by your inner reflection?

When you are under stress, are you able to see God's hand in every circumstance? Do you know the inner tranquility that Jesus promised (my peace I give to you) or are you anxious and you just can't let it all go?

6. Do you look for outward approval by men instead of inner recognition by God?

Does your reputation count more than your quiet service before God? Do you look for recognition from others? Do you keep "score"?

7. Are you struggling to find your destiny or are you striving to bring about God's purposes?

If you wrote down the top three desires for your life, where would devotion (not service) to God be?

8. How hard is it for you to admit your mistakes, genuinely ask for forgiveness and make apologies?

Once you answer these questions, you may find that you are much more Greek than you are Hebrew. That might explain why you find frustration in your spiritual life. When Paul tells us that we must become like Christ by the renewing of our minds, he is speaking about much more than just changing our religious beliefs. We need to start seeing the world from God's perspective, and that perspective does not come from the top of Mt. Olympus.

Today's cultural orientation is based on Greek thinking and assumptions. If we are going to express our faith in this Greek world, we need to know when we are facing fundamental differences in viewpoints. This does not mean that we can't be Christian in the workplace, in civil and social settings or in education. Obviously, God is the God of all creation and sovereign over every circumstance. So, God expects us to behave like His son in every situation. But we usually try to do the right thing without even knowing how to make the changes in our own minds first. We need to get God's viewpoint regarding our situation before we can put His purposes into action. And that means taking a serious look at what we really believe by looking at how we act, not what we say.

For example, we teach our children that success in life is the result of education. We tell them that knowledge and study is the way to happiness. This concept is Greek. God's way is quite different. First, life is not measured by material gain and success. Secondly, life is not about education; it is about wisdom. Thirdly, knowledge is valuable only if it produces a submissive attitude toward God. Degrees on the wall, sales awards, career promotions and corporate titles mean nothing if they are not part of God's purpose for us. This does not mean that we take an anti-educational stance. It means that we take a position that looks beyond this world by acting on the basis of eternal values. We do what makes sense for a much bigger picture. We are not limited by the horizon.

It's time to unmask the enemy. Our minds are fertile ground for all sorts of self-defeating behavior. As Pogo said in that favorite cartoon, "We have met the enemy and he is us."

Other Greek – Hebrew paradigm shifts include:

Greek		Hebrew
Individual	vs.	Tribe (Community)
Education = information	vs.	Education = right living
Names as labels	vs.	Names as identity – essence
Personal Worth: Commodity	vs.	Value granted by God
Money, Effort	vs.	Devotion, Dependence
Organization	vs.	Community
Hierarchy	vs.	Family
Religion as ritual	vs.	True worship
Fate and luck	vs.	Sovereign Direction
Balanced life	vs.	Centered Life
Desire for control	vs.	Dynamically Powerless

These pairs only scratch the surface of the shift in perspective, but they may be useful by helping us with the concept of opposing paradigms. As we explore these differences in the selected verses that follow, we will discover that a great many of our presuppositions about life are really built on the sandy foundation of Greek thought. That should come as a warning. Every past civilization that attempted to build on this kind of foundation failed. It was swept away by time and tide. God's eternal kingdom is not of this world. That only means it does not operate on the same principles that we find in the Greek perspective. If we try to live according to the worldview that rests on this beach, we too will be washed away. Unfortunately, most of us aren't even aware that we are building on sand. It's time to look at what's really under our feet.

Chapter 1

Word Work: Re-Examining Biblical Interpretation

"*L*et's play the alphabet game." If you've ever traveled long distances with bored children, this little mental and visual exercise can break the monotony. Each player is challenged to find all the letters of the alphabet in order on signs or other words outside the windows of the vehicle. As you can imagine, some letters are particularly difficult to find.

You might think that this is only child's play, but the truth is that our understanding of Scripture is quite a bit like this little game. There are about fifteen thousand different words in the Greek and Hebrew texts of the Bible. Of course, some of these words are used an enormous number of times. For example, the Hebrew word *shuv*, usually translated "return" or "repent" is used nearly 1000 times. It has more than three dozen different nuances. Every time we translate this word, and hundreds of other words like it, into our contemporary language, we run the risk of leaving behind some important element found in the original language. Sometimes it doesn't matter much, but there are many occasions when not knowing the full meaning in the original has serious side-effects. And there are times, as we shall see, when the contemporary translations have been altered because the translators decided to change the original for theological or cultural reasons. The problem is that most of the time you and I simply aren't aware of these alterations. Consequently, we are robbed of the treasures hidden in the text.

It's time to change that! It's time to start uncovering what has been buried behind the translations for centuries. In an age when there are ample resources available to even the casual reader, there is no longer any excuse for relying on your favorite Bible version. **No English translation can be considered totally reliable.** When you really want to know what the passage says, you'll have to do a lot of comparison shopping. This book is the result of doing some comparative shopping for a long time. Hopefully, it will spur you to look deeper. To begin with, we will look much deeper into the assumptions that are buried in contemporary translations; assumptions that re-direct your understanding about God, His purposes and your salvation.

In this regard, reading the Bible is an Olympic event. If you want to really understand it, you'll have to be in peak literary condition. Sure, you can page through this book as an amateur. You can play the biblical game in the backyard or the minor leagues. But you won't discovery the beauty and majesty that comes with an Olympic performance. If you want to get the gold, you'll have to practice reading this book just like you would practice for an Olympic medal.

The Bible is the simplest most difficult book to read in the whole world. That's because it isn't like any other book. In its pages you will encounter several millennia of human history, many different cultures and a wide array of different types of literature. It's not a novel or a handbook or a life-guide. It's the love story between God and Man – and its filled with every kind of venue that encompasses the divine-human encounter. It takes practice to read the Bible, lots and lots of practice. Most of us probably open the Bible to some passage and read the translated words without giving a second thought about the type of literature we are reading, the original context of that literature or the theological assumptions we bring along with us. We forget that the Bible is a collection of narrative, civil and spiritual regulations, letters, poetry, prophetic utterance and theological history. We are inclined to think that everything in the Bible is contemporaneous rather than progressive revelation. We imagine that it is all meant for us in our current culture and time. Most of all, we tend to read the Bible with a particular set of assumptions, like thinking that football always means the American version of the game. Too often, our previous theological training, even if it was only Sunday School, lets us skim over the texts that we think we know, rather than carefully paying attention to the smallest details. No Olympic athlete can afford to ignore the details. Medals are lost for lack of attention. Reading this book is exactly the same. Ignore a word or an allusion or a metaphor and you'll be left behind.

These common ways of approaching the Bible prevent us from really grasping its deepest meanings and its incredible consistency. There are things in this Book that we haven't discovered because we haven't slowed down enough to examine the actual words. We think we know what faith means, or forgiveness, or salvation, or grace, but most of us are relying on what someone told us rather than what the text says. We think we can understand what the Bible says by reading our favorite translation, but we haven't considered the fact that translators also have bias, that too often our English words don't really capture the nuances of Greek or Hebrew and that usually we convert the meaning in the ancient world into something contemporary, like the prose of *The Message*.

We have stopped *learning* what the Bible says because we don't ask enough questions. We just want something easy to read.

If you want just a glimpse at how deep this treasure really is, consider the fact that Hebrew was originally a pictographic language, much like Egyptian hieroglyphics. Sometimes the pictographs that form the letters that are now part of the biblical Hebrew text have their own story to tell. For example, the Hebrew word *dabar* means "word" or "speech." It's consonants (Hebrew is a language for the most part without written vowels) are D B R. The pictograph behind these consonants give us "D = pathway, tent door, B = in, into a house, and R = person." We arrive at a pictograph for "word" meaning "a pathway into a person." Imagine what that means when it comes to understanding God's *words*. How important they become when we see them as God's pathway into who we are as people.

On this treasure hunt, we'll look at just a few issues in biblical interpretation. We'll slowly examine some verses that uncover things we didn't know were there. This isn't a systematic theology. We won't develop doctrines. We're only looking at a few verses. But we will pry back the lid just enough to take a peek at a world that exists beneath the contemporary translations. After all, what God says is incredibly important and demands careful examination. The goal here is to seriously think about it. So, let's start practicing and see what we find.

(Note on the transliteration of words: Hebrew and Greek have sounds that are hard to reproduce in English spelling. For example, Hebrew has a guttural sound like the German "ach". This is usually spelled as a "k" or a "ch" or a "c". However, there is a lot of variation in Hebrew phonetics, so some conventions need to be adopted. Just remember that no matter what the spelling, the phonetic is that guttural "ach". There are similar issues in Greek. So, you might find some variations in the English spelling of these words, but don't worry about it. The Greek or Hebrew word didn't change. All that changed was the way we try to say it.)

1.

*And when some of the bystanders heard it, they began saying, "Behold, He is calling for **Elijah**." Mark 15:35*

Unraveling Translations

Elijah – My theological education led me astray. In spite of the commonly held belief that Jesus spoke Aramaic, and that His words in the Greek New Testament are a translation from Aramaic, I have discovered that this is a mistake. The evidence says that this idea simply isn't true. It's amazing what you can learn when you get old enough to admit your mistakes. But my confession to you has a much bigger implication than just that the teacher learned something new. The implication changes a great deal about how we understand the New Testament – and the teachings of Jesus. So, bear with me. We are about to make some startling corrections.

This word, *Elijah*, is the interpretation that people placed on the words of Jesus spoken from the cross. According to Mark 15:34, Jesus said, "*Eloi, Eloi, lama sabachthani.*" Mark tells us that this is translated as "My God, My God, why have you forsaken me?" We often take this to be an *Aramaic* phrase. That's why we think it needs translation. But if it were in Aramaic, then it would have been impossible for the crowd to confuse Jesus' words with the name for Elijah, since *only in Hebrew* does the word *Eli* have the double meaning of "my God" and the shortened name for Elijah. If Jesus spoke the words in Aramaic, no one would have been confused at all. But Mark records that they were confused. They thought Jesus was calling Elijah. That means that Jesus *must have uttered the words in Hebrew*, not Aramaic.

You may say, "So what? What's the big deal?" The big deal (and it is a very big deal) is that if Jesus conversed in Hebrew as His native tongue, then it is simply impossible to understand what He taught without knowing the culture and grammar of Hebrew, not Greek or Aramaic. We already know that Jesus used Scripture (the Old Testament) exhaustively. But if He commonly *spoke* Hebrew, then all of His thought forms, expressions and idioms will have to be understood from a *Jewish* perspective. That is a very big deal. It means that Christians are much closer to Jewish thinking than we have commonly believed. It means that Jesus was the greatest *rabbi* who ever lived, and that He taught in the fashion of the rabbis. It means that if we are going to practice what Jesus commanded, we will have to enter into the Jewish worldview in order to understand what those commands really mean. We will have to throw away centuries of segregation between Jewish thought and Christian thought and re-discover the Judaism beneath the soil of Christianity. This will rock our world!

Concepts of the church, evangelism, discipleship, tithing, prayer, blessing, confession, repentance and many, many more will have to be reconsidered from an Old Testament perspective. When Jesus said that He did not come to abolish the Law, we will see this in a radically new light. God has not changed. The plan is the same as it has always been from before the foundation of the world. Jesus came to open our eyes to what God had already been doing for thousands of years with the Hebrew nation called Israel. The Christian Bible starts in Genesis, not *Matthew*. So, I'm sorry. We have so much to learn – again. Are you with me?

A reference note: The idea that Jesus spoke Hebrew, not Aramaic, and that most of the original gospels were written in Hebrew, not Greek, is radical, but not unjustified. For a scholarly treatment of the evidence, see *Understanding the Difficult Words of Jesus: New Insights from a Hebraic Perspective* by David Bivin and Roy Blizzard, Jr. (Destiny Image, 2001). These men cite the evidence that will lead you on a new path of discovery. There is a lot more to say about this. The implications for our understanding of the New Testament are staggering. While Paul wrote his letters in Greek, it appears that Matthew, Mark, John, Peter and James wrote in Hebrew. If we want to know what they really meant, we will have to begin with an Old Testament worldview. This changes everything!

2.

*Behold, the soul of him is puffed up and is not upright, but the just shall live by his **faith**.* Habakkuk 2:4

The God Bottle

Faith – We all know the second part of this verse. Paul quotes it in Romans as the centerpiece of the theology of grace. "The just shall live by faith." We don't *earn* our way to God. We come to Him by faith. Ah, but now there is a problem. Just what is this *faith*, anyway? Does this verse say, "The man justified by faith shall live," or "The just man shall live by his faith." You might have to read this twice to see the difference. Is "faith" something that I have to acquire and accumulate in order to live a life pleasing to God?

You might say that the first reading is correct. We are justified by faith (whose?) and for that reason we live. But listen to the way Christians usually talk. "God will remove the barriers in your life if you have enough faith." "You need more faith in order to see God bring about a miracle." "She had great faith, so God answered her prayers." All of this kind of talk makes it seem like "faith" is some sort of elixir in a God bottle. We need to collect more of it to be prepared for crisis. If we can just purchase an additional supply (say "Hail Mary's", put in some extra offering, do a few more good deeds), then we will have it on hand when we need it the most. We want more "faith," but we're not quite sure how to get it. It's definitely *not* on eBay.

In order to understand how we should read this particular text, we need to look at the idea of faith in the context of the whole Bible. What we discover, of course, is that "faith" is not like medicine. In fact, it's not a *substance* at all. It is a code word for a relationship, and just like any other relationship, you can't bottle it or store it or acquire it *except* in interactive exchange. The relationship exists *only* in the exchange. You don't have a "relationship" with someone you never speak to. The idea that "faith" is something that I *acquire* is as misguided as the idea that children are something I own. In fact, the Hebrew word, *'emunah*, is typically a word about *character*, the utter reliability and fidelity of someone, particularly God. **Faith is my *active* attitude and behavioral results of total reliance on God's absolute trustworthiness.** That means that my "faith" is demonstrated in the *action* of putting myself in His care, no matter what the circumstances! Until and unless I act on His reliability, I just don't have faith. I might have a set of written beliefs that I can recite, but I won't have any active relationship. **Faith is only found**

in the action, not the declaration. Israel claimed to have "faith" in God, but their actions revealed denial of His claim on them. The truth is that they were faithless. Jesus asks the same of us. "Why do you call me Lord, Lord, and do not do what I say?"

How much faith does it take to please God? The question itself is wrong-headed. If faith is the action of trusting Him, then I either *act* or I don't *act*. I either trust Him, or I don't. There is no "half-full" measurement here. So, how do I get this faith? God grants it, freely, abundantly, continuously. From God's side of the relationship, nothing impedes your trust in Him. All you have to do is *act* accordingly. Of course, that doesn't mean just *thinking* about doing something, does it?

3.

because by the **works** *of the Law no flesh will be justified in His sight*
Romans 3:20

It's Not All Grace

Works – Most Christians believe that the Law has no place in the process of salvation. It is *grace alone* that brings us into fellowship with the Father. There is little doubt that God's action towards us, and not our attempt to appease Him, is the true foundation of our redemption. But is that the end of the story? Is there no *further* obligation on our part once God has gifted us with restoration to His company?

Verses like this one might be understood in a way that would confirm that the Law no longer has a place in the life of a believer. Nothing could be more mistaken! Paul was Jewish, in thought and expression. What he means in this verse is not in conflict with the rest of the Bible, and the rest of the Bible, including the words of the Son, follows the path of Deuteronomy 30:11. God saves us *in order that we might obey His commandments*, not so that we might ignore them. In fact, He tells us that what He asks is *not too difficult* for us to do. It is *expected*! Keeping the commandments will not save us. The Law leads us to the saving work of Jesus. But once we have been adopted into the family, we are obligated, and expected, to live according to the commands of the *paterfamilias*, God the Father. In fact, if our actions do not display evidence of a commitment and willingness to obey Him, it just might be the case that we were never adopted.

The Greek word here is *erga*. It is "work, task, occupation, enterprise." But Paul is not thinking in Greek. Paul is thinking in Hebrew. And why wouldn't we expect that? Paul is a Pharisee of the Pharisees, a member of the tribe of Benjamin, a *torah*-observant follower of the Messiah. Paul is thoroughly Hebrew. He would have it no other way.   Therefore, what he means is that a slavish, mechanical, legalistic observance of the rules of religion in order to *obligate* God to perform is useless misunderstanding of the Law. It is work, not life! Without a heart devoted to the author of the Law, all rule-keeping is worthless.   God wants circumcised hearts, not regulated hands. Christianity is a religion of volunteers, not rules for conscripts. What Paul means, from a Jewish perspective, is that a legalistic application of the Law justifies no one. Such an application is a mistake. The Law is a contract for enjoying *life*, not a set of rules for controlling behavior.   Too often we allow our interpretation of the Hebrew word *torah* to be governed by the culturally-sensitive word "Law" rather than by the more appropriate translation "instructions." God's *instructions* are designed for our benefit right here and right now. That is why God can *expect* His children to keep His commandments, joyfully!

Am I supposed to follow the Law (instructions) of God? Of course I am! God redeems me so that I can become part of His great family of those who are devoted to Him. And if I am devoted to Him, I will rejoice in His commands. They are an expression of the character of our Father. No follower of the Messiah sees the Law as a means of *earning* God's favor, but no Christ-follower sets aside the Law as a means of displaying devotion to the Lord.   The Law helps me understand the nature of the God I serve. I keep it because I love Him. It is not a yoke around my neck. It is liberty in my heart.

Is the Law for me? You bet! God asks me to observe it, empowers me to observe it and delights in me when I observe it. Keeping the

Law because I am devoted to Him is my way of saying, "Thank You, Father, for rescuing me."

4.

The word of the LORD which __came__ to Micah of Moresheth in the days of Jotham, Ahaz and Hezekiah   Micah 1:1

Inspiration

Came – How do you receive communication today? Today we probably think about e mail. I could have sent you a letter, or called you on the phone, or sent a telegram (how quaint) or traveled to your house and told you in person. Does any of this help me understand how God communicates His message? That's the issue that confronts us with the doctrine of inspiration. How does God communicate *exactly* what He wants to say to human beings?

This Hebrew verb gives us a clue, but it is certainly *not* what we were expecting. You see, the verb is not *bo'* ("to come to a place, to arrive"). It is *hayah,* and *hayah* means "to exist, to be, to become, to happen." The translation, "the word of the Lord *came* to," isn't quite right. The word did not arrive like this message you're reading. God's word came into existence in Micah; it happened to him. And here's the best part. This verb, *hayah,* is the same verb that is behind the *name of God,* Yahweh. YHWH (from Exodus 3:i4) is the great I AM. God's very personal name is tied to the verb "to be." His word is *manifested into existence* by the same mysterious process that all existence becomes what it is. Would you have expected anything less?

Does this help us understand divine inspiration? Yes, and no. Yes, it makes perfect sense that God's creative process is behind His word manifesting itself in Micah – and in lots of other people. However it happens, it has God as its origin. So, Paul tells us that all Scripture is *God-breathed.* Of course it is! That's how God created us. But, this doesn't really help us answer the question, "How?" That's because we have no more rational explanation for how life began than we do for how inspiration occurs. It is the *question* that is wrong, not the answer. The question assumes that there is some clearly defined specific, rational process that can be dissected, analyzed and replicated. The question is *Greek*. It is a request for technical information. But the Hebrew concept is *organic*. It is a description about how the happening appears to Micah, not a description about a technical manual on God's communication.

Why is this important (other than to theologians)? Well, how many times have you heard someone say, "God spoke to me," or "God told me"? Did they mean that God whispered something in their ears? Or did they mean that somehow, by some mysterious means, God's word became a reality in them?

Did you think that God stopped *being manifested* when the last of the apostles died? If that were the case, why would Paul (and others) provide us with instructions to *test* what is revealed? What is in Scripture is the complete standard and accepted rule of practice for believers, but inspiration continues. God is not silent. He is still *being* God.

5.

*and man **became** a living being* Genesis 2:7

Manifested in the Flesh

Became – The Bible is without doubt the most fascinating book in the world. Why? Because it is simply beyond reasonable inference to imagine that all of the intricacies woven into its fabric could have been concocted by human beings. From beginning to end, the language of the Bible is filled with surprises, deep insights and tasty linguistic treats. None are more fascinating than the implications provided by the use of the verb *hayah* (to be, to become). We just discovered that there is a marvelous connection between the idea of God's word *becoming* in Micah. At the very least, this implies that God's verbal instruction to His people manifested itself in the prophet. How that occurs is a mystery, but no more mysterious than another use of *hayah*, found here in the story of the creation of Man.

Man *became nephesh* (the Hebrew word that encompasses will, emotions, mind, body and spirit – a total person). The same creative manifestation demonstrated in God's word in the prophets is at the bottom of what it means to be alive. God's breath manifested itself in the dust-formed creature and *ha.a.dam le.ne.fesh ha.yah* (literally, "the earth-made person was manifested"). It's almost as though the text says, "Personal life happened in this lump of formed dirt." How life came to be in Man is not essentially different than how God's word came to be in Micah.

God's personal name, YHWH (Yahweh), is also formed from the verb *hayah*. When God manifests His word in Micah and when He manifests His life in Man, He merely makes tangible what He is. Take that thought and read John 1: 14 from a Hebrew perspective. "The Word *hayah* flesh." The very essence of God, the I AM (*Hayah*) is manifested as *basar* (a tangible body). This says a lot more than that Jesus was born as a man. This says that the great "TO BE" now appeared in bodily form. The I AM now existed as the same kind of living being as human bodies. God's mysterious *hayah* is demonstrated in yet another unparalleled way.

Think about what this means for human life - for you and me. No, it does not mean that each of us has a spark of divinity. That is pure Greek philosophy. What this means is that you and I are in some respect vehicles by which God is manifested in His creation. We are fully equipped to reveal His glorious *hayah*. Whatever it means to be created in His image, it at least means that God plans to use my *nephesh hayah* (living person) as a demonstration of His glory.

How far is God from manifesting Himself in your life? Take a breath. That's how far.

6.

*and man became **a living being*** Genesis 2:7

The Earth-made Being Who Prays

A Living Being – God fashioned from the dust the body that He animated with His breath - man manifested as *nephesh*. There is a bit more here than we might think. The Mishnah (specific teachings of the rabbis usually transmitted by oral memorization) uses a synonym for *nephesh*. The word is *mav'eh*, derived from the root *ba'ah*, a verb that means, "to ask, to seek, to request – as in prayer." Rabbi Scherman comments, "In other words, the Talmud defines man as 'the creature that prays.' Furthermore, the Talmud teaches that even *nephesh*, the life-sustaining soul, is synonymous with prayer." What would happen to our thinking if we translated this verse about the creation of Man as "and man was manifested as a praying being?" Would we suddenly realize that we are human *only insofar as* we are engaged in relationship with the Creator? What is prayer if it is not the essential *me* in contact with *Him*?

If I am going to become human, I must move in the direction of the divine design in me. That does not happen by random chance or automatic pilot. I must *decide* to become human. That is essentially what it means to have free will – the ability to choose. I can move toward God's design innately implanted in me, or I can move away from His design forging a self-made creature fashioned by lesser purposes. I am equipped to manifest God's design. He has insured that I lack nothing necessary for this project. But accomplishing the task of becoming human requires a continual connection to the Maker. My humanity depends entirely on how His life is manifest in my *nephesh*. Therefore, prayer (in all of its wider Hebrew meaning) is the absolutely necessary ingredient for being what God intended. The man who does not pray will soon not be a man.

Prayer existed before the Fall. The one formed from the earth communicated with the Creator and in the process received life-enhancing purpose, balance and instruction. In a fallen world, prayer is even more important. Now the world itself is under the power and influence of the inhuman. The systems of this world are designed to remove your humanity because they are designed to remove you from a relationship with your Creator. Whatever is self-driven leads to inhuman behavior. True humanity is found in humble submission to the Creator. The closer I get to selfless obedience, the more human I become. How do I know this? Because God manifested Himself in His Son and demonstrated what truly being human actually looks like. Being truly human looks exactly like Jesus.

There is only one living model for being human. That model is Jesus. If I want to be human, I need only look as far as Him to see what humanness means. Now you know why Jesus spent hours in prayer. He knew that being human means being connected to the source of Life. He wasn't on His knees begging the Father for blessings, power or instructions. He was in the company of the Father enjoying being fully human. Don't you long for that too?

7.

*and man became **a living being*** Genesis 2:7

Carrier

Living Being – Are you a carrier or a producer? In a world where the emphasis is on *productive* living, we need to take a step backward and ask this question from the biblical point of view. The world's performance expectation is not what it seems.

The prophet of God is a messenger, not a producer. What he proclaims is *not* his own creation. In fact, the mark of a false prophet is the proclamation of his own ideas. What is manifested in the prophet comes from God. The prophet gets no credit at all for the content. His role is only the delivery. He carries what is manifested by someone else.

The same principle applies to us. When God created men and women in His own image, we became carriers of that image. It is not ours. Just like the word happened in the prophets, God's image happens in us – and we are carriers of His glory for His benefit and His purposes. Our role is to deliver God-*embodied* messages to the world. The original plan to place human beings as vice-regents in creation, acting on behalf of the Creator, only underscores the fact that the plan doesn't come from us. We are the vehicles by which God stewards creation. We are not the owners.

If this is true, then the claim that I am the originator of my destiny, the captain of my soul, is a false representation of what it means to be human. That is the equivalent of being a false prophet – the one who claimed that the message was his own. This world loves those who take credit for their production. The father of all lies loves this lie because it cuts right into the heart of what it means to be a bearer of God's image. If God designed me to be the vehicle for His expressed use, carrying His purposes out in His creation, then anytime I act with disregard toward Him or take credit for myself or imagine that my plans are my own, I align myself with the father of lies.

To be human is to be a carrier of God happening in me. The message is far more important than the carrier. The message is the sovereign rule of the Holy of holies. If I lose sight of my role as carrier, I will be seduced into believing that the package is more important than the contents. I will start to believe that human life is measured in terms of my production – what I accomplish, accumulate, enjoy and influence – rather than how elegantly I carry the image. If true humanity is the *manifestation* of the image of God in me, then any peripherals that do not contribute directly to the message really don't count, do they? So, I ask you: How do you measure your humanity? Are you living as a carrier or did you think you were the content?

(Just a fascinating note: The Hebrew words for "living being" are *both* feminine nouns. So, Man (*adam*) who comes from *adamah* (the earth) is manifest as a living (feminine) person (feminine). You can't make a case based solely on the gender of nouns, but it certainly makes you wonder why "living person" is feminine. That should throw all the male-gender advocates into a tizzy.)

8.

If you will not take heed to do all the words of this law which are written in this book, to fear this glorious and fearful Name, Yahweh your God, then . . " Deuteronomy 28:58

The Law

If You Will Not Take Heed – An email I received one day expressed real concern. "Are you saying that the old law is not dead? Wasn't the old law before nailed to the cross? We live under a new covenant, don't we?" asked the writer. He could not imagine that we are still bound by the commandments given to Israel so many centuries ago. He was taught that the law was rendered null and void with the death of Christ. After all, didn't Paul say that we were no longer under the law, that we were dead to it? It is quite popular for Christians to speak this way, suggesting that we have severed the ties to Old Testament roots because we live under the banner of grace.

Oops! There is a lot of confusion here. Some of it has some tragic consequences.

How can Jesus say, "I did not come to abolish [the Law], but to fulfill it" (Matthew 5:17), or proclaim that not the smallest part of the Law will pass away until "all is accomplished"? Did you think that He meant until He died? Is that *all* that God has to accomplish? How can He teach from the Law, draw inferences from the Law, and hold His audience accountable to the Law, if He knows that it is no longer applicable? Are we to say that God's character, revealed in the Law (for the Law is simply an expression of Who God is) has changed? If you think that the law is dead, then how do you know how to live today? Do you just sit around waiting for God to give you "a word"? If now you live according to the Spirit, not the law, then do you believe that the Spirit does not endorse the character of the God who gave the law in the first place? And if the Law is no longer applicable, which of the Ten Commandments are you ready to stop doing? Which of them doesn't matter?

No, my friends! Jesus was nailed to the cross, not the law. Jesus died, not the law. The reason that Paul can say that we are dead to the law and that the law no longer has effect is not that the law is null and void. It is the **consequences** of the law that are null and void. God has accepted the substitution of Jesus' sacrifice on our behalf so that we no longer are cursed by the requirements of the law. **That does not mean that the law is abolished. It means that the punishment I deserved under the law is abolished.** Now I am free *to obey the law*. Jesus says that He came to "fill up" the revelation of God in the law. He *fulfilled* the law by providing a complete revelation of its meaning, not by setting it aside.

Before you run out and join a synagogue, remember that all human beings are a product of time, culture and circumstances. So, some of those Levitical rules for living might not apply now that we have antibiotics and passports. But that does not mean *all* of the law is discarded. God revealed Himself to the Jewish people for a reason. We would do well to think long and hard about His choice. When God says "if you will not take heed" (*imlo tishmor*), He is serious. Dire consequences follow the thinking that God's directions for life don't count anymore. The phrase literally means, "not watch over, keep, guard or care for." Jesus set you free to be an *obedient slave* to the God of law and order. He didn't give you a pass to ignore God's character. He simply made it possible for you to stand before the throne and say, "Here am I, Lord. What would you have me do?"

Now don't get scared. No one can ever *earn* salvation. My obedience to the Law *never* earns my way to God's favor. That is not the purpose of the Law. But throwing away the Law because it could not save me is ridiculous. It is my guide to living after I have been restored to fellowship by grace. God never changed His mind about how we should live. Why should He? His word was perfect then; it is perfect now. Living according to the Law has a different purpose, as we shall see.

9.

*"Be **faithful** unto death, and I will give you the crown of life."* Revelation 2:10

Solid As A Rock

Faithful – What does it mean to be faithful? What do you think of when you hear these words? Do you think about a marriage vow or a promise to someone? Do you think about unwavering commitment or loyalty? If we look at the way John uses this word, we find some other imagery that helps us understand what faithfulness really is. Then we will know why Jesus can say, "Be faithful unto death."

John uses this word only one time in his gospel. When Jesus confronts Thomas' disbelief, Jesus invites Thomas to examine the nail prints and the scar from the spear. Jesus says, "Come and look, and as a result, *be believing*." That is the Greek word *pistos*. It is an adjective, not a verb, so our English translation sounds funny. We would like to say, "Come and believe," but that would make *pistos* a verb, and John doesn't use "believe" that way. When John talks about *believe*, he always uses the verb *pistis* (92 times). For John, belief is an action, not a set of statements. To be faithful is to *act* in a certain way.

How do I act when I am faithful? For that answer, we need to look at the Hebrew thought behind this Greek word. We arrive at Numbers 12:7, for example, where the Greek word *pistos* translates the Hebrew word *'aman*. This Hebrew word paints a very tangible picture. Its primary meaning is to provide stability and confidence. It is used to describe the foundation of a house, the support of pillars, a nurse holding a baby in her arms, a nail driven into a post. It is about things that can be relied upon; things that are solid as a rock. Suddenly faithfulness is no longer simply mental affirmation. It is no longer just about what I think. It is about the concrete actions of unshakeable trust. It is building on granite instead of sand. It is trusting that nurse not to drop the baby. It is knowing that the pillars will hold up the roof. To be faithful unto death is to be steady as a rock no matter what the storm may bring.

Faithfulness is not found in my signature at the bottom of a list of beliefs. Faithfulness is found in the behaviors that reflect those beliefs. Yes, I must know what I believe, but until my head knowledge is converted into real, tangible actions, it is not faithfulness.

The Old Testament uses *pistos* for another Hebrew word, *ne'um*, a word that means "an oracle or prophetic saying from God." You can find this in 2 Samuel 23:1. Why is this also *pistos*? Because it comes from God's mouth and it is totally and undeniably trustworthy. You can act on it. It is rock-solid truth. Accepting the oracle of God means more than simply acknowledging that God spoke it. It means hearing and *acting* on it. I cannot be faithful until I put it in practice.

God is a Rock. Imitating that rock-like quality is being faithful. So, polish the granite in your life. Sculpt the marble. Shine like a diamond. You were called to be a geological marvel.

10.

*who executes judgment for the **oppressed***   Psalm 146:7

The Mission of Jesus

Oppressed – How can we imagine that we understand what Jesus came to do if we do not know the Scriptures? And I don't mean the books from Matthew to Revelation. None of those New Testament passages make any sense unless they are surrounded by God's revelation to Israel – the Old Testament. Christianity does not begin with Matthew. And not a single author of the New Testament was very far removed from the God of Genesis to Malachi.

For example, look at Psalm 147:3-6. If you know Jesus' quotation in Luke 4, this should jump off the page. Did you think that Isaiah was the only one who announced that God's mission among men had a social context? Centuries before Isaiah, David told us that *God was at work in the world* bringing justice, healing, encouragement and protection. When Jesus quoted Isaiah, He simply connected His mission to the things God had been doing since the Fall of Man. Oh, and by the way, since every Jew in the synagogue knew this connection, what do you suppose they understood when Jesus made it? Only one thing could come to mind. Jesus just claimed to be God! (Go read the psalm again and see if that isn't obvious.) No wonder they were upset.

Now we get to ask the application question. If Jesus announces that His mission is the same in the first century as it was in the tenth century BC, do you supposed that it has somehow changed twenty centuries later? Do you think that just because the Father sent the Son to redeem us that we are no longer called to execute that mission? Is it now all just love and forgiveness without fighting for justice, feeding the hungry, opening the eyes of the blind, lifting the broken, and guarding the strangers and widows? Not a chance! When Jesus calls us to be like Him, He means that we are to take up the same mission. We are to be God's representatives in the fallen world – and that is accomplished by doing the same things God has been doing in the fallen world for a very long time.

We celebrate the birth of *Yeshua*, salvation among us. We put on holiday attire, give presents, overeat and entertain ourselves while we claim to be adherents of The Way. Most of our activities will reflect none of His mission. We won't recognize that Jesus' proclamation of His divinity was couched in *actions toward the oppressed of the world*. We will enjoy the Christmas plays and the choral music and never think that Jesus came to bring God's comfort to those in real need. We have long ago removed Christmas from any serious consideration of the *'ashuqim* (the Hebrew word for "the oppressed"). But Psalm 147 will not let us forget the "catalog of the wretched." They are the true recipients of Christmas joy. God came for them, not for the comfortably affluent and creditworthy middle class. The gift of Christmas is not found at Macy's or an on-line retailer. It is found in the midst of poverty; in the straw of temporary shelter; in displaced people; in birth without hospital sanitation; in fathers who cannot provide; in the tears of the outcasts.

Where will you spend your Christmas – at the mall or in the manger?

11.

*Yahweh loves **the righteous*** Psalm 146:8

Location, Location, Location

The Righteous – Where will you look for a righteous man? God tells us exactly where to find this most important role-model follower. Right between the bowed down and the strangers (verses 8 and 9); right in the midst of the hungry, the prisoners, the blind and the fatherless; right where injustice and discrimination seem to prevail; right where the wicked have their way.

What does this mean? It's really pretty obvious. The righteous man is just like them. He is found in the company of the sick, the hurt and the oppressed.

Let that arrow penetrate deeply into your heart. Let the Spirit of the living God cut into that carefully crafted confident portrayal to the world. Let God bring you to your knees in sorrow and sin-sick pride. When did we decide that the righteous were the ones driving a Mercedes or writing big checks for the mission fund? God's location is certainly *not* what we expected.

Gerstenberger points out that the inclusion of the *tsaddiyqim* in the midst of the catalog of the wretched is no accident. The righteous are themselves part of the exploited, the poor and the suffering. Why? Because God's grace comes to those who understand their own poverty and need. Why doesn't God lift them out of the mess? Because grace is a function of dependence. If God's grace is sufficient, it will not share space with a better investment portfolio. No wonder Jesus told us it was nearly impossible for the rich to enter heaven. The righteous are at home with the poor.

We must rethink the Bible. We have assumed that it is a book about being a follower in order to be successful. So, we underline the passages about God's blessings. We have forgotten that the Bible is for the broken. It is not a "Ten Steps To Success" bestseller. It is a guide for those who spill their blood for others because God's heart of compassion tears them apart. It is a story of weeping over the world. It is a glimpse of the greatest tragedy and the greatest rescue the world will ever know – at unimaginable cost. **It is a love letter for the undeserving.**

Can you ask forgiveness for your aggressive exploitation in pursuit of human achievement? Has the Spirit shown you the deepest pride in a heart that really wants recognition? Can you put your arms around a leper in Calcutta and *love* him?

God's righteous real estate is not easily purchased. It will cost you your life as you know it. But what good is a deed for property on Park Avenue if God is working in the slums of Mexico City?

12.

*"**Sanctify** them in truth; Thy word is truth."* John 17:17

Sandals

Sanctify – What is the first thing that comes to mind when you read this verse? Do you think that Jesus, in the prayer before the crucifixion, is asking the Father to keep His followers morally and ethically pure? Does sanctification for you mean sinless perfection – or at least an attempt to reach that goal? If we don't really understand what Jesus says, then we will be confused about the second part of this prayer. How is sanctification (whatever that means) directly connected to God's Word (the Old Testament Scriptures)?

Let's do some detective work. First, the Greek term here is *hagiason*, from the verb *hagiazo*. You can see the connection to the English word *holy*, and that is just what it means, "to make holy." In Greek, Jesus is asking the Father to make his disciples holy. But Jesus is not speaking Greek. So, when we look for the Hebrew equivalent, we find the word *qadash*. The root *qds* is used about 900 times in the Old Testament. Its principle meaning is to consecrate, to set apart, and, as a result, make holy. You can find a clear example in Exodus 20:8, where God makes the Sabbath day holy. There are some important nuances to this word that cannot be overlooked.

First, when this Hebrew verb is used *reflexively* (an action applied to the subject, like "He watched himself"), God is the only subject. Only God is holy in Himself. That means that whatever holiness is applied to any person, place or thing, it is *derived* holiness, not inherent holiness. It owes its condition to the only One who is truly holy.

Second, *qadash* does not imply moral or ethical conditions. The word is about consecration and separation, not about moral and ethical behaviors. So, places can be holy. So can utensils, garments and ox carts. More importantly, people can be made holy by being set apart to God, dedicated to God's purposes. This does not mean that they are holy because they have ethically pure lives. It means that they serve God alone. They are His possessions. How they express that consecration might involve ethical purity, but they are set apart for God before ethical considerations enter the picture. Therefore, God can require that the first- born be consecrated to Him before a child has made a single moral decision.

How does this help us see what Jesus asked the Father? It corrects our misunderstanding about moral purity. **Sanctification is not about becoming perfect. It is about becoming perfectly His.** It is about giving more and more of my life over to God for His possession. When Moses met God at the burning bush, he took off his sandals to show that he had no ownership of the ground he stood on. It belonged to God. That's what we must do – transfer ownership to Him, give up our claims and consecrate ourselves to His purposes. God is not asking for the perfect life. He is asking to set aside the life we have entirely for Him.

Qadash corrects our vision about perfection. I can't make myself holy, but I can give myself completely to Him. I can stop pretending that my life is mine to control and turn ownership over to God. Jesus prays that the Father will separate us – for His use. Now you and I get to assess the ownership issues in our lives and ask, "Have I taken off my shoes?"

13.

*"Sanctify them in **truth**; Thy word is truth."* John 17:17

Right Conduct

Truth – Pay close attention. Why does Jesus say, "Sanctify them *in* the truth" rather than "Sanctify them *with* the truth?" (By the way, the definite article *the* is in the text, but left out in English translations. You might want to ask why?) We wouldn't say what Jesus said. It doesn't sound quite right. But there is a very important reason why Jesus' words sound funny to our ears. Once we understand what He is really saying, He makes perfect sense.

One of the fundamental differences between the Greek worldview and the Hebrew worldview is the place of reason and the place of conduct. For the Greeks, reason was the supreme path to salvation.

"As I think, I am," would be a very Greek motto. The Greeks believed that correct *thinking* was the solution to life's problems. Therefore, the truth was found in correct thought, in understanding with my mind what the real problem and the real solution is. Greeks are thoroughly committed to intellectual analysis in pursuit of freedom.

But the Hebrew worldview takes a completely different approach. It is about correct *action*. From the Hebrew perspective, dependence on thinking alone is dangerous. The Bible cautions us not to lean on our own understanding. Why? Because men are not innately good. They are not prisoners held in corruptible bodies, waiting for illumination to free them. From a Hebrew perspective, men are riddled with sin and so is their thinking. **The truth is not discovered by thought. It is appropriated by action** – and that action must be in accordance with what God says is true. From the Hebrew perspective, I do not have to think my way out of the box. I have to obey God who has already told me the right actions to get out of the box.

Jesus is thoroughly Hebrew. He does not ask the Father to enlighten the minds of the disciples with correct thinking. He asks the Father to saturate them in correct action. He asks the Father to bring them to *obedience*, not apprehension. The only kind of truth that sets you free is the truth that you obey. So, this Greek word, *alethia*, needs to be understood in the Hebrew context of *'aman*. That means it is about faithfulness, not statements of faith. It is about reliability, not accuracy. It is about God's words backed up by God's actions, not my thoughts justified by my arguments. To be sanctified is to be trustworthy. To be sanctified *in truth* is to be completely obedient and dependent on what God says. Period.

We live in a Greek world. Only the thinnest icing of Judeo-Christian morality tops the thoroughly Greek cake of our civilization. Wherever human reasoning replaces God's revelation, the icing melts away to reveal a commitment to the glorification of the intellect. But thought without action is dead (does that sound like James?). Sanctification comes in only one flavor – take off your shoes and obey!

Do you want the truth? Notice that I did not say, "Do you want to *know* the truth?" I am not interested in what you *know*. I am interested in what you *do*. You either *do* the truth, or you are a liar. Which is it?

14.

*"Sanctify them in truth; **Thy word** is truth."* John 17:17

What Is Truth?

Thy Word – We reach the end of this amazing verse with the capstone of the Hebrew view of reality: the Word of God. From a Hebrew perspective, the goal of life is devotion and obedience to God. How can I know what to do unless God tells me what to do? I simply cannot *think* my way into correct action because all of my thought is tainted by my sin. I must depend on God's revelation of true and faithful behavior. Therefore, if I am to be set apart and consecrated to Him, I must obey all that He reveals. He is the only One Who sees that full picture. For me to rely on any other source for decisions that affect life or death is not only utter stupidity, it is outrageous arrogance.

Have we settled this? To *do* the truth, I must commit myself to God's direction. Now we can ask, "What did Jesus have in mind when He said, "Thy word?" Where would Jesus look to find the directions for correct action?   The answer is obvious. To Scripture - the 39 books of the Old Testament, the only Scripture that Jesus ever had.

Contemporary Christianity seems to think that the New Covenant begins in Matthew. Impossible! Jesus prays that we will be sanctified in the truth of obedience to Scripture – the Old Testament. The New Covenant really begins the moment God asks, "Who told you that you were naked?" Even before that terrible primal choice ushered in the need for crucifixion, God had prepared the New Covenant. It was not inevitable, but it was necessary.

Now, at this last moment, Jesus prays that the entire declaration of correct action revealed by God will so saturate his disciples that they will be truly separated and consecrated to God's purposes. And all that they need to know about what to do is found in only one place – Scripture. God's Word is *'emet*. It is totally reliable and trustworthy as the basis of my decisions. If I do what God says I should do, I can't go wrong.

Our Greek text uses the phrase *ho logos ho sos* (the word of you). This is equivalent to the Hebrew *devar ha emet* (you can see the phrase in Psalm 119:160). Once you see that Jesus is using the Hebrew word *'emet*, all kinds of changes in our thinking must occur, because *'emet* is not about *correct thinking* at all. It is about *correct relationship* seen in *right action*! The best general translation for *emet* is not "true facts," but rather "completely reliable." Jesus tells us that truth is very personal, always relational and about what is so solid that I can base my living decisions on it – it is simply the *faithfulness of the character of God*. Entire books could be written about this shift from accurate propositions to reliable behavior. Unless we see that Jesus is thoroughly Jewish here, we will miss the point about sanctification. Sanctification is about the *conduct* of a person, not the facts he believes. Sanctification is about placing my entire life in the hands of the only truly reliable person – the Holy One of Israel. And that means that I accept His word as the only measure of my actions, without deviation. What is at stake when it comes to the truth is the *character* of God. How I show that I rely on His character is demonstrated in my actions!

Be sanctified. Live according to the Book – all of it. It is God's character revealed.

15.

Blessed be the LORD, the God of Israel, from everlasting to everlasting.
Amen *and* **Amen***.* Psalm 41:13

Making It My Own

Amen – Did you know that "Amen" is a Hebrew word that has moved into our language *untranslated*? Every time you say, "Amen," you are speaking Hebrew. You are saying something in the language of the Scriptures that has an enormous meaning. But the chances are that you don't know what you are really saying. It's time to find out.

Amen is a form of the Hebrew root *'mn*, which is also the root for *'emet* (true, that is, reliable, trustworthy, permanent and secure), and *he'emin* (lasting, to prove faithful, to be constant), and *'emeth* (stability, reliability, faithfulness and truth). You can see right away that the context of all these thoughts center around the permanence and stability of the character of God. All of them are about *personal* actions that come from trustworthy character. Now you know what Jesus meant when He said, "I am the truth," not "I *know* the truth" or "I *have* the truth." Truth is not facts. It is personal engagement.

Amen is related to all of these thoughts. It is literally the personal endorsement of God's actions. It is like saying, "What God says, I accept and submit myself to." It is making God's will my will, like a shorthand way of saying, "Thy kingdom come on earth (in me) as it is in heaven."

Amen is a part of prayer, not because it is some magical formula or because it is a nice closing, but because it proclaims that I commit myself to God's will declared in the prayer. You cannot say, *Amen*, and simply walk away. *Amen* is your spiritual signature on the holy contract. It is your word that what you have prayed is what God wants – and what you must do to see it happen. *Amen* is saying, "This is the absolutely reliably truth for me! I stake my life on it!"

Amazingly, *amen* is not used very often in Old Testament Scripture; only 24 times. Twelve of those occur in Deuteronomy. That makes perfect sense when you know that the book of the Law (instructions) requires consent and submission. *Amen* to that! What is a bit more startling is the way that Jesus uses *amen*. You see, *amen* is normally found *after* a declaration of God's will, but Jesus says *amen before* IIe gives His teaching (see John 1:51. 5:19 and 6:26 for examples). Now what does that tell you? Who can possibly give an endorsement to God's will *before* God's will is revealed? Only God, of course, because only God knows what His will is *before* it is spoken to men. So, Jesus is not being just a good orthodox Jew. He is declaring His divinity whenever He begins a statement with *amen amen*. What a shame that our English translations often change these words to "truly, truly" or "verily, verily" or "I tell you truly." Such translations lose the real impact of Jesus' use of *amen* by converting it from the

Hebrew endorsement of God's uncontested will to some kind of emphasis on what is true.

So, now you know. Now you can use *amen* correctly. Say *amen* and sign on the dotted line.

16.

For a child will be born to us, a son will be given to us; and the government will rest on His shoulders; and His name will be called **Wonderful Counselor**, *Mighty God, Eternal Father, Prince of Peace.*
Isaiah 9:6

What's In A Name

Pele-yoez – So, you're looking at these words in bold and thinking, "What is that? What is *pele-yoez?*" The answer, of course, is that *Pele-yoez* is His *name*! We have read this verse in translation so long that we don't realize that Isaiah is telling us the *name* of the child, not the translated *meaning* of the child's name. The full name of this child is *Pele-yoez-el-gibbor-Abi-ad-sar-shalom*. That's right. His name is "wonderful counselor-mighty God-prince of peace."

What difference does it make if we have the translation of the meaning or if we have the name itself? Well, in the Hebrew world, it makes a tremendous difference. You see, naming is not just a random act of selection in the ancient world. To name something is to designate its true essence. So, when we read the name "Adam," we know that the root word *adamah* means that Adam is a man from the ground (the dust). That is his true essence – and in the end, that essence will prevail. Adam will return to his true essence – dust. Of course, Biblical names are generally like this. So, a name like Balaam (Numbers 22:5) is not just the name of a prophet who is to utter a curse against Israel. It is his essence – to swallow or devour the people. You will find these kinds of examples throughout the Old Testament.

Now, are you ready for a shock? "Jesus" is *not* the name of this child. This child has many names, as we can see from this verse in Isaiah, but Jesus is not one of them. You see, Jesus is a Greek derivation from a translated meaning of the Hebrew name. We end up with this word *Jesus* because the sound of the Y in Hebrew is phonetically a J sound in English. The real name of the child born to Miriam (Mary's *Hebrew* name) is *Yeshua*, which, of course, has a specific meaning that describes the essence of this person (by the way, this is *not* the same as Joshua, *Yehoshua* in Hebrew – "The Lord is salvation"). *Yeshua* means "salvation," not "the Lord is salvation." Why this change? Because this child **is** *salvation*. In other words, in the context and culture of ancient Israel, this child's very name expresses His divinity.

Isaiah gives us another name of this child; a name of divine titles that describe the character of the one born to us. The first title is *pele-yoez*. *Pele* means "a miracle, a marvel, a wonder." It is a word about the extraordinary, the astonishing and the tremendously significant. This word is always used in connection with God (except once in Lamentations). The second term, *yoez*, means not only to counsel and advise, but also to plan and execute. Both ideas are combined in the same root. The child that is born to us will be an astonishing and miraculous advisor who will also marvelously execute His plans. He will be someone totally unique, combining God's purposes with miraculous counsel. He will know God's perfect will and perfectly bring it to pass. His name is not two separate ideas, "wonderful" and "counselor." It is a single unity of miraculous plan and execution. That is what we celebrate today.

And that's only the *first part* of the name.

17.

*For a child will be born to us, a son will be given to us; and the government will rest on His shoulders; and His name will be called Wonderful Counselor, **Mighty God**, Eternal Father, Prince of Peace.* Isaiah 9:6

Warrior, Champion and Hero

Mighty God – Now we discover that this child is the champion of the universe, the supreme warrior of all creation. But how would you know that unless you knew His next title, *el-gibbor*? This part of the full name of the child combines the title of "God" (*el*) with the adjective *gibbor*. We translate it as "Mighty," but there is much more to this adjective. Some of it is hidden in the construction. Some is hidden in the usage. But, of course, it is only hidden from us, because we do not speak or read Hebrew.

Let's put this word under the magnifying glass and see what happens.

First, the root is *gbr* (the consonants that form this word). Did you notice that if we look at the consonants of *gibbor*, we see two *b*'s, not one. This is called "doubling the middle radical." It is a technique to add emphasis to the word. So, this is not just a mighty God; this is a *very mighty and particularly powerful* God. It's like having an exclamation point in the middle of the word! Second, we discover that most of the uses of *gibbor* surround military conquests and actions. *Gibbor* is a word for someone who carries out great deeds – a hero. Third, by looking at the other instances of *gibbor*, we find that only men who demonstrate prowess, strength and exceptional accomplishments are called *gibbor*. No women or children are ever included in this group, nor are ordinary men (but don't be upset if you are a woman. God has another heroic description for you – *'eshet hayil* - see Proverbs 31). Now you can see why this name is so startlingly unusual. This is a *child* who is *gibbor* from birth! He is *born to power*, something that marks Him as totally exceptional. Finally, this name recalls other names of God that incorporate *gibbor*. You will find some in Psalm 24:8 and Deuteronomy 10:17. These uses of *gibbor* tell us that this God is *terrible* in His power and might, shattering His enemies and causing dread and fear among those who oppose Him.

Part of the name of this baby, born among the livestock in a backwoods village, shouts out His true identity – THE ALL MIGHTY GOD FOR WHOM NOTHING IS IMPOSSIBLE! Yes, babies are cute. Yes, there is a certain softness to newborns. But never let the depiction of the manger scene rob you of what is really happening here. *El-gibbor* has arrived among men, and His presence will change everything. This is a birth for which there is no parallel. This is the creative power of the universe wrapped in hand-woven cloth, sleeping in Mary's arms.

If that doesn't make you fall on your face in worship, nothing ever will.

18.

*For a child will be born to us, a son will be given to us; and the government will rest on His shoulders; and His name will be called Wonderful Counselor, Mighty God, **Eternal Father**, Prince of Peace.* Isaiah 9:6

Irrevocable

Eternal Father – Did you think that Jesus was the first to call God *"Father"*? Were you taught that the God of the Old Testament was a stern, fearsome and unapproachable monarch? If you are under the impression that Jesus was the one who changed our view of God from Lawgiver to Sin Forgiver, then you never really understood the meaning of *abi-ad*. In the middle of this child's name the Hebrew word combination *abi-ad* signifies more than Eternal Father. It tells us about the character of God and about the Messiah who comes as the fulfillment of these qualities.

Abi-ad combines the word *ab* (father) with the word *ad* (perpetual, continuing, eternal). Often this second word (*ad*) is found in conjunction with *olam*, meaning "forever and ever" or "everlasting." Behind this designation is the theological idea of trust in the character and promises of God. *Ad* is the context for trusting God. I can trust Him *forever* because His promises are irrevocable.

Followers of the Messiah proclaim God's eternal promises. We put our hope in what God says will come to pass. We believe His word. But often the circumstances of life seem to deny God's claims. Often we are left with the question, "Why should I trust you, God?"

The name *abi-ad* gives us the answer to this important question. *Abi-ad* tells us *why* we can trust Him. In ancient Semitic cultures, the father's responsibility for the welfare of the family and all those who depended on him included provision, protection and promises like inheritance and destiny. God as Father insures that all of these requirements will be accomplished eternally. The *abi-ad* is more than a figurehead or a propagator. The *abi-ad* plays a crucial role in the continuation of the entire family line, and, of course, with God that line goes on forever. Of His kingdom there will be no end.

When Isaiah uses the term *abi-ad*, he is not employing a special, technical, theological term. He is using a word combination that anchors God's actions and promises in the center of family life – right where the Child is born. This Child, the one who is the *Abi-Ad*, comes to us in the most ordinary way. But He comes with the mantle of the Father Forever, with all the consummate responsibilities, obligations and abilities that belong to the Father of all Mankind.

This Child is the namesake and, consequently, the exact identity of the Father Forever. He secures the irrevocable promise of the Father by bringing that promise to its fully revealed existence.

Worship is the only appropriate response.

19.

*For a child will be born to us, a son will be given to us; and the government will rest on His shoulders; and His name will be called Wonderful Counselor, Mighty God, Eternal Father, **Prince of Peace**.* Isaiah 9:6

The Help Desk

Prince of Peace – The last title in Isaiah's name for the child is the most startling of them all. Today, we are so used to the "Prince of Peace" appellation for the Messiah that we no longer see how out-of-place this translation really is. We don't realize that the Hebrew word *sar* (in *sar-shalom*) is almost always a designation for a vassal king or a subordinate authority. Isaiah does not want us to make this mistake. In fact, this is the only place in all Scripture where the combination *sar-shalom* is used. That should tell us to be very careful about how we translate this title. It is not to be translated in the usual way. This child is *not* a subordinate or lesser official in the

Kingdom, as are all the rest of the *sarim* in the Old Testament. When Isaiah coins the title, *sar-shalom*, he is not thinking of *Yeshua* as a subordinate god. Isaiah is thinking of the further purpose of the Messiah, and that further purpose is not just about "peace" or about who has authority over peace.

How do we know that Isaiah doesn't think of *sar* in the typically Hebrew way? Because Isaiah has already given us two other titles that can only be ascribed to God Himself, *el-gibbor* and *abi-ad*. The same child who is "mighty God" and "eternal Father" is also *sar-shalom*. So, "prince" cannot be correct. Some other translation is required.

To determine what *sar* means, we must think about the word *shalom*. Of course, *shalom* does mean "peace," and the alliteration "Prince of Peace" has a pleasant sound. But "peace" is far too limited an understanding of *shalom*. *Shalom* is a word that really means well-being in all aspects of life; physically, emotionally, mentally and spiritually. When one Jew greeted another with the word "*Shalom*," it need not mean, "Have a nice day." It meant, "May all that you need for your well-being today come to you this day." That's *shalom*. This child is the official in charge of all *shalom*. This child is the "well-being authority." If you really want *shalom*, then you must come to him, for he is the one divinely ordained to give it.

Of course, this means that Yeshua grants peace with God. But that is not the limit of His authority. All that is necessary for men to find well-being is under His care. When Jesus said, "Without me, you can do nothing," He meant it. No effort toward well-being is accomplished without the expressed authority of Jesus, even if no one ever acknowledges His power over this effort. All that I need for a life well-lived is to be found in Him.

No, "Prince of peace" is not enough. His authority is much bigger than that. John tells us that His authority extends to all creation; that everything came into being through Him. This is no subordinate ruler. This is no prince. This is the King of glory, the absolute monarch of the ages, the *Alpha* and *Omega* of all that is. This child is

Pele-yoez-El-gibbor-Abi-ad-Sar-Shalom. Quake before Him! Kneel in submission!

And then remember this: Amazingly, He *loves* you. Now you can rejoice!

20.

Hear, *O Israel, the statutes and judgments which I am about to proclaim in your hearing today; and you will learn them and you will take care to do them.* Deuteronomy 5:1 (translation by Peter C. Craigie)

The Beginning

Hear – When it comes to God's order, everything begins with *shema.* "*Hear*, O Israel" carries the sense of listening attentively and obeying what you hear. God's order always starts with His word. He speaks. We obey. It's that simple. God doesn't make it difficult. But we certainly seem to.

If we understand that God knows what's best, and if we hear what God says about the organization and operation of life, then why don't we just do it? The answer can only be this: we don't trust what He says. Any other explanation is an indication of insanity. To know what is the best thing for me to do and then to do something else is an indication of mental collapse. That's why sin is ultimately inexplicable. Sin is the choice to do what I know is not in my best interest. It is irrational and suicidal. But we do it anyway, don't we?

So, the only real *reason* why I don't do what God tells me to do is that I don't trust His word. How utterly foolish that is! Do I think that I know better than God? Actually, I do. That's why I don't take His advice. In that moment of disobedience, I think that I really do know better than He does. I am not willing to listen and obey because I believe that I know what is right for me. When we sin, we deny God's sovereignty *and* His omniscience. We act as though He doesn't know and He isn't in charge. We suffer from a serious and dangerous mental defect. Maybe that's why Paul tells us to renew our minds. You can be human and live rationally by following God's statutes and ordinances, or you can become insane and follow your own heart.

There is one other *legitimate* explanation for our voluntary insanity. It could be that we have never heard what God says. We don't act according to His design for the universe because we don't know what it is. This is legitimate but inexcusable. Why? Because what God wants us to do is not hidden in secret code or mystery religion. It is *written in the Book*. Therefore, you and I are accountable even if we haven't read it because *we have access to God's word* on the subject even if we don't avail ourselves of the opportunity. Don't ask me about the poor child in Ethiopia who has never heard of Jesus. Ask me about the man or woman who carries a Bible, attends church, lives in a "Christian" nation but has no idea what God has to say about loans, education, family quarrels, business practices, law suits, government, holy days or sex. We make up the rules as we go along rather than listen and obey the rules God put in place centuries ago. It's time to change.

So, we begin at the beginning. Are you ready to listen, or would you rather be insane?

21.

*The Lord our God made a **covenant** with us in Horeb.* Deuteronomy 5:2

Contract Renewal

Covenant – God is a God of promises kept. That's why you can trust Him. He is not like men who give their word and then don't do it. When God speaks, He commits His character. He never lies and He never fails to fulfill. If we are going to hear and obey, we must first understand the absolute reliability of God. Since there are no human beings who have ever been completely and entirely faithful to us, we must take a step beyond our personal and corporate experience. We must look at the *past record of God* to determine His unwavering trustworthiness. That's why the Biblical record constantly reminds us that this is the God Who rescued Israel out of Egypt, the God Who parted the Red Sea and the Jordan, the God Who sent the prophets, judged Edom and controlled Babylon. You can't trust a person who does not present you with a history of faithful actions. You can *hope*, but you cannot have settled confidence. God knows this. So, He provides ample evidence of His constant stability. He is faithful.

That is the essence of the word *beriyth*. The basis of an agreement between God and Man is God's faithfulness and reliability, not ours. God promises *Himself* that He will fulfill His agreement to rescue His creation from its own insanity. We are the beneficiaries of His *beriyth*.

Every *beriyth* contains obligations. Perhaps you can appreciate the seriousness of such an agreement if you knew that the verb preceding *beriyth* is often *karath*, meaning "to *cut*." When I enter into an ancient Semitic covenant, I cut into my forearm, leaving a visible scar for all to see. I carry the mark of my agreement, demonstrating my obligation to another. God stipulates this same kind of symbolic reminder of His covenant, only He places the "cut" on the human instrument of propagation. God's mark establishes that He is the God of life. The covenant is *not* a license to do whatever we please. It is a standing order to obey what God says.

Notice that Moses tells the *present* generation that God made a covenant with them. These are not the same people who heard the voice of the Lord at Horeb (Sinai). Nevertheless, the same agreement pertains. It is a *permanent* agreement made by God but it requires constant *renewal* by the human partners. That's us! We are the children of Abraham. Consequently, we must renew our obligation under God's covenant. We have to *cut* the covenant into our hearts and minds if we are going to live under God's provision and protection.

Covenant agreements *demand* trust. Without trust in the reliability of the parties, nothing happens. So, do you trust Him? You can't submit without answering that question. You might comply until you have a chance to act independently but that isn't a covenant, is it? Renew the cut today! Renewal is not a feeling. It's a decision to act according to the obligations, no matter what. Cut deep. Let the scar show.

22.

*You shall have **no** other gods besides Me.* Deuteronomy 5:7

Absolute Fidelity

No – It's too bad that we can't read this verse in Hebrew. If we could, we would see that it begins with the most important word in the verse and that word is not *You*. It is the Hebrew word *lo*, which means "no." In other words, the verse really reads "Not shall you have other gods." The emphasis is on the power of the exclusion. This is demonstrated in two ways. The negative is first, in the place of priority, and the word used is *lo*, the Hebrew unconditional negative. There is another Hebrew word for "no" (*'al*), but it is expresses urgent, personal prohibition, not legislation. You can see it used in Proverbs 22:22 ff. Here the negative shouts out the Law!

So, the first word of the first command sets the tone for all the rest of the covenant. Nothing is to take the place of the Lord. No other thing - no relationship, no service, no worship, no suzerain - is to command more fidelity or more obedience. This God, the God Who brought you out, is to be the only, exclusive Master of your life.

But we already acknowledge this, don't we? We all claim that God is first in our lives. We can't imagine worshipping some idol or serving some other false god. At least that's what we say. But when it comes to critical examination of our loyalties, things look a bit different. The point of a covenant relationship is not the acknowledgment of the words but the fulfillment of the acts. God doesn't put a lot of stock in what I say. He looks at what I do.

So let's do a little fidelity self-check. Since God is my suzerain Lord, *all* that I have is His, right? That means that I gladly and without remorse make all my possessions available to His service whenever He asks. The first test of fidelity is this: Is there anything – any possession or relationship – that I am holding back from Him? The second test is similar. God is interested in obedience. He has given us the handbook for living that is pleasing to Him. Are there any requirements that I am dodging, ignoring or rationalizing? Am I making all of my life choices on the basis of His point of view? And just for fun, let's add this one: God is the Lord of time. Every moment belongs to Him. He graciously loans some to me but He is constantly on the look-out to see if I will *redeem* my loaned moments by inviting the presence of the divine into my temporal reality. Am I so conscious of His hand on my existence that every breath I take is a blessing to Him? Or do a take little vacations from God a minute at a time as the opportunity presents itself?

We could go through the usual money, sex and power items but most of us know only too well how we struggle with those. I suspect that the issues are deeper – that "*other gods*" is really an orientation away from the Lord's sovereignty over my life. Sure, money, power and sex trip me up, but I can be legally righteous and not practice the spirit of the covenant. God first is strikingly simple – and profoundly challenging. What comes first determines everything else in life. If you aren't aware of God's presence, maybe you'll need a priority examination.

23.

"What man is there among you who has a sheep, and if it falls into a **pit** *on the Sabbath, will he not take hold of it an lift it out?"* Matthew 12:11

Theology of the Ditch

Pit - Jesus gave us the proper perspective on theology when he asked the Pharisees about the fate of an animal that had fallen into a pit. The purpose of theology is not to explain *how* the animal fell into its pitiful state. The purpose of theology is to get the animal *out* of the condition it is in. As my good friends in AA will quickly remind us, "It doesn't matter how you got into the ditch. It only matters that you get out." Christianity is ditch theology. It is designed to rescue you from the pitiful state of a broken relationship with God. It is not designed to explain *how* you got into such a pitiful state. It simply assumes that you are already *in the ditch*. Now you need rescue!

Therefore, you won't find an explanation for the origin of evil in the Scriptures. Neither will you find a carefully worked-out rational for issues like the Trinity, the incarnation, the end of the world, election, predestination or a host of other theologically knotty problems. Of course, you will find *some* information about these things. After all, ditches exist. But the major themes of Scripture, and the place where the Word of God is most clearly effective, is not in these areas. It is rather in extracting us from misery. God's Word gets us out of the ditch. When you find yourself contemplating the nature of the ditch, the size of the ditch, the angle of its walls or the texture of the mud, you are probably in need of a therapist, not a theologian. The purpose of God's Word is rescue and restoration, not eloquent explanation of extraneous information. Maybe that's why theology is so difficult. It's like trying to decipher a mechanical blueprint for an automobile engine from a driver's manual. There's just not enough information available. If you want to understand the Biblical perspective, you must first realize that you need rescue. You need to get out of the ditch. But once you are out, you need a guidebook that will help you avoid stepping into the next ditch along the road. What is the point of being pulled from one pit only to fall into another? Once rescued, you and I need instructions for avoiding further catastrophes. We find precisely such directions in the Bible. Since God designed the universe, He is quite familiar with its layout. He willingly tells us how to navigate in this world. He explains the location of pitfalls and the procedures for dealing with them. It isn't always the way we would do it but God isn't the one who needs rescue, is He? The best course of action is to listen to the one who is *not* in the ditch.

Biblical instruction is ultimately practical application. There is no point in explaining the nature of rescue and the process of ditch-avoidance if you and I aren't going to put the advice into action. That's why so much of the Bible is filled with rules for living and stories about people who followed (or didn't follow) the rules. It's not legalism. It's simply avoiding ditches. Today is an excellent day not to end up in the mud. If your theology is any good at all, it will keep you high and dry. If it isn't, you probably need a bath before you visit the shrink.

24.

*You shall have no other gods **besides Me**.* Deuteronomy 5:7

The Ground of Morality

Besides Me – In Hebrew literature, this is the first *word* of the Ten Words; those saying that we commonly call The Ten Commandments or The Decalogue. The first *Word* is all about loyalty and exclusivity. This phrase in the first "word" is very difficult word to translate, even though the general meaning is quite clear. In Hebrew it is *al-panai*, a combination that could mean "beside me," or "above me," or "in preference to me." What is clear is this: God will not share His glory with *any rival* (see Isaiah 42:8), whether man or beast or inanimate object. Spoken to a congregation that had just come out of a culture where men, beasts and objects all represented gods, this was a powerful declaration.

If we break down the two combined Hebrew words, we discover that the preposition *al* is followed by the word for "face" (*paniym*). Hebrew is a tactile language, rooted in practical experience. When Hebrew uses words to describe intangible concepts, it often turns to the *visible* symptoms of the invisible. Thus, "before my face" describes the idea of presenting oneself in an audience with the King. To stand before the *face* of God is to account for one's attitude and actions in the presence of the Holy One of Israel. This commandment implies that God will determine where our true loyalty lies in a face-to-face examination.

What He finds is of utmost importance.

Perhaps our Greek-based intellectualization of God's person (omniscience, omnipotence, omnipresence, etc.) could use a little "in-your-face" correction. Imagine standing before the King, the Creator of all things, the One Who gives you your very breath. This is a fearful event since everything you are and everything you have is really a loan from the King. You exist only because of His grace. Now, while you are contemplating your essential dependence, God asks you about your loyalty. But, of course, He does not ask you what you *think* about it, or how you *feel* about it. He asks you what

55

you have *done* to demonstrate this absolute loyalty. He asks you to give an account of your actions. Do they exhibit fidelity to Him, or do they point toward obedience to His rivals?

All men have gods. It is the nature of men to serve some higher power, whether that be a person, a cause or a dream. In the final analysis, there are no atheists. There are only those who refuse to serve YHWH, the God Who brings you out. The first *Word* commands clarity of devotion. Any substitution in public or private worship violates this commitment and denies the essential worthiness of the character of God Himself. This is the basis of *all* morality, for either I live according to the character of God or I do not. Therefore, every one of my actions can be measured according to His character. When I have no other gods, there is nothing in my life that points away from His holy being. The question is this: where do your actions point? No wonder discipleship requires such exacting assessment of our lives.

25.

You shall not make for yourself an **image** Deuteronomy 5:8

The Idolatry of the Future

Image – It's all connected. Let me show you how. Idolatry is the substitution of devotion to something other than God. Keep that in mind as we look at a story from the life of Moses. In Exodus 33:23, God fulfills Moses' request to see His glory by passing before Moses and allowing Moses to see *et-achorai*, usually translated "back part." But when we examine the word, we find that it is derived from the same root (*achor*) that give rise to the word *acharyith*, the Hebrew word for the future. This is a crucial difference between Hebrew and Greek. For the Greeks, man faces his future, looking to complete his destiny as he captains his soul into the unknown. But for the Hebrews, we are like men in a rowboat. We face the past, not the future. The future is toward our backs, unknown and unknowable. But we have clear slight of the past. And we have to do is line up our lives with those markers of God's interactions in the past and keep rowing. When we are in alignment with the way God has worked in the past, we can be assured that our course is correct *even if we* *cannot see it.* The Hebrew word *achor* is about *direction*, not body parts. God does not show Moses His back. He actually shows Moses *the direction where He has been.* In other words, when God's glory passes by, Moses is allowed to see where God has already been. From the human perspective, God's glory is seen *after the fact.*

This is critically important, because we live in a Greek-oriented world where we are encouraged to look to the *future* for our security, meaning and significance. We live under the idolatry of evolution, thinking that the best is yet to come, that the world is headed toward advancement and that God has yet to finish His plan before His work is complete. We worship the future in every concern about tomorrow. The world pushes us to ask what we will *become*, what tomorrow will be like and where we are going. None of this is the direction that God wants us to incorporate into our being.

Moses sees God in the *past.* He sees where God has already been. In exactly the same way, God asks us to look at the past to see who we really are, who He is and worship Him on that basis. In the Hebrew world, God created everything good. It was not incomplete, waiting for some future date to be finished. It was done, finished and good at the beginning. If you want to see what being human is supposed to be like, you don't have to peer into the next century. You have to look back to Adam and the original creation. We started out perfect. We are not moving toward perfection. We are moving toward *redemption and restoration*, toward recovering what we once were. Social evolution suggests that the past has nothing of value because it has been eclipsed by today and tomorrow. We have bought the lie. We think that our real meaning lies ahead of us in time. But God wants us to get re-directed and see that who we are has been established in Creation and in the resurrection of Jesus. God has already given us our identity. The problem is that we are looking the wrong way.

Please notice that if your true identity lies in the future, it will depend on you. However, if you are who you are because God has already done His work in the past, then there is nothing for you to earn in the future to make you complete. Imagine how important this is the next time you ask a child, "What do you want to be when you grow up?"

You think that you are not an idol worshipper? Look again! Look at all those things in your life that point you toward a future fulfillment, a future significance, a future destiny. Ask yourself how many of your actions are dictated, dedicated and directed by future issues. Then read the *history* of Israel. Look where God has already been and recognize that who you are and what you are is settled in His past actions, not your future plans. Stop worshipping where the world insists you are going to be and start living according to the God Who has directed all that has come to be. Look to the past. That is the only clear directional finder you have.

When we cut ourselves off from the history of God's actions in the past, we are like men trying to walk with one leg. There is going to be a lot of falling and stumbling. Is that how you want to get through life?

26.

*You shall not **bow** yourself to them nor **serve** them, for I, Jehovah your God, am a jealous God* Deuteronomy 5:9

Idolatry in Action

Bow – Serve – Idolatry comes in two related flavors. The first is *shachah*, to bow down in submission or reverence or worship. Hollywood has exploited this flavor of idolatry with its scenes of pagan rituals. Of course, that external obeisance is only a small taste of the real heart commitment to another god. Isaiah 2:12-17 uses this same word to show us that all who are proud and arrogant are licking the *shachah* flavor – and they will all be judged because of this. You don't have to flop before a statue in order to retain pride and arrogance in your heart, do you? In fact, if we think about those actions and attitudes which elevate us above others or contribute to our disdain of others, we might just discover that the *shachah* tendency runs deeper than we thought.

But that isn't the end of the story. God tells us that there is another flavor mixed into this lethal brew. It is *avad*, a very important word in Hebrew thought. *Avad* is the umbrella word for labor. It includes both work and service, and in the context of this commandment, that means that work can also be seen as worship. When work is dedicated to the Lord's purposes, it becomes worship. When it is not dedicated to the Lord's purposes, *avad* is service to false gods. The commandment prohibits providing economic leverage to those idols that oppose God's plans. The attitude of arrogance and pride will find its expression in opposition to God, even if the false gods are telling you just how "good" the work is. Work and worship are intimately connected.

What does this mean for the daily grind? First, it implies that a follower of the Way sees all daily activity in a spiritual context. I don't go to work just to fill my time so that I can get money to fill my desires. If I am a follower of the Way, work is the place God puts me to experience His engineering of my life. I come with contentment because I know that He orders my day. I serve with gladness because I am where He wants me to be, whether at the register in Target or at the gas pump or at the boardroom table. If I am not there because God wants me there, then my *avad* probably serves another god.

The same can be said for my purposes. No matter where God places me, I still serve (work for) Him. Isn't this exactly what Paul suggested? If I find that what occupies my effort is directed toward desires that are not in line with the will of the Father, then my *avad* is passive rebellion, denying God's authority and ownership of all my endeavors.

David said that all the earth will worship (fall down and serve) the Lord. If the sun, moon and stars sing His praises, and if every hill and valley, ocean and stream shout out the magnificence of the Holy One of Israel, can we do any less and claim that we are obedient to this second commandment?

Today, you may walk humbly before your God. You may serve Him with contentment and joy. Or, you can look to other gods in your *attitude and actions*. It's really up to you, isn't it?

27.

and you shall love the LORD your God with all your heart and with all your soul and with all your **strength**. Deuteronomy 6:5

Circular Reasoning

Strength – Most Christians think that this verse is about *parts* of my spiritual anatomy. So, we refer to the quotation of this verse in Matthew 22:37 or Mark 12:30 or Luke 10:27 and we end up with my heart, my soul and my mind (or something like that). That's a real stretch, especially when this Hebrew word (*me'od*) isn't even a noun. It's used 300 times in Scripture, and almost always as an adverb, something that *modifies an action*, not a thing. Most of the time it means "exceeding" or "great" or "much", like the way it is used in Genesis 1:31 or Exodus 1:7 ("exceedingly good"). Literally, we might translate this commandment like "love the Lord your God with all your heart and soul and exceeding-ness." Of course, that contorts the language so badly we can't stand it. Rabbinic scholars opt for "with all your resources," but that's just another noun in place of a modifier. What are we supposed to do?

You might say, "So what? I get the idea. Isn't that good enough?" You might be right, but what if God has something really important in mind here and we miss it, just because it is difficult to grasp? Jesus quoted this as the *greatest commandment*. That should be motivation enough to dig deeper. Fortunately, someone already did the digging for us.

McBride suggests that this commandment is not about parts of my body at all. It is rather about concentric circles of interest, like a bull's eye target. The deepest, inside circle is the "heart." The Hebrew is *lev*, the seat of my will, emotion and intellect – in other words, my entire personality. The next circle is "soul", how we commonly translate the Hebrew *nephesh*. This is not the "soul" in opposition to the body. That idea is Greek. *Nephesh* is the full embodiment of the person, the whole self, the unity of flesh and blood that I call "me." Then there is one more circle – the *me'od*. That circle covers all that I influence, all that I have stewardship over in the world. In other words, all that my person and my body affects – the *extension* of who I am in the world.

Seen this way, the commandment is totally encompassing. It is not just about the parts of me. It is about me in relationship to myself, my presence in this world and my effect on the world. The commandment is the call to let God be the Lord of *all* that I am, embodied here and now, in community and interaction with what is.

Do you suppose that Jesus made a little play on words (in Hebrew) when He said that this is the *greatest* commandment? It is the *me'od* commandment about *me'od*.

Now you will have to go back to Matthew, Mark and Luke and re-write those verses. You might even have to ask forgiveness for restricting God's sovereignty to some Greek idea of body parts.

28.

*You shall eat of it **in sorrow** all the days of your life* Genesis 3:17

The Midas Touch

In Sorrow – Why do I need to live according to God's commandments? Why can't I determine my own rules for living? It's my life. What's the matter with the "do what I want as long as it doesn't hurt anyone" philosophy? I'm smart. I'm creative. Why can't I adapt to the way things are and do what's best for me?

How many times have you heard some version of this argument? It's played out in movies, novels and politics. Do you know how to answer without getting moralistic? Do you know the real reason why God gives the commandments? It's all wrapped up in the Hebrew word *atsav*, the word for "sorrow."

The reason why all human beings need to adopt God's point of view is not to be "saved." Salvation is not about moral living. Salvation is God's option, not ours. The reason why all human beings need to

61

align themselves with God's point of view is because this world is a mess. It has fallen from a state of grace into a state of sorrow. And there's nothing any human being can do about it.

The world teaches a big, fat lie. It tells you that life can be controlled, that things will get better and that you can be the master of your own destiny - *carpe diem* and all that (along with the *secrets* of success). But reality bites! The Bible is the ultimate book for a realistic approach to life. It doesn't pull punches and it doesn't sugar coat the truth. Life is filled to the brim with *atsav*. No matter how hard you try, you can never get everything working just right at the same time (and don't deny it). God knows the world is a mess. That's why we need Him so desperately.

None of the original mission objectives for human beings has changed. The image of God resident in men and women hasn't changed. But now everything is subject to distress, destruction and destitution. Everything that we do, everything that we are is touched by sorrow. We don't turn everything to gold like King Midas. We turn everything to rot like the Second Law of Thermodynamics. Just think about it. Man's struggle outside the garden is to use his talents, skills and creativity to overcome sorrow. But he never succeeds. Oh, sometimes we can *delay* the effects of sorrow. We can employ technology, medicine, economics, psychology and hedge funds. But these are only delay tactics. Sorrow always wins. Jesus told the absolute, unmitigated truth when He said, "In this world, you will have trouble." "Life is difficult," starts a well-known book. The Bible starts with the *answer* to the problem - "In the beginning, God." Imagine what life would be like if God did *not* give us commandments. We would spend our years trying to figure out how to get the universe to cooperate. And then a hurricane comes along. No, God is filled with grace. He actually tells us, in words we can understand, what to do – and what He tells us isn't too difficult either. God knows that sorrow is the constant companion of life on earth, so He volunteers to share that sorrow with us, and tell us what to do about it. Now, if we would only listen!

29.

*Now therefore, O kings, show **discernment**; take **warning**, O judges of the earth.* Psalm 2:10

The Shift

Discernment / Warning – The first rule of proper interpretation of Scripture is the rule of historical context. If I don't know what the words would have meant to the audience that first heard them, then I don't know what they can possibly mean to me. That means that I must do all that I can to understand the words within the context of their historical setting. I simply cannot apply my post-modern Christianity to the text and declare its contemporary meaning as though it were written yesterday.

This might seem obvious to you. After all, in this psalm, the historical context is from 1000 BC. The first place I need to look to determine what the psalmist is saying is to the language and culture of 3000 years ago in Israel. What you might not realize is that the very choice of words in translation often subtly affects how we understand the meaning. Unless we work hard at gaining a Hebrew, 9th Century BC perspective, we will miss the whole point.

Hebrew is a language that is rooted in *active obedience*, not mental assent. Greek, and the Greek-based culture we live in, focuses on rational and mental control of the world. We are taught to understand the "facts" and draw rational conclusions as the basis of decision-making. We believe we can *think* our way out of the problem. But not the Hebrew. The Hebrew looks first to action and obedience, not to rational explanation. Why? Because the Hebrew knows that man is frail and finite. No man sees the big picture well enough to know how to solve the problems of life. What man can do is listen to God and obey Him. The orientation is radically different. Rather than rely on my mind, I must rely on God's word, even if I don't always understand what God is doing.

Now, when we translate the Hebrew words *sakhal* (show discernment) and *yasar* (take warning), we must be sure that we remain *Hebrew* and not slip into *Greek* meanings for these words.

63

That's why the King James translation, "be wise" and "be instructed" is hopelessly inadequate. The King James implies that the words are about *information and rational understanding*. The translation is Greek even though the words are Hebrew. The New American Standard is better, but still misses some of the impact. Yes, *sakhal* is about discernment, but the basic idea is to *act in such a way so as to avoid evil consequences*. This is not primarily a mental choice, the way we think of discerning the right solution. It is about my *behavior*, not my reasoning. The case with *yasar* is even more misdirected. *Yasar* is a verb about punishment for the purposes of correction, discipline and chastening. Of course it covers warning. But warning is verbal and rational. Punishment is tangible and emotional. We must move from the cerebral to the physical if we want to appreciate this psalm written in the 9th Century BC. "Now, therefore, O kings, be prudent in your actions; discipline and punish, O judges of the earth." Why? Because you are to serve the Lord with fear and trembling (the very next verse).

If you want to read the Bible for all its worth, ask the Lord to remove the post-modern blueprints in your mind, the patterns of this age. That's what Paul meant in Romans 12. It's time to seriously re-consider *how* you read.

30.

*You shall not **add** to the word which I am commanding you, nor **take away** from it, that you may keep the commandments of the LORD your God which I command you.* Deuteronomy 4:2

Basic Arithmetic

Add / Take Away – Do you think that God is serious when He says we are not to add or subtract anything from His commandments? The Hebrew verb for "add" is *yasaf*. It is used to describe increasing, repeating, continuing and enhancing actions. So, Israel's sins are piled one on another and her guilt is *increased*. The Lord *added* sons to Jacob and Rachel. Solomon *increased* the tax burden on the people. It's pretty easy to understand the meaning of *yasaf*. Since that's the case, I wonder why we don't seem to pay any attention to it.

Do we add to God's commandments? Well, we might start by asking if we increase or enhance the requirements. For example, a society that expects and awards massive punitive damages certainly adds to God's civil justice. We do the same thing in the church, adding tradition to church governance and requirements. That pushes us in the direction of legalism. Just think about all the behavioral rules that govern your life. How many of them are really grounded in Scripture? How many of them are extensions or additions? Does God command you to go to church every Sunday? Does He obligate you to give the tithe to the local church? Does He compel you to wear specific clothing, speak with particular phrases or use certain prayers? Does He regulate your social contacts or your choice of career? We really need to know; but my guess is that most of us have never looked closely to see what God says and what He doesn't say.

On the other hand, God is just as concerned about taking away from His word. Here the Hebrew is *gara*, a verb that means "to diminish, to reduce, to remove and to cut short." We're much better at subtraction than addition. That's because reducing and diminishing God's word doesn't require so much investigation. All we have to do is do what we want. For example, God commands us to honor the Sabbath and keep it holy. Hard to get around that, isn't it? Pretty black and white. When did we decide as Christians that God really didn't mean what He says? Do you suppose that happened when it became *inconvenient*? After all, do we really think God actually cares what we do *after church* on Sunday? If we don't understand what God means, subtraction is pretty easy. Of course, the great Christian excuse is this: these laws were only for Jews. We have so saturated our theology with grace and forgiveness that it has become the perfect excuse to do whatever seems morally correct. So, in spite of the fact that God says the Feast of Unleavened Bread is to be kept forever, most Christians have never participated in such a feast, nor even imagine they ever will. There's something wrong here. **God is not interested in moral correctness. He is interested in obedience.**

Living according to God's Word is dangerous. It's dangerous because it demands a razor-sharp understanding of God's freedom in the midst of human structure. God is neither legalistic nor antinomian. Rules do not make a relationship with Him. Neither does the denial of rules. You and I have to walk on the edge of the blade if we are going to serve our Master *according to His desires*. If you're not sure about adding or subtracting, maybe you need to get back to first grade and start over. **It's not what's "right" that matters. It's what He desires.**

31.

Rise Lord! **Rescue me**, *my God* Psalm 3:7 (translation: Robert Alter)

Salvation!

Rescue Me – "*ho.shi e.ni*." Say it again, out loud! This one is worth remembering. The Hebrew root is *yasha*, "to bring help to those in trouble." The pronoun "me" is attached directly to the verb. That's what I want – direct connection to my helper. Save *me*!

Why is this word worth remembering? Not only because it is the cry of every man and woman who suddenly faces the reality of the broken world. Not only because it admits our own insufficiency. The word is worth remembering in Hebrew because it is the basis of the name of the Savior. Yes, *Yeshua* (the name of our Lord in His native tongue) is derived from the same root, *yasha*. When I call out to God for help, He answers me with the name of His Son. If we translated it into English, we would stop saying "Jesus." "Jesus" is the substituted phonetic transliteration from Hebrew to Greek to English. Since neither Hebrew or Greek has a "J" sound, we substituted that phoneme from Germanic roots. But the meaning of His name is "Salvation!" When I call out for help, I use the name of the Helper. "Salvation, come save me!"

Life needs a lot of rescuing. The broken world just doesn't work. How could it? Sin has infected every part of our earthly existence. That's why Paul tells us not to be conformed to the blueprints of this world. We need rescue from a world that is insanely headed to destruction. But here lies an important distinction. *Hoshi eni* does not mean escape out of trouble. It means help *in the midst of* trouble. In our case, rescue doesn't mean getting out. It means being empowered to act as redemptive agents in the mess sin left behind. Of course, that means constantly coming into contact with the infection – without hazmat suits. Salvation comes to my aid, giving me hope, help and heart to accomplish His will through my hands, right here, in the middle of trouble. This is important. In spite of the wonderful music, there is a real mistake in the idea that "this world is not my home; I'm just a' passin' through." If you understand the concept of Hebrew *yasha*, you would never be fooled into thinking it only means getting to heaven. The Hebrew worldview is about here – on the earth where my Father's will is to be done just as it is in the heavenly realm.

This is hard to take. So much of our contemporary theological dreamware is about escape. We long for heaven. We fix our eyes on the other world. We want out! How many times have you thought, "Lord, I get it. I accept you. Why can't I just leave here now?" That's not part of the Hebrew mindset. *Yasha* is a word for *this* world, not the next. Salvation is not about heaven. It's about help. How can God accomplish His purposes for the restoration of your true humanity and the redemption of His creation if all we want to do is find the escape hatch?

What are you looking for – heaven, or help?

32.

*The one who says he abides in Him ought himself to walk **in the same manner** as He walked.* 1 John 2:6

The World According to Jesus

In The Same Manner – Here's an interesting phrase: *kathos ekeinos.* Literally, it means "according to the same." It comes *before* the verb "walk" in the Greek text. This places the emphasis on the duplication of the way Jesus conducted Himself. Of course, you have probably heard this exhortation dozens of times. But have you ever stopped to ask yourself what it means?

The typical answer to the question, "What would Jesus do?" is based on some moral or ethical presupposition that fits our contemporary religious persuasion. In other words, we are not likely to actually *do* what Jesus did. We are likely to interpret what Jesus did through our own religious filters and then develop a *principle* of action. So, we say that Jesus acted with *agape* love and we apply that principle to our own circumstances. But what if John has something else in mind – something far more pragmatic and definitive? What if John is not pointing us toward ethical principles but rather toward specific, obedient actions?

John is a Jew. By the way, so is Jesus. That means that the word "walk" has a very special significance in the thinking of both John and Jesus. To "walk" is to form a habitual pattern of actions that determine *and describe* someone's life. To walk in God's way, the goal of every observant Jew, is to form a habitual pattern based on the Torah. It is to do, over and over and over, precisely what the Torah prescribes in every circumstance of life so that eventually my reaction and my character are determined and described as godly. Here's the catch. From a Jewish perspective, it isn't possible for me to derive a general principle of life that will guide me to this conclusion. I am intrinsically and fundamentally confused and belligerent. The only hope I have of walking in this way is to conform my life to God's *revealed* truth, not to my own conclusions about God's truth. This is precisely what Jesus did. He conformed His life, in every respect, to Torah. He walked in God's way.

Not surprisingly, John recommends that we do the same thing. Does that mean that we have to be puzzled about what Jesus would do in any given circumstance? Does it mean that we need instruction books on contemporary Christian ethics? No! What we need is to bring our lives into compliance with the same set of walking instructions that Jesus used – the Torah! If we are going to walk *kathos ekeinos*, in the same manner as Jesus, then we will be as Torah-observant as He was. How could it be any other way? Jesus did not sin. That means He must have been *perfectly* Torah-observant, right? And if John tells us that we should walk according to the same way as Jesus, how is it that we generally *ignore* most of what He did to remain sinless? John wrote this verse decades *after* Jesus' ascension. Does John imply anywhere that it is no longer necessary to walk like Jesus in observance of Torah? I don't think so!

33.

*Beloved, I am not writing a new commandment to you, but an **old** commandment which you have had from the beginning;* 1 John 2:7

How Old?

Old – Just how old is John's "old commandment"? Does John start counting with the teaching of Jesus, or does his reckoning begin earlier than that? Does John think that Jesus' commandment, "Love one another," is the beginning of a new way of living, or does John see a much longer history?

If you listen to most Christians today, you would surmise that John's "old commandment" was introduced about sixty years before he wrote this sentence. Most Christians seem to think that Jesus introduced *new* material and that we are now to live according to this new information. But John uses a Greek word, *palaios*, that means "long standing," not "antiquated." What would we think if we realized that everything Jesus taught started in Genesis, not Matthew? Then the "old commandment" takes on a different look, doesn't it?

Consider this: If Jesus is God, then the message that He brings while He is in human form is going to be consistent with the same message He provided before the incarnation. How could it be any different? God does not change His mind about the means of redemption, does He? He does not alter His will about how the righteous shall live, does He? So, Jesus' teaching must be in alignment with the will of the Father *from the beginning*. After all, don't even the *New* Testament writers tell us that the Messiah was slain *before* the foundations of the world? That means that Jesus is providing *corrective commentary* on the proper understanding of God's will. In other words, God in human form is clarifying and demonstrating what God as spirit has always taught. If Jesus is God, then there is no better person to tell us exactly what the Father meant.

Of course, when we really look at the teaching of Jesus, we discover that it all comes from the Old Testament. How could it be any other way? Jesus is Jewish. His sacred Scriptures are the scriptures of the

Hebrew Bible. His culture, religious experience and thought forms are Hebrew. Jesus is *the* Old Testament man. That means that if we want to understand the *old* commandments, we need to pay close attention to what Jesus says about them. That's the equivalent of reading God's commentary on God's word. When John says that he is not writing a new commandment, he excludes any human addition to God's will. No man can add to the work or word of God. Instead, John wants us to look back – way back – to the will of God found in the commandments we have had *from the beginning*. So, my friends, it's back to Genesis. If you want to know what Jesus said, and why He said it, you will have to start at the beginning.

How *old* is the commandment that you follow?

34.

*"The world **is not able** to hate you; but it hates Me because I witness about it, that its works are evil."* John 7:7

Can't We Just Get Along

Is Not Able – Did you really read these words? If you go too fast, you might think that Jesus says, "The world *does not* hate you." But that isn't His point. The Greek expression is *ou dunatai*, from the verb *dunamai*. Every word that is derived from this stem has the sense of power or capacity or ability. It isn't that the world doesn't hate its own as a matter of happenstance. It is that the world lacks the power or ability to hate its own. It has no strength to discern what isn't right about evil. It's like trying to see the shape of the dark in the dark. The world is *blind* to its own condition.

It's no use in trying to show those who are part of the systems of this world where they are mistaken. They don't have the capacity to see it. It's no use trying to negotiate with evil in order to get some perspective. There is no power to make a difference. Nothing in the world's systems provides any differentiation that allows someone to rise out of the mire. When it comes to rescue, the world is utterly powerless. If you adopt the systems of the world as your measuring stick, you won't be able to tell the difference between night and day.

Sometimes we treat Jesus' radical claims with perilous indifference. This is usually one of those times. We think that we can operate in *both realms*. We think we can conduct our typical affairs within the systems of the world. After all, the world has a vibrant economy, a political structure, a kind of morality and a social fabric. Those things work, don't they? We make money. We govern. We have high standards. We love our friends. What's wrong with all that? Why can't we just get along – and still worship the King on Sunday?

Living in the dark might feel very comfortable. After all, living in the dark has a kind of security to it. No one can see you and you can't see anyone else. That's the essence of tolerance. Just leave me alone in the dark. That way I can do whatever I really want to do and no one will see me – until someone comes along with a light. If I like living in the dark, I will hate the one with the light. But I will be perfectly content to have everyone else live in the dark along with me – just as long as I can't see them. We can all just get along quite nicely that way.

A disciple of Yeshua brings light to the dark. That is grounds for instant hatred. That's not getting along. That's not tolerance. That's exposure and confrontation and embarrassment and humiliation. The light shows everyone who I really am, and that is simply unacceptable in a dark world.

Jesus makes it very clear that the world will not tolerate Him. So, what does that say about us? Does the world tolerate you or me? Do we bring light – and feel the pain of rejection and animosity? Or do we just try to get along, keeping one foot in the dark?

35.

The Lord made garments of skin for Adam and his wife, and **clothed** *them.* Genesis 3:21

Second Skin

Clothed – The first principle of atonement occurs immediately after the first sin. That principle never changes. It is this: the innocent die for the guilty. When Adam and Eve sinned, they lost something irretrievable. They lost the original covering provided to them by God. They lost the covering of transparency in relationships. Once they were naked and unashamed. Now they were exposed and needed covering. But this catastrophic shift is not about covering genitals. It's about vulnerability. Now they have something to hide.

There's a lot to learn in this short verse. First, we see that the covering that Adam and Eve attempt to make for themselves is totally inadequate. Human effort to cover up broken relationships and vulnerability is as useless as leaves tied together. What men and women do to hide themselves is hopelessly inadequate. The truth of their nakedness can't be concealed.

Second, we see that God's action is the only adequate solution. If God doesn't cover our brokenness, we will remain naked and ashamed despite our efforts. God has to dress us with a covering that only He can supply.

Finally, we discover the horrible truth of sin. God had to slaughter and skin an innocent animal in order to cover the guilty. The Hebrew verb, *labash* (to dress, to put on clothing), clearly means that God fashioned garments for sinful Adam and Eve at the expense of taking the life of an animal. This is the first killing, initiated by God for the sake of guilty humanity. This is the first experience of death, the first witness of bloodshed, the first smell of extinction. Now Adam and Eve *wear* a reminder of the loss of glorious transparency. Their second skin comes at the price of taking life away from the innocent. **In God's divine economy, the innocent pay for the guilty.**

Today, believers wear second skin. Of course, we don't wear animal hides these days but we are all either covered by the death of the Innocent Christ, or we walk naked in the world. We are either dressed by God, or we are exposed and broken. There is no hope of making our own clothes just as there was no concealing Adam's sin with leaves. If we have not been clothed in the evidence of an innocent death, we are naked and ashamed.

Just one more thing. Did you realize that Adam didn't think of killing an animal for clothing? Adam's solution did not involve the sacrifice of another. Only God's provision required the death of the innocent.

Believers are called to follow the principles that God has written into the moral government of the universe. This is the first one with costly significance. *The innocent pay for the guilty*. How have you made that a reality in your life?

36.

"Behold, days are coming," declares the LORD, "when I will make a **new** *covenant with the house of Israel and the house of Judah."* Jeremiah 31:31

Change of Venue

New – You and I are part of the family of Israel and Judah. We are part of the family by *adoption* (unless you are Jewish, of course). We have been grafted in. That means that this promise in Jeremiah is also ours. The announcement of the new covenant applies to us. The only question left is this: what is this new covenant?

The answer is not as difficult as it might seem. God actually describes the effects of this new covenant. Of course, if we don't pay attention to the words that He uses, we won't understand what it really entails. Let's start at the beginning (always a good place to start). Then we can discover what it means to say that this is a *new* covenant.

The Hebrew word is *hadash*. It is certainly the same word that Jesus used when He spoke about the new covenant in His blood. It's a crucial word. When we look at other instances of this word, we discover something startling. The word *hadash* is most often connected with the idea of the *new* moon. In fact, in example after example, the word *hadash* is not about something absolutely new but rather about something *renewed*. It's the moon seen again after a period of darkness. It's used to describe the psalms of *renewal* and the new song to the Lord (Isaiah 42:10). It's even used to describe the *rebuilding* of ancient ruins (Isaiah 61:4). The conclusion is inevitable. The *new* covenant is not a change in the content of the covenant itself. It is a *renewal* of the covenant by placing the old covenant in a new venue. The original covenant, the same one given to Moses, is renewed because it is moved from tablets of stone to inscription on the heart. In other words, God is going to move the covenant from an external declaration of right living to an internal orientation toward right living. Obedience will become a matter of the heart.

Isn't this exactly what Jesus said? Religion is not a matter of outward compliance. It is a matter of inner submission. It is attitude that generates action, not simply living according to an external set of rules. Jesus shows us what this new covenant will be like. It will be like total submission to the will of the Father. It will be loving God with all your heart, mind and strength. When Jesus says that He is the new covenant, He points us toward His relationship with the Father as the paradigm case of *renewed* relationship.

But – there's always one of these, isn't there – this *renewed* covenant does *not* put away the content of the original. The moon is not recreated each month. It's only seen again in a fresh way. The covenant instructions, the right way to live before God, are exactly the same. The only thing that changes is *where* these instructions reside. Once they were written on stone. Now they will be written on the heart. Once they were external prescriptions. Now they will be internal desires. Under the new covenant, men and women will live according to God's instructions *because they desire to*.

There's a lot more to say here. Hold onto your hat!

37.

and that from **childhood** *you have known the sacred writings which are able to give you the wisdom that leads to salvation through faith which is in Christ Jesus.* 2 Timothy 3:15

Training Days

Childhood – The next verse is the famous one. "All Scripture is inspired by God." Of course, lifted from the context, the statement about inspiration is reshaped to fit contemporary theology. That's why we need this verse first. Before we get to the doctrine of inspiration, we need to have the context of life-long training. When Paul says that Timothy already has a long history with the sacred texts, there is only one book that fits the bill – the Hebrew Bible – the Old Testament. What Paul says about those sacred writings should cause us to take a serious step backwards.

The first thing that we acknowledge is that Timothy never knew the writings of Matthew, Mark, Luke or all the rest of the New Testament authors *from childhood*. Since those documents didn't exist, it's simply impossible that Paul has them in mind. What Timothy knew was the Tenakah, the collection of the books that make up the Hebrew Bible. Paul's use of the Greek word, *brephous* (a newborn), makes this pretty obvious, doesn't it?

Then we come to the second "obvious" conclusion. Paul says that Timothy's exposure to the Hebrew Bible is able to give him the wisdom he needs to lead him to salvation *through faith*! What? I thought that the Hebrew Bible was a religion of works' righteousness. Didn't the Jews attempt to appease God with works? The Old Testament is based on rules. Only the New Testament presents the "salvation by faith" message. Right?

Apparently the answer is "No." Paul himself, the author of those great letters about salvation by faith alone, says right here that the Hebrew Bible teaches salvation by faith, not works. Of course, that doesn't mean that men and women won't misunderstand and distort the teaching. That same kind of misunderstanding and distortion can happen today – and it does with any form of legalism, even if the words are about membership and tithing instead of about sacrifice and temple worship. What Paul makes absolutely clear is this: the real basis of salvation has *never* changed. God's plan is the same, from Abraham to John. When Jesus expounded the Scriptures to the men on the road to Emmaus, He demonstrated that the Old Testament was a "faith only" document. That's exactly what Paul says here.

This verse, coming before the famous one, is too often neglected. But what it says is crucial. It says that the Tenakah is sacred, inspired and absolutely consistent with salvation by grace alone. That means, among other things, that the entire sacrificial system *cannot be about salvation*. The sacrificial system is about something else. The sacrifices do not save. They never did and they never will. Whatever is going on with the sacrifices, it isn't about salvation.

So, this verse should cause us to ask a very penetrating question. If the sacrificial system isn't about salvation, then what is it about? And if it's about some other aspect of my relationship with God, then why don't I follow it today?

Training days. Oh, how they disturb our nice, tight assumptions.

38.

"until heaven and earth pass away, not the smallest letter or stroke shall pass away from the Law until all is **accomplished***."* Matthew 5:18

The Beginning of the End (1)

Accomplished – When is it all accomplished? If you're like most contemporary Christians, you think that it was all accomplished when Jesus died on the cross. In fact, many English translations of Jesus' final words ("It is accomplished.") certainly could lead you to that conclusion. What the translators don't tell you is that the word here is not the same Greek word used in Jesus' last statement – and the difference is very important. The word used here is *ginomai*, usually translated as "become" or "come." You will find it in John 1:6 in the phrase, "There *came* a man, sent from God, whose name was John." The word means "to come into being, to become," not "to finish or end."

So, let's ask the question with the right verb. When will it all come to be? When will it all become reality? Now we see that Jesus' statement on the cross cannot be about the end. Everything in the law did not pass away when Jesus died, did it? We still live by the Ten Commandments, don't we? We haven't thrown them out. We still struggle to uphold the law of love, don't we? We still follow the instructions of Paul and James and Jesus. Of course, when Jesus said that not a single part of the *law* would pass away, He didn't use the Greek word *nomos* (law) either. He used the Hebrew word *torah*, and as we know, *torah* does not mean Law, with a capital L. That is another interpretation by the translators. *Torah* means instruction. *Torah* is *all* the instructions of God about how to live found in the first five books of the Hebrew Bible. That's what Jesus meant in Matthew 5:18. None of God's *instructions* will be set aside until everything comes to be.

Now we have a real problem. It's easy to dismiss the Old Testament instructions if you think that Jesus said that all those insights from God ended when He died on the cross. But now you know that He didn't say that. Now you know that He said *none* of the *torah* would pass away until *all* has come to be. What Jesus says is shocking to us (but not to His first century audience). Jesus says that the *torah* is still God's way of living. You can't push it aside just because of the death and resurrection of the Messiah. Heaven and earth are still here, so the *torah* is still the standard.

That leaves us with an even bigger question. What is the *all* in "all has come to be"? For the answer, we have to take a serious look at the *new* covenant. And guess what? The *new* covenant isn't found in Matthew, Mark, Luke or John. It's found in Jeremiah. Jesus' reference to the new covenant is an Old Testament reference. Of course it would be. After all, the Hebrew Bible is the only Bible Jesus knew.

Are you ready to listen to what Jesus *actually* says? It's the beginning of the end of a lot of things you thought were true. But don't be afraid. It's gloriously liberating. We will discover just how *old* the new covenant really is.

39.

*"until heaven and earth pass away, not the smallest letter or stroke shall pass away from the Law until **all** is accomplished."* Matthew 5:18

The Beginning of the End (2)

All – What must come into existence before the *torah* ceases to be? We have to know the answer if we are going to understand the relationship between the old and new covenants. We can't simply go on our way, thinking that somehow this new covenant is all grace while the old covenant is all rules and regulations. That won't work anymore. We have to pay more attention.

So, we look for the *new covenant* in the only place that Jesus would have looked – in the Old Testament. And we find it in Jeremiah 31:31. "Behold, the days are coming when I will make a *new covenant* with the house of Israel and the house of Jacob." Certainly this is what Jesus has in mind when He speaks of the *new* covenant. Now all we have to do is look at the description of this new covenant to see what must be accomplished. Here's what we find: The old covenant was written on tablets of stone; the new covenant will be written on the hearts of men. The old covenant needed to be taught to men; the new covenant will be understood intuitively by everyone. The old covenant was practiced by a few; the new covenant will be practiced by all.

There you have it. This is what must be manifest before the *new* covenant is fulfilled. So, what's different between the old covenant and the new covenant. It's simple. The new covenant is the *divine action that inscribes the torah into the heart of every person.* When that is accomplished, *everyone* will know the Lord directly. Then the external law will no longer be needed for all will obey Him from the heart.

Do you know when this will become a reality? Sure you do. It will become a reality when Jesus returns to reign in glory. The new covenant is fulfilled when the Lord is ruler of all and not before.

Why did Jesus use the words "new covenant" to speak about His death and resurrection? He used Jeremiah's words because a covenant must be sealed with a sacrifice. Just go back to Genesis 15. Animals were sacrificed to seal the covenant with Abraham. A promise of this magnitude required the *death* of the innocent. A promise like this had to be written in blood. That is exactly what's happening on the cross. Jesus is the innocent sacrifice that guarantees the new covenant. His blood seals the deal. And when the new covenant is finally fulfilled, everyone in the house of the Lord will serve Him from the heart. Jesus' death *inaugurates* the new covenant. He is the first fruit, the evidence, the proof that God will bring it all to pass. Jesus' death and resurrection point us toward the day when we will serve the Lord naturally. But until then, until all has come to be, the *torah* is still God's guide for living.

Now you have a new perspective on the death of the Messiah. His death is not simply a substitutionary atonement for your sins. It is the sacrificial seal, the guarantee that the day will come when God will rule over every heart - and every heart will gladly serve Him. Jesus' death and resurrection *starts* it all. It's not the end. It's the beginning. That glorious day when it is finished is still to come. In the meanwhile, we have the *torah*.

40.

"Brethren, though I had done nothing against our people, or the **customs** *of our fathers, yet I was delivered prisoner from Jerusalem in to the hands of the Romans."* Acts 28:17

Paul's Confession

Customs – This verse is squeezed into a story about Paul's imprisonment before being shipped to Rome. It is very bothersome. If you pay close attention to what Paul says, you will find it very difficult to reconcile his statement with the contemporary separation of Law and Grace. Here is Paul, the apostle who has more to say about grace than anyone else in the New Testament, claiming that he has never violated any of the customs of his forefathers. The Greek word is *ethesi* (plural of *ethos*); a word that means "established practices." What Paul is saying is this: he has always been a scrupulously observant Jew. He has always followed the instructions of the *torah*. He has never violated or set aside any of his religious practices.

If that doesn't bother you, then you haven't been paying attention in church.

No one will claim that Paul is lying. No one asserts that he is exaggerating for effect. If Scripture is inspired, and Paul is truthful, then what he says is that he has *always* practiced the rules and regulations of living that are found in the Hebrew Bible. How can this be? Isn't Paul that man who set aside circumcision, who said it is all about grace, who left behind the "fulfilled" law? Obviously, we have a problem (and this isn't the only place where the problem comes to light). If Paul keeps the *torah*, then the *torah* must belong in the life of a man saved by grace. Otherwise, there is no reason for this claim.

We have made a terrible mistake. Somewhere along the way, from the cross to the contemporary church, we didn't pay attention to statements like this. We were so anxious to put the Jewish way of life aside that we pushed our theological framework right out of the synagogue. We were so concerned about not being under the Law that we failed to understand the relationship between law and grace. We threw the baby out with the bathwater, and then we couldn't understand why we felt so alone and confused.

Paul didn't make this tragic mistake. Paul knew that grace saves and law fulfills. It has *always* been that way. Since the first sacrifice in the Garden, when God killed an innocent animal to provide grace to a sinful couple, grace has always been the way of salvation. And law has always been the way of fulfillment. Law puts a hedge around God's people so that God can bless them and use them for His purposes. Law doesn't save. Grace doesn't fulfill. **If you want all that God has to offer, you come to Him for His grace *and* you submit to Him to have purpose.**

Oh, you can live as half a person, surviving on grace alone or attempting to live a life of law-keeping. But you'll spend a lot of time wondering where the baby went.

Paul tells his friends, after all his service to the Kingdom, that he is a *torah*-observant man. It is who he is: saved by faith, useful through *torah*. I wonder if we could say the same.

41.

*In that day, YHWH **made** a covenant with Abram* Genesis 15:18

Unbreakable

Made – Today you need an attorney but in ancient Semitic cultures contracts between two parties were signed, sealed and delivered with sacrifice. God tells Abram (later Abraham) that He wants a contract between them. This valid contract obligates two parties to certain actions. Furthermore, breach of contract means that the offending party will be punished – severely. In this case, cut in half, just like the animals that are sacrificed to seal the deal. Abraham is all for this arrangement. After all, God promises to make him into a great nation. It seems like a good deal.

Unfortunately, Abraham doesn't account for human failure. Fortunately, God does. While Abraham sleeps, God completes the covenant agreement. Literally, God *cuts* a covenant (the Hebrew word is *karat*) with Abraham. The imagery could hardly be more graphic. God passes between the rows of slaughtered animals. There is a lot of blood. Life has been taken. This covenant is sealed with cutting. It's as powerful a covenant as you could get. But here's the clincher. God obligates Himself to *both* sides of the agreement. Abraham never walks between the slaughtered animals. God takes on His part of the agreement *and* Abraham's part. This covenant is *unbreakable*!

Why is this so important? First, it establishes the entire foundational agreement between God and His people. God chooses Abraham as the father of the eventual nation of priests. This covenant guarantees that God's work through Abraham will absolutely come to be.

Second, this covenant tells us that Abraham's failures and disobedience (and by extension, the failures and disobedience of all of Abraham's children of the promise) *do not nullify the covenant*. Human sin cannot break God's promise because God's promise is *not conditional*. In fact (and this is very important), God Himself cannot nullify this covenant. Why? Because He obligated Himself to *both* sides of the agreement.

We need to let this sink in. What it implies will change your views about a lot of subjects. The covenant with Abraham *will never be broken*. It is just as valid today as it was on the day that God cut it. God still considers Israel His true and only child. Israel is still the vehicle through which God will bring the nations to Himself. Israel is not rejected, displaced or superseded. The church does not stand as the successor to Israel. The church is merely grafted into Israel in order that God may accomplish His ultimate purposes *for* Israel.

Don't get confused. The political entity called Israel is not the same as the line of the children of promise called Israel. You and I, as believers and followers of the Messiah Yeshua, have been adopted into the family of the true Israel. We are Gentile proselytes joined with Jewish believers. Our father is Abraham too. But this means that the ways of God revealed to Israel must be our ways because we are now part of Israel. God hasn't changed His mind about what He wants or how He will get it. The covenant *cannot be broken.*

42.

and all who dwell on the earth will worship him, every one whose name has not been written from the **foundation** *of the world in the book of life of the Lamb who has been slain.* Revelation 13:8

Fundamental Shift

Foundation – In English, I prefer the New American Standard Bible but I was quite surprised when I read this verse. All the words from the Greek are here but the order has been significantly altered. The result is a fundamental change in the idea of the covenant. Unfortunately, you would never know it unless you read the Greek text.

The Greek text places "from the foundation of the world" as a modifier of "the Lamb who has been slain." In other words, a normal reading of the Greek leads us to the conclusion that Yeshua, the Lamb of God, was sacrificed before the world came into existence.

However, the NASB shifts the placement of this modifying phrase to match a similar phrase in Revelation 17:8, making the modifier apply to the writing of names, not to the sacrifice of Yeshua. The way the NASB reads, we would conclude that the names of the apostates and the names of the faithful have been written in the book of life since the world began. That's a *big* shift. The NASB gives us a theology of individual predestination. The Greek (and the NIV) puts the focus on the eternal sacrifice of Yeshua. But without an explanation, you would never know. This is not a mistake. It is deliberate alteration of the translated text to match a prior theological position. It's equivalent to the NIV consistently translating *sarx* (flesh) as "sinful nature".

Once we've cleared up the English translation, we can pay attention to the implication. Read correctly, this verse makes a startling and powerful claim. Yeshua's sacrifice occurred *before* the creation of the world. Of course, in earthly physical reality His death on the cross occurred in the first century AD. But as far as the Bible is concerned, the real sacrifice happened the moment Yeshua took on the role of redeemer, and He volunteered for that role before the world began. God didn't make up the plan of redemption on the fly. He didn't think it up *after* the Fall. It was all conceived and executed in advance. There was always a provision for sin.

Let's push this one step further. Since the perfect sacrifice was initiated before the world began, all of the sacrificial provisions found in the *torah* are merely shadows of the greater reality. The real sacrifice happened in heaven. The progressive revelation of God's plan of redemption introduced many sacrifices as pointers, symbols, representations and tokens of the heavenly reality. Here's the fundamental shift: **every sacrifice given by God in the *torah* exemplifies and exhibits some element of the full complexity of the heavenly sacrifice of the Lamb.** The peace offering, the sin offering, the cereal offering, the freewill offering, the burnt offering and more – all of them reveal some aspect of the sacrifice of the Lamb. Jesus' death on the cross is truly the *fulfillment* of all of those elements, but *it does not replace them*. Every time a sacrifice is offered, it underscores some aspect of the full and complete sacrifice that occurred in heaven *before the world began*. Earthly expressions of the heavenly sacrifice are incomplete in themselves, but they are not invalid. They all say something important about the full manifestation and eternal complexity of the Lamb slain before the foundations of the world.

Maybe the next time you read Leviticus it won't seem so confusing.

43.

*For God has not given us a spirit of timidity, but of power and **love** and discipline.* 2 Timothy 1:7

Phenomenal

Love – We all know that the word "love" covers a wide range of feelings and actions. Greek has four different words to explain it. Hebrew has three words. But the number of different words isn't the most important factor in understanding what Paul means. To really grasp Paul's proclamation of God's gift, we have to get into the Hebrew mind.   And that requires suspending some long-held presuppositions about the world as we know it.

The big difference between Greek and Hebrew is the way the languages view reality. Greek views reality as organized bits. It is the language of *analysis*, breaking down each new element into smaller and smaller pieces. When you adopt the Greek worldview, you see the world as a sum of parts.   In order to understand something, you have uncover all the underlying the parts.   That's why "love" in Greek is broken into its separate pieces: love for brothers and friends, love for family and children, love for things and love for God.

But Hebrew doesn't see things this way. Hebrew is a *phenomenal* language. It describes the world *the way it appears* to the observer. As a result, love is about emotions, choices, consequences and activities. One concept, even in three words, contains the whole range of human observations about love. In Hebrew, love is not a series of discrete elements but rather the whole sweep of spontaneous feelings, choices and actions no matter how it shows up in human expression. Now you know why the Old Testament draws continuous analogies between sex and worship. Both are part of the *continuum* of the Hebrew concept of "love."

OK, so why does this matter? Well, Paul is a Hebrew. When he write his letter in Greek and uses the Greek word *agape*, he isn't thinking about the exclusive category of religious love usually ascribed to *agape*. In fact, the New Testament authors actually used *agape* in novel ways, not relying on the classical Greek definition. In order to understand Paul, we have to think like a Hebrew. That means Paul is pointing his readers to the entire scope of the spirit of love, from the spontaneous feelings of passion to the impulse for self-giving, from the desire for pleasure to the nobility of obedience. Wherever human emotion or action touches the heart of the personal God, you and I experience love. It can just as easily be found in an embrace with my spouse as it can be found in fighting injustice among the poor. Old Testament love is jealous but self-denying. It is exclusive but embraces everyone. It is volitional but intensely emotional. It is sacrificial but self-interested.

The Hebrew word, *ahav*, is a *phenomenal* word (pun intended). If you want to find the spirit of love, don't rush to the psychoanalyst. Don't bother digging into your inner thoughts. Just observe humanity touched by God. You'll see everything you need to know about *ahav*. That's the point, isn't it? When I *see* it, then I know what to do. That's why I look at Jesus when I want to see *phenomenal* love.

44.

so that what was spoken through the prophet might be fulfilled, saying, "I will open my mouth in parables; I will utter things hidden since the **foundation of the world**." Matthew 13:35

A Little Inspiration

Foundation Of The World – There are a lot of quotations of the Old Testament in the books of the New Testament. We never think too much about them because we *assume* that the quotations are accurate representations of the Old Testament texts. But have you ever really looked? Take a deep breath. You might be surprised.

Matthew's quotation of Psalm 78:2 is an example of what we usually find. The verse in Psalms doesn't quite say what Matthew says. In fact, the verse in Hebrew literally says, "I will open my mouth in a parable. I will utter dark sayings from of old." You will notice immediately that Matthew's quotation changes *parable* to *parables* and *dark sayings from of old* to *thing hidden from the foundation of the world*. How is this possible? How can Matthew believe that Psalms is inspired by God, right down to the very letters, and still make all these changes?

Most of us *assume* that Matthew is just quoting from the Septuagint (LXX). We don't bother to ask what that tells us about the issue of the inspiration of the LXX. We just think that Matthew was writing in Greek and the problem is in translation. But that won't quite do it. Why? Because the LXX doesn't say what Matthew says either.

Maybe the problem is just in the English. Maybe our translations are *dynamic* instead of *word-for-word*. A dynamic translation captures the meaning of the text and converts it into the translated language whereas a word-for-word translation tries to be accurate in each word of the original. That might explain the problem, except that Matthew is Jewish and he clearly knew what the original words were, yet the Greek passage here isn't even close.

The usual explanations fail. Does that mean that we have to give up the usual doctrine of inspiration? Not at all! We just need to understand what inspiration means from a Hebrew point of view. After all, that famous text (2 Timothy 3:16) uses a Greek word for inspiration that Paul had to *make up* because there was no Greek word available that would capture what he was trying to say about God and God's revelation. The issue is really not so trivial, especially since most of the New Testament authors seem to play fast and loose with Old Testament quotations.

So, let's get a few of the basics straight. First, the Hebrew view of inspiration applies right down to the letters of the words (and even more than that). That's about as strong a concept of inspiration as you can get. No New Testament author ever doubted the divine authority and accuracy of the Old Testament. Neither should we.

But, second, rabbinic methods of using Scripture are very different than our Greek-based ideas of accurate quotations. We tend to think that quotations must be exactly correct. We provide citations in order to show the reader that we have accurately *copied* the original author's words. This is not the way a rabbi thinks. From a rabbinical point of view, it is possible to alter a text to fit the needs of an argument *without* implying any degradation of the authority of the original because the point of the argument is not the accuracy of the quotation but rather the impact of the conclusion on the life of the believer. There is a lot more flexibility in the Hebrew idea of inspiration *in its application*, but there is even more rigidity in its authority and divine authorship.

What does this tell us? It tells us that the way we look at the world from our Greek "has to be exactly right" point of view might not fit the Hebrew worldview. Just as Hebrew is a language of flow and action (while Greek is a language of fixed and static entities), so the Hebrew idea of inspiration has a fluid quality in its application that we don't usually recognize in our doctrinal positions. So, when you read the New Testament, you are really reading a *commentary* on the Old Testament. Try that on for size and see how it fits.

Chapter 2

Education: The Enlightenment of Highly Intelligent Fools

*I*n a Greek world, education is based on the transfer of information. Just give me the *facts*! As long as I have the correct information, I can make a rational and truthful determination. Therefore, education is really gathering information about everything there is to know in the universe. Our ideal Man is a figure from the Renaissance; someone who is acquainted with the widest possible collection of correct information and is able to use all this knowledge for noble purposes.

Contemporary educational models endorse this Greek ideal. That's why we force children to learn algebra, chemistry, art history and economics even if they are terribly frustrated in the process. We believe that *everyone* should be as fully informed as possible regardless of their individual gifts, talents and proclivities. We think of our children as blank slates waiting for teachers to write imparted information on their minds. In our Greek-based society, knowledge is power. Cognitive excellence is prized as the mark of a great person.

The Hebrew world is very different. In the ancient Hebrew world, obedience comes first. The goal of life is not to know as much as possible. It is to live in holiness under the shelter of a holy God. Therefore, knowledge means nothing if it does not produce godly action. What I *do* is far more important than what I *think*. Of course, that doesn't mean that the Scriptures endorse blind obedience. They do not! God is a God of order, reason and logic. But reason does not stand apart from God and His world. The proper, rational perspective begins and ends with the God Who acts. If I want to reason correctly I must start with a conversation with my Maker. That conversation enables be to become human. It results in obedience and fellowship. Anything else is animal existence, no matter how "intelligent" I become.

In the Hebrew world, children are educated in order to bring their lives into conformity with a relationship with God. Nothing is more important than this, so this educational process begins at birth and continues for the rest of life. Algebra, chemistry and economics are interesting, useful and challenging, but they are seen as inquiries into the riches of God's creation, not essential gateways to a better life. Better living doesn't come about through electricity. It comes about through worship and obedience.

1.

*All Scripture is inspired by God and profitable for teaching, for reproof, for **correction**, for training in righteousness* 2 Timothy 3:16

Once Is Enough

Correction - The Greek word *epanorthosis* occurs only once in the New Testament, right here in this verse about the effectiveness of the Word of God. Did you notice that it is closely associated with teaching and training, but that it is distinguished from reproof? That leads us to ask, "What is the difference between "reproof" and "correction?" If they were the same, then Paul would not have employed this unique word in order to make his point.

"Reproof" is a word about *conviction*. It describes the inward and outward experience of acknowledging our sin. It is the manifestation of the fact that God's Word confronts us with the truth – and we are far from meeting the standard. Reproof is what happens when I open to a passage of Scripture and am suddenly struck by my disobedience and guilt. Reproof has but one object in mind – repentance.

On the other hand, "correction" has a different objective. Correction is about setting the right course. It comes from a combination of Greek words that literally means "to set up straight again." Paul may be thinking of the Hebrew counterpart – the idea that aligning myself with God's Word will almost always require some form of chastisement (Hebrew *musar*) because my heart is powerfully deceitful, even to me! Again and again, Proverbs exhorts the use of *musar* (correction – both mental and physical) in order to keep us on the straight and narrow. God employs exactly the same tactics. In order to bring our lives into alignment with His purposes, He must often apply the rod. How He does that can vary from pressing circumstances to outright punishment but why He does that always has the same goal – holiness.

Reproof brings repentance. If God's Word is striking conviction in your heart, drop to your knees and ask His mercy. Correction brings holiness – and usually at great cost. This is the stripping away process that God uses to remove what does not edify. This is the agony of discovering that our lives are riddled with compromise. This is the painful experience of self-denial and cross-bearing. God's Word is designed to bring this suffering into our lives for the express purpose of conforming us to the image of the Son.

Why do we need to go through all this? Why doesn't God make this transition easy? The answer is really our problem. God does make it easy – as easy as is absolutely necessary to bring us into full fellowship. God restrains *all* that could be used to correct us by using *only* what is minimally required. He could have knocked us flat, but He would never do so. He only brings just enough to set us straight again. Of course, He has to turn up the volume if you pretend to be deaf.

How's your hearing today?

2.

*This wisdom is not that which comes down from above, but is earthly, natural, **demonic**,* James 3:15

You've Been Fooled

Demonic – There's no doubt about it. James considers the wisdom of this world *daimoniodes* (literally – like the Devil). Doesn't that seem a bit outlandish? Does James really intend for us to think that all our science, economics, philosophy, politics, etc. are *demonic*? Look at all the good these fields of human inquiry have done? Doesn't that count in God's book? Aren't human beings created for progress?

In order to understand what James is saying, we have to have the same perspective that James enjoys. James is an eschatological pragmatist. That means he is focused on the here and now but with the vision of the eternal in mind. What he notices is that the very structure of this world and all of its systems, designs, achievements and dreams, are under the pervasive power of the prince of darkness. All human wisdom has been perverted to serve a false master. It may not have been totally corrupted. Not everyone is a

Hitler. But the schematics of this world are bent just enough so that if I live according to even the highest human morality I am still serving an imposter god. The problem is not that I can't do very good things with all this information. The problem is that no collection of facts from this world is purified holy, fit for the King of kings. My greatest works are as filthy rags in the sight of unblemished holiness. To think otherwise is to be fooled. And most of us have been fooled – big time!

Proverbs 26:12relational and always about discerning what attitudes and actions bring me into alignment with the Creator. But my world is riddled with delusions, dead-ends and difficulties. Left to myself, I just simply cannot find my way to the personal God. His holiness is completely beyond me. I don't have that "spark of the divine" within (a very popular lie). What I have within is the result of thousands of generations of distilled disobedience. I was born in the swamp of human arrogance and I have been drinking and breathing that environment since conception. Unless God reveals the wisdom I need *from above*, I am lost, even if I win one Nobel Prize after another. This is James' perspective. If I don't see the *final* purpose, I will be fooled into thinking that my understanding and knowledge is quite good enough.

James knows that the only real *wisdom* must come from God. It must come from a pure and holy source. It can never be discovered from the bottom up because the bottom-up process is always tainted by its source – me! Just ask the boys in theoretical physics about the influence of the observer. Pure? No way!

So, don't be fooled. Don't go off thinking that good is good enough. The only thing good enough is 100% holy. That's why this world is the devil's playground. He rules the swamp and everything in it for the time being! If you want real wisdom, you will have to look elsewhere.

3.

*Do you see a person who is **wise** in his own eyes? There is more hope for a fool than for him?* Proverbs 26:12

No Room Left

Wise – Biblical wisdom doesn't come with degrees on the wall. The word *hakam* covers a host of *practical* living skills, from builders and metalworkers to leaders and counselors. But the basis for all these practical applications is *given* by God, not earned in a university. The wise person is one who heeds God's law, accepts rebuke and correction, speaks with appropriate humility and recognizes the Source of his good fortune.

Of course, there is another kind of "wisdom." It is what the world calls "wisdom." This kind of wisdom attempts to find its source in the skills and cleverness of men. Its goal is to find a way to make it on your own. Its result is a subtle arrogance. "I've got this one down pat." "I know my way around." "No one's got anything on me."

Solomon was the wisest man in the world; a wisdom that came as a gift from God. None of his insight was born from himself. Realizing that his understanding was nothing but a gift, he gives us a warning. There are plenty of people who think themselves wise. They believe that they have life in their grasp. They are the "go for it" guys. Solomon tells us quite sternly that these people have less hope of true relationships than the fool and the fool was pretty far gone. Why is Solomon so harsh? Because he knows that the first step toward disaster is self-reliance and self-sufficiency. If my dream is to be my own man (or woman), if I resonate with Frank's tune, "I did it my way," then I am surely worse off than the fool. Even the fool has the hope of severe punishment leading to repentance. But the man who thinks he is his own god is doomed. The fool has a little left to be saved but not the arrogant man.

Amazingly, our culture idolizes the arrogant. Of course, we don't fawn over those who push their arrogance in our faces. Nevertheless, we all want to be famous, free and fortunate. We love the tabloids, the celebrities and the rich and famous. Why? Because we put the self-made man on the world's pedestal. We worship at the feet of those whom we believe grabbed life by the horns. Who's the bigger fool: the one who believes he controls his own destiny or the one who worships the arrogant man?

Christians, unfortunately, are not immune from the terminal disease. It has been infecting men since Eve thought she could do her job better with a little outside help. Even those of us with the best of motives can quickly fall victim to the big A (for arrogance) when we start to think we are better, faster, smoother and more capable. God's gifts come with awesome responsibility; usually best displayed in those who are reluctant to use them. If you get comfortable with God's hand in your life, watch out. You just may be leaning toward "I can do it myself, thank you," thinking.

4.

For wisdom is better than jewels; and **all desirable things** *cannot compare with her.* Proverbs 8:11

The Wisdom Genie

All Desirable Things – You get one wish. What is your desire? Wait, don't think small. Really let it go. What is your *greatest* desire? Of all the things that you can think of, what appeals the most? Do you have it in mind? Now read this verse again. Whatever it is, it can't even compare to what wisdom offers!

The Hebrew phrase is *khol-khafatsim*. The root is *khafets*, a word for delight and pleasure. All the delights and all the pleasures and all the wants that you might entertain aren't even in the same category as wisdom. That is a very strong statement. Some very wise people don't seem to have much in life that is pleasurable. They seem to live on the edge, often poor, often abused. How can wisdom be better than a full, satisfying life stuffed with the delights of the senses? The author, Solomon, once pursued *khafatsim*. He wrote all about it in Ecclesiastes. His conclusion? After denying himself nothing, he discovered a terrible revelation. In the end, all his desires had no meaning. He would die just like the most wretched of men. Game over.

Wisdom offers a different kind of genie; not the one consumed with my next greatest desire but one focused entirely on the truth – the truth about me, about life and about purpose. The reason wisdom is better than any genie from a lamp is quite simple. Wisdom gives me God's point of view. If I want the very best, I must be aligned with His plan and purposes. The beginning of wisdom (did you get that? – the *beginning*, not the majority) is proper reverence and relationship to the Lord. In fact, beginning anywhere else is foolishness. *Fear* of the Lord is the first *axiom* of wisdom. If you don't start there, you simply cannot get anywhere.

What would you rather have – a life filled with your desires or a life satisfying to God (which, by the way, you will discover to be entirely satisfying for you)? Solomon tried the first alternative. He found genuine disappointment even when he had everything he could want. So he advises us to take the other route. Seek wisdom! Begin with a proper attitude and respect for Who God is. Buy the truth, whatever the price, and never sell it. Hold on to the Lord's commands for your life depends on them. Listen! And obey! Every insight given you from the Father above is designed to bring about eternal change in your perspective, your appreciation and your application. If you find yourself wishing for a *khafets* genie, think deeper. All things desirable are not good enough to bring about what God has in mind. Choose the better part. You'll be glad you did.

Today someone will approach you with an offer of worldly advice. It will sound reasonable – even appealing – because it will satisfy one of your *khafatsim*. When you realize just how much it appeals, turn to this verse. Seek wisdom. Satisfy your soul.

5.

*"For this commandment which I command you today is **not too difficult** for you, nor is it out of reach."* Deuteronomy 30:11

The Secret of Life

Not Too Difficult - Our culture is saturated with the Greek idea of hidden, secret knowledge. In ancient Greece, popular Gnostic and mystic religions proclaimed various secret understandings about life.

To join these sects and become illuminated meant taking a death vow. If you revealed the secret to an outsider, you could be killed.

We don't take such extreme measures today but we still hold on to the Greek mysticism that endorses the "secrets" of life. A casual walk through the bookstore says it all. Secrets of success. Secrets to great sex. Secrets the government doesn't want you to know. Secret ways to get what you want. Secrets to losing weight. On and on it goes. Don't you ever wonder, "If all of these things are secrets, how did we ever manage to survive this long?" Our Greek, post-modern culture loves the idea of secrets because secrets feed the ego with power and control. If I know something you don't, I can take advantage of situations you can't. Therefore, I am better than you.

But what if life isn't really like that? What if it's all a metaphysical smoke screen designed to entice you to lust for power? What if we had a Hebrew view instead of a Greek perspective? We would suddenly discover that life is really pretty simple. There really aren't any *secrets* for gaining power over the way life is. From the Hebrew point of view, life is pretty much just what it seems to be. God designed life so that anyone who asks will know what to do. In fact, God gave instructions about living before we even asked the questions. He provided the Law; a code of conduct that governs relationships with Him and with all other people and the rest of creation. God never left us in the dark, wondering how we were going to survive without the *essential secrets*. He told us straight up what life was all about and how to conduct ourselves accordingly.

From the Hebrew perspective there is no hidden reality deeply buried behind the appearances we encounter with our senses. Instead, there is life as it is. And God, Who is not hidden away in the transcendent other world, is right here in the midst of it all, interacting with us, guiding us, providing for us and protecting us – in the midst of life as it is. In fact, God tells us plainly that what He gives as the guide to life is *lo-nif.let hiv mim* (not too extraordinary or too difficult). God's instructions are plain and simple. No secrets.

What would happen to the way you behave if you knew that life is exactly what life appears to be; that the good, the bad and the ugly

96

are all factors woven into God's order of existence for the fallen world? How would your thinking change if you knew that what God has already revealed about Himself and His purposes is sufficient for living a full and satisfying life right here in the middle of systems under the control of the evil one? What if you realized that finding the *right* solution was really a myth? The right solution was never covered up at all. It was right there in front of you, in His Word. Would you be relieved? Would you rejoice? Would you stop feeling so guilty for not knowing the *secrets* of life? Now, let me tell you a secret. There aren't any secrets. Just go read the Book!

6.

*punishing the iniquity of the fathers on the children, and on the third and forth generation of those that **hate** me.* Deuteronomy 5:9

Educational Responsibility

Hate – What happens when we bow down and serve false gods? Among other things, our children suffer. Why? Because our attitudes and actions demonstrate that we do not need God. They copy us. As a result, they become God-haters.

Oh, I don't mean that they will be atheists. The Hebrew word here never suggests that. It is *sane*, the opposite of the Hebrew *ahav* (love). Remember that "love" is not about feelings. It is about *actions*. In Hebrew, *ahav* means that I do what God commands. I obey Him. That demonstrates my love for Him. So, those who hate God are simply those who *disobey* Him. It doesn't matter if they are nice people. It doesn't even matter if they have good feelings about the existence of God. If they do not bow down and serve Him, they are God-haters. They do not keep His covenant. They are not loyal to Him. They are His enemies.

How did they get that way? Their parents failed to fulfill the mission and purpose of the Law. Their parents, who were redeemed out of bondage by a compassionate Lord, failed to instruct their children about the ways of God. And the result is terrible. Not only the children but the grandchildren and the great-grandchildren are lost in the process. All because the first generation thought that a few rules didn't really matter.

Do you see the absolute truth behind this? If your life is like my life, you will see it in graphic reality among your own children. There is no greater pain than that of parents who finally see that the life they led results in tragic destruction for their children. That's when regret can only turn to weeping and beseeching God to straighten out what we have bent. And even God tells us that this is no easy task. Unless God intervenes the consequences will go on for three and four generations.

All you have to do today is look at the state of the world's young people - floating free on a sewer of abandoned relationships, to God and to each other. We have failed them because we did not take God's word seriously. But how could we? There was a generation before ours that left the divine educational plan behind as well. God put the education of His ways in the hands of fathers and mothers. Fathers and mothers sent their children off to the professionals while they pursued their own desires. We all reaped what we sowed.

The Law was supposed to accomplish God's plan of evangelism to the nations. It was also supposed to secure the message of His goodness and mercy *within* the household of His people. It hasn't changed. It is still designed to do just this. We simply stopped using it. Maybe it's time to re-think how we educate our children. God forgive us before it's too late.

7.

*But Jesus said, "Allow the little children and do not prevent them to come to Me, for **of such** is the kingdom of heaven."* Matthew 19:14

The Quality of the Kingdom

Of Such – Honor your parents. Why? Because they have the God-given responsibility to present you with the covenant relationship with God. So, what do parents do? Well, if you were in the crowd on the day Jesus met these children, you would have seen something quite shocking happen. Parents brought their children to the Master because they were trying to fulfill God's command. They might not have known that Jesus was God but they certainly knew that He was very close to God and they naturally wanted their children to experience the presence of a man who walked with God. But, much to their amazement, those accompanying Jesus prevented them.

Our usual theological interpretation of this verse concentrates on Jesus' remark about the character of Kingdom citizens. But what we might not see is that the fourth commandment is being broken here. The disciples are not honoring the relationship between parents and children. Jesus does not simply speak about citizen character. He corrects a tragic mistake. The covenant responsibility must not be blocked.

In the Greek New Testament, the word *toioutos* ("of such") is unusual. The common form is *toios*, meaning "such", like "such as this kind." But the Greek here adds emphasis. This little word puts some qualitative stress here. These are not just any kind of children. These are children who carry a critically important role. They are representatives of God's plan for communicating the covenant. Their status – dependent, unimportant and vulnerable – represents all of those who would enter into the covenant. No one comes to God carrying a glowing resume. We come dragging life's ashes. We come without self-sufficiency, or we do not come at all. God's plan was always to use the family to bring His grace to those who were most vulnerable. The enemy goes after the powerful, holding them up as icons of human success. God looks the other way - to the ones who gently rest in His sufficiency, who think nothing of tomorrow because they want to play today.

And how will they know that there is a God Who cares for them with such deliberate intensity? God entrusts that responsibility to parents. Jesus knew all about this divine delegation and He would not allow the socially zealous disciples to interfere. The disciples thought only of protecting their esteemed Master from the annoyance of the unworthy. The Master saw that God's plan begins and ends with those who have no advocate for themselves.

I wonder if we aren't more like those disciples than we would like to admit. I wonder if we stand in the way of the vulnerable, the helpless and the dependent because we are "protecting" Jesus from the unworthy. I wonder if we realize that we are breaking a commandment.

8.

*And YHWH **called** to Moses and spoke to him out of the tabernacle of the congregation, saying,* Leviticus 1:1

Kindergarten

Called – If you had to decide which book of the Bible you would use to train your children in the ways of God, would you choose Leviticus? Probably not. You would probably decide on some New Testament book; most likely the gospel of John. That seems to be the evangelical choice of the last century. But when you think about it (from God's perspective), John is really not a very good place to begin, is it? It's far to complicated. It assumes a great deal of prior Jewish theology. It has a peculiar vocabulary (which most of us don't appreciate in English). And it really doesn't tell us what we need to know, does it? Yes, it proclaims the divinity of Yeshua the Messiah but it doesn't really tell me what I have to do. It leaves me with verses like, "keep my commandments," and "love one another." But what do those statements mean in *practical application*? We can't afford to guess, can we? After all, eternal matters are at stake.

Maybe that's why the education of a Jewish child begins here in Leviticus. Leviticus is the great book of the details of sacrifice. It spells out *exactly* what I have to do. It tells me precisely how I must live if I am to honor the God Who set me free. Without all this background, it's hard to say if the gospels really come to grips with the biggest issues in life. Unless I know what Yeshua learned when he was a child in synagogue school, I really can't appreciate what He tells me as my Lord. It's time to go back to kindergarten and learn to read by learning Leviticus.

Most of us will have quite a bit of resistance to this idea. We think we know what the Bible is all about. It's about faith and grace and forgiveness and mercy. Leviticus is all about peace offerings and cereal offerings and purification offerings and all those things that don't really matter anymore, right? Why should we be bothered with ancient rituals when we are *free*? Who cares if the Lord smells a sweet aroma? We're forgiven, right? We don't have to practice all those strange customs now. Or do we?

Why did the children of ancient Israel learn to read by studying Leviticus? The answer is simple – and startling in its condemnation of our blindness. The children of ancient Israel were taught to read through the study of Leviticus because the *most important thing in life is my service and submission to God*. If I don't start with this focus all the rest of my education is really pointless. If I don't learn right from the beginning what God wants and how to serve Him, what is the purpose of learning anything else? Parents in Israel knew something we have forgotten. God comes first! Training children in God's word begins the moment they can talk. The purpose of education is to enter into His presence and enjoy His fellowship, not to get a better job!

God *summoned* Moses. That's what this Hebrew word *qara* means. God is going to deliver the perfect instruction for dealing with sin in His family. It will all lead to the perfect sacrifice. But unless I know the details, **unless I practice obedience**, I will never understand how extraordinarily significant the death of the Messiah is. Time to get back to school. When God summons, don't be tardy.

9.

*And YHWH called to Moses and **spoke** to him out of the tabernacle of the congregation, saying,* Leviticus 1:1

The Word of the Lord

Spoke – Why did God wait until His presence rested over the tabernacle before He spoke to Moses about the sacrifices? Some contemporary translations of this verse omit the word "tabernacle," but we shouldn't! The tabernacle represented the presence of God among His people. It was not a *dwelling* place. God didn't reside in the tabernacle. It was a visible symbol of God's glory in the midst of the camp; a reminder that God elected this community. From this holy manifestation, God instructs Moses. The fact that God communicated out of the tabernacle raised the communication to its most sacred level. What God says next is *critically important*. It has the same authority as the voice from Mount Sinai. What God says involves all the details of how we are to stand before Him.

The Hebrew word *dabar* means both "to speak or to say" and "what is spoken, a word or speech." The same consonants (D B R) are used in both forms. What God speaks is His word. Once we have that securely in mind, then we need to ask the next question: How are we to treat God's word? The answer is obvious. God's word is the very substance of life. Not only must we have it in order to live ("Man shall not live by bread alone but by every word that proceeds from the mouth of God"), but it is also God's word that calls everything, including us, into existence. God's word is the instruction that will not disappear even if heaven and earth disappear. God's word is the permanent declaration of His will, His character and His authority. When God speaks, the angelic hosts revel in His majesty. So, when God summoned Moses and spoke to him, you can bet that Moses listened very attentively. Makes you wonder about us, doesn't it? Do we treat this portion of God's word with the reverence it deserves? Do we recognize it with the same power and majesty as the speaking of the Ten Commandments? Are we as careful to obey it? Probably not, but it makes you wonder, doesn't it? When did we decide that some things God's says are more important than others, that some are more spiritual than others?

There is one other element to this voice from the tabernacle. When God does tell Moses about the system of sacrifices, we discover that the offerings cover a very wide range of human situations and attitudes. Yes, that's right – attitudes. God's instructions acknowledge no difference between civil and spiritual "laws", no difference between what is moral and what is legal, and no difference between my heart and my hands. Of course, there are different civil punishments and different elements of sacrifice for those who exhibit inner attitudes in ungodly outer behavior but the *torah* is the only ancient code that actually legislates what I *think* as well as what I do. When it comes to the Word of the Lord, *all* life falls under His purview. Sometimes we forget that God has an interest in *everything* about us. Maybe that's why Leviticus is so detailed. Maybe that's why we usually think it boring. Maybe we're the ones who don't like the routine but it is in the routine that God is so wonderfully present.

Next time you wish you were climbing mountains, look around at the valley where you're standing. God is sitting in those shadows, ready to greet you.

Additional Thoughts on Godly Education:

Devolving: Evolution as Social Theory

I'm not about to enter into the creation debate. Personally, I believe it takes considerably more "faith" to posit a random, chaotic origin than it does to believe in a personal God who spoke everything into being. We could debate the issue but unless you are prepared to argue for the verifiability of inferential empiricism (the epistemological foundation of all current science) as something more than a probability that approaches zero (an inherent difficulty with verification), then we would be wasting our time. My disagreement with Darwin's proposal is not rooted in the so-called inferential evidence. My objections are about the *logic* of such a proposal. But if you're dying to argue the case, you can spend thirty years studying the philosophy of science (like I have) and then we'll talk.

No, I don't want to debate the creation issue. But I do want to point out some rather interesting problems with evolution as a *social theory* for I also believe that the *carte blanche* acceptance of evolution as an explanation of progress has deeply affected our thinking and, subsequently, driven us into an alley that clearly has (as Sartre would say) "no exit".

To begin our inquiry we must ask the question, "What are the basic assumptions of evolutionary theory concerning progress?" The answer is straightforward. Systems (whether they are simple organisms or complex communities) that adapt survive. Those that do not adapt do not survive. Therefore, what exists presently on the planet must be occurrence of systems that were capable of adaptation or else, *ipso facto*, they would not exist. This simple assumption has the following corollaries. Surviving systems are of a higher order than failing systems. Those systems that exist in the world today are of superior quality and mechanism than the systems of the past since the systems of the past are now extinct. From this we may draw the conclusion that whatever exists presently is in some respect better than what has come before. This must be so since evolutionary theory requires that only the superior system remains in existence. Therefore, what is now is the best it could be.

Of course, today is not the end of the chain. Tomorrow's systems will by a matter of logic be of a higher order than today's systems simply because they will be in existence tomorrow. Evolutionary theory posits that as time progress what is inferior is bred out of the world. Since the world has not yet ended, we can therefore look forward to a better tomorrow. *Voila*. Utopia is just ahead (on a cosmic scale, of course).

When this logic is applied to microbes and amoebas, we might actually have some reason to imagine it to be true. After all, microbes do adapt to antibiotics. New strains survive. Old strains die. But a quantum leap occurs when such thinking is applied to the more complex systems of the world. This quantum leap has shocking implications, yet it seems to have become the acceptable *raison d'etre* of contemporary culture. With little appreciation for the dilemma it creates, the post modern world has adopted a social evolutionary theory that has propelled the entire world into a Sartrean alley.

What happens when the simple logic of evolution is applied to society and culture? First, of course, we must revise the expectation of progress. Evolution tells me that what now exists is superior to what used to exist. This is simply an inescapable result of the logic of evolutionary progress. What exists today, i.e. the shape and mores and values of the culture, must be the product of higher functioning *because it is.* Of course, today's cultural systems will be replaced by tomorrow's, but right now, this is as good as it gets.

What implications result from this new utopian logic?

First, we must note that the past, its history, people and societies are relegated to useless status. After all, they didn't survive. What can we possible learn, much less apply, from people and societies that were the product of *inferior* adaptation? At best, all they can show us is how far we have progressed. At worst, they can be completely dismissed or, more likely, rewritten according to our enlightened understanding. Why should we want to learn anything from mistakes?

The consequences are obvious.

Ancient wisdom is nothing more than unenlightened mythology. Past history has nothing to tell us of contemporary worth. The previous generations are less capable, less informed, less insightful and less equipped than our generation. Previous social systems based on old morality have little if any relevance. Parents know less and are less competent than their children. Grandparents are further down the ladder of inadequacy and irrelevance. The moral values of the past generations are outdated and unenlightened. The understanding of the human beings in the world, their purpose, place and relationships must be based on the latest thinking, not on defective past constructions. The only hope of human kind is to be found in the future.

If you didn't see the signs of this evolutionary theory in action, then you weren't paying attention when Disney produced movies that systematically portrayed children as smarter and more capable than their parents, when the judiciary rewrote the law to fit the current cultural morals, when technology replaced relationships, when marriage between opposite sexes became a symbol of an antiquated morality, when sex as recreation was detached from ethical responsibility, when the church became a business instead of a change agent, when the Hollywood agenda became the politics of the land, when educational texts rewrote history to reflect political correctness. This list goes on and on. General Electric has no idea how relevant their motto was when they used to say, "Progress is our most important product."

Buried in the implication of evolution as social theory is the shipwreck of society. Why? Because evolutionary utopian logic disconnects the culture from any and all of its past moorings. The culture is in a mad rush to seek meaning in the future, and, since the future is as yet unknown and unknowable, all stability due to historical precedent is demolished. Culture becomes a ship without rudder or anchor, adrift on the sea of change for the sake of change, going wherever the tides and winds take it. And since the sailors on this ship have thrown away the compass, they have no idea where they are going either.

What really happens when the culture adopts evolution as a social theory is the devolution of society. Amazingly, this is not our first encounter with such madness. Even in Biblical times, the prevailing culture flirted with letting go of the past. In those days, "every man did what was right in his own eyes". If we weren't so myopically fixated on the utopian future, we would know that the time of the judges in Israel was followed by social collapse, tyranny and captivity. But who reads history these days?

James Black, in his book *When Nations Die*, demonstrates that the collapse of great civilizations in human history have followed a fairly consistent pattern, from ancient Rome to post-modern Europe. In every case, traditions were abandoned for progress. Darwin did not invent the evolutionary model. It has been alive and well in the world's greatest empires and in the world's greatest failures. When economic systems, political systems, educational systems, social systems and religious systems become disconnected from an historical perspective and a traditional mooring, the society waivers, gasps and falls.

What is so interesting about this pattern is its fundamentally *spiritual* root. The shift to the utopian logic of evolution as a social theory cannot occur until men are released, by will or circumstance, from a higher authority that governs the world. This higher authority cannot rest in Law as conceived by the Greeks. That authority is nothing more than a refined summary of the will of the citizens. It is the expression of the *polis*, modified perhaps by enlightened cooperation, but ultimately dependent on the contemporary mores and values. As such, it must change as the will of the people (however one decides to define this term) changes. Today's Western world judicial morass is a perfect example of the logical conclusion of such thinking. Without a philosopher king, the mob eventually rules.

The Hebrews, through no effort on their own, avoided this logical inevitability, at least until they too succumbed to the world's system of government. They operated under a *theocracy*. God was the Law. That is to say, God did not simply reveal the Law. He was the figurative expression of the Law itself. In such a system, there is no court of appeals, no popular referendum, no impeachment, no recall. God's word establishes the absolute boundaries of social and ethical behavior without exception. God's word revealed to men becomes the final and absolute foundation of human expectation and social interaction. Quite simply, it does *not* progress. It is, as it is, perfect.

It is instructive to note that the Jewish orthodox culture has remained more or less intact through thousands of years while most other Indo-European cultures have gone through amazing metamorphosis and, in some cases, ceased to exist. I wonder if historians might not draw the conclusion that this resilience and constancy over time finds its explanation in the Hebrew's *spiritual* commitment.

The God of the Bible claims an authority over the world that is antithetical to any evolutionary utopian logic. In Biblical terms, the world *began* perfect. Its present state of decay is the ironic conclusion of Man's decision to usurp the order put in place by a perfect God. From this perspective, the world is not evolving. It is devolving. It is departing more and more from its intended and original form, destroying itself in its "progress" toward oblivion. Anyone with the slightest awareness of the history of human ethical behavior must agree that Man's compassion for his fellow creatures and for the planet as a whole is rapidly moving toward entopic death.

In opposition to evolutionary logic, the Biblical view posits the need for a complete reconstruction of a presently doomed universe. Progress is not only our least important product, it is the very thing from whom the bell tolls.

We have touched on the judicial dilemma. The same can be said for economic enterprise. The current version of capitalism is fundamentally based on the presupposition of the right of gain. In its evolutionary model, the delivery of gain outweighs any consideration of cost unless and until the exploitation of the sources of supply prevent such exploitation. In other words, evolutionary theory says, "What survives is better than what does not survive. Therefore, if I consume the environment in order to survive, I have only exercised my right to prove that I am of a higher order." This will continue until my use of the sources of gain cause me to not survive (a state that we are approaching). Aided by technology, the evolutionary progress of consumption expands wherever gain can be achieved. But as an example of the other side of the equation, we must take note of the diminishing of raw resources and of human capital. At some point, the quest for gain outstrips the resources and the system collapses.

The Biblical assumption under girding capitalism is fundamentally different. In the Biblical paradigm, gain is a function of stewardship and compassion. In other words, gain must reflect the character of the authority that I serve. I am not the owner, the possessor of resources. I am the caretaker acting on behalf of another. The authority specifically instructs me to "work" and "carefully watch over" the owner's property. It is interesting that the two Hebrew words associated with this primal task of Man are words associated with worship and protection, concepts that are meaningless to a survival logic.

The analysis could go on. Education, family structure, social responsibility, ethical values, cultic behavior, political organization – all of these and more are affected by the shift from personal and divine higher authority to progressive and utopian success. We might usefully explore them, but the case for analysis has been made. The world faces two fundamentally opposed logical tracks. One proposes advancement as the sweeping solution to Man's grief. The other points toward the past, asking us to come to grips with our own inhumanity. One tells us that the final meaning lies in the yet unknown. The other says that once we knew the truth and we lost it along the way. One posits belief in progression. The other claims authority in a Person.

There is a *krisis* before us. The Greek makes it clear. A turning point. A moment of decision. Will you choose survival or submission? You can't have both.

Chapter 3

Leadership: Failing to Solve the Real Problem

*I*t's the latest business fad. Everyone seems convinced that *leadership* is the solution to all our problems. Furthermore, it looks as though the collective genius of the age thinks that everyone can be a leader. All they need is training.

Of course, the idea that absorbing correct information will convert us into leaders is just one more example of the Greek educational model. Add money and you have the world's best recipe for success. Information and money can solve any problem.

Leadership is critical, but what leadership looks like, who functions in the role of leader, what motivates a leader and how we measure success depend a great deal on the embedded worldview. Without a critical assessment of how leadership works, who leaders are and where they are going, we are just as likely to follow Stalin as we are to follow Gandhi. World history proves that. Jesus might be touted as the world's best leadership model, but too often our understanding of what He did and what He said are couched in Hellenized language, goals and mission statements. Despite the popularized suggestion, Jesus was *not* a CEO. He didn't manage by any standards common to the world of top executives. In fact, as a CEO He would probably be fired.

We will need a new look at the Jewish Jesus before we can truly appreciate and copy His approach to leadership. Jesus is simply the human being that God created in the beginning, now made manifest to us in flesh and blood so that we can see what the fulfillment of the Old Testament model of leadership really looks like.

1.

*Now to Him who **is able** to establish you according to my gospel and the preaching of Jesus Christ*   Romans 16:25

Resident Reluctance

Is Able – God is the power. If I am in His will, then He directs that power *through* me, not *to* me. God is in the power *distribution* business. He gives in order that it might be given. God does not create batteries. There is no such thing as *stored up* divine energy. The power that I receive is always intended to flow out of me to others. When I stop the flow, I stand opposed to God's design.

By the way, this principle applies to *all* of God's creation. The *dynamic* (remember *dynamai*?) of creation is the constant *flow* from one thing to another. Batteries are human inventions, not divine ones.

Consider this principle in leadership. God provides the power, not me. When a leader begins to think that it is *his ability* and *his vision* that makes the difference, all the followers are in trouble. The mark of a godly leader is his *reluctance* to accept the job in the first place and his continuing *discomfort* with the call. Godly leaders know that the job is bigger than they are. They often feel overwhelmed and inadequate. They should! After all, if I feel up to the task, I don't need that total, voluntary reliance of God's power to get me through. The day a leader starts to think his position is perfect for him is the day he should leave. Godly leadership always stretches us beyond ourselves because it is all about being poured out every day. The godly leader has no reserves. He must come to God every morning for that day's abilities.

Everywhere we see a different view of leadership, even inside the circle of Christianity. We see people who aspire to be leaders, who grasp at the opportunity and pursue the prestige. They are seeking to be batteries – storehouses of accumulated power. God never endorses such clamoring. You will find God's leaders among those who know their jobs are too much for them, who would prefer to be somewhere else, who are obedient to a call not of their own choosing. You will find God's men and women among those who cry out to Him for help, who have nothing left of their own reserves and who know the heartache of obedience. Those are the ones worth following.

God is able. I am not. That is the motto of a leader. Leave the battery people behind. Follow the reluctant ones who are emptied each day.

2.

Now to Him who is able **to establish** *you according to my gospel and the preaching of Jesus Christ* Romans 16:25

Power Applied

To Establish – There is a bit of buried treasure here. When an Greek infinitive (like "to establish") follows the verb *dynamai* (is able), the sense is a *continuous action*, not a one-time event. Let that sink in a minute. Paul tells us that God is continuously operating with power to cause us to stand firm. What a tremendous relief! This is just what I needed to hear.

Our world loves the phrase, "it's up to you." We take the Greek position of individual responsibility (when we aren't falling victim to entitlement thinking). We adopt the view that my life is in my hands, for better or worse. If I fail, it's my fault. I should have done something differently. If I succeed, then I get the credit. I did the right things. This seems so *natural*, until we confront sin. Then the reality of the world crashes in on us. Even if I want to do the right thing, I soon discover that I have no power to do it. I end up doing the very things I know are wrong (just take a look at Romans 7). The real truth is this: if it's really up to me, I am doomed to failure. There is nothing in me that will guarantee my success because I do not have the resident power to succeed – even when it comes to holiness and sin.

Paul speaks the truth. God establishes us. His power is applied to our weakness in order that we might live in ways that delight Him.

When I try to fight sin in my own strength, it's like turning the sword on myself. Even if I win, I die.

The Greek word *sterizo* comes from a root that means, "to stand." God's power applied to me allows me to *stand*. The result of His power application is seen in my steadfast obedience, my renewed mind, my confirmed convictions and my strength to submit. By the way, this word has links to the idea of resurrection – to stand again. If I want the resurrected life, I will have to let God apply His power to me. No man can lift himself from the grave.

Now let's look at the grammar. Standing is a daily activity. God's power is applied continuously in order that I may be a conduit for His will. Standing is not storing. Today's bread is rotted tomorrow. The only way God's power can be applied is in continuous connection. That means life is either standing through a power not my own or falling because I am disconnected. God is *continuously able*. I am not.

The discovery is to let Him apply the power.

3.

*"Do not work for the food which perishes, but for the **food which endures** to eternal life, which the Son of Man will give to you, for on Him the Father, God, has set His seal."* John 6:27

Maslow Reversed

Food Which Endures – Contemporary psychology tells us that the basic priorities of life must be our first concerns. Only after we have achieved some level of sustainable food, clothing, shelter and security can we turn our attention to the question of self-fulfillment. Maslow's hierarchy of needs captures this common system of beliefs. Start with the basics and progress up the ladder. In an affluent society, that means taking care of my short-term and long-term expectations first. So, financial advisors tell us to make sure we have retirement accounts in place, to insure ourselves against loss and to create a "wealth management" plan. Then we can pay some attention to those other issues like charities, spiritual growth and noble causes. Reduced to its simplest form, this view of the world is "me first – everything else second."

But Jesus has something else to say about food that endures (*brosin ten menousan*). Did you notice that Jesus turns Maslow upside down? In Jesus' view, the most important priority is the *final* result, not the intermediate steps. My "essential" needs take a back seat to God's will for me. Unless I am doing what He wishes, nothing matters. When I am doing what He wishes, nothing else matters. **When I do what God intends, I free God to do what He commits to do – protect and provide.** If I do not obey Him, I essential tie God's hands. He almost never overrides my will. That doesn't make Him less than God. It just makes Him a God who is not a tyrant. The fact that we attempt to act as protector and provider for ourselves really usurps God's authority. When we pay attention to God's order of priorities, we honor God with trust in His control over our lives. But when we take the Maslow approach, we push God aside and pretend that we are in charge of our own arrangements.

Maslow views self-actualization as the *last* step in human development. God views it as the *first* step. "Seek first the Kingdom and My righteousness," says God, "and all of these will be added." Do it the other way around and spend life trying to act in God's place. God's order of priorities is backwards. But then, who knows best? Me or Him?

Few of us truly break the world's mold when it comes to priorities. We succumb to the constant pressure to take care of business. What a shame! When will we let God do what He promises? Wouldn't it make life *easier*?

4.

*"Not everyone saying to me, Lord, Lord, will enter into the kingdom of heaven, but he who **does** the will of my Father"* Matthew 7:21

Terrifying Truth

Does – In case you thought you knew Jesus' words, I would like to challenge you to read His statements again – exactly for what they say. Set aside the preacher's application, the theologian's argument and the Sunday school teacher's feelings. Read it as it is. Jesus was one very scary prophet.

First, notice that He addresses those who claim that He is their Lord. This passage is not for the rebellious pagans or the defiant backsliders. This is for you and me, the ones who do the right religious things and hold our heads up in church. This is for the morally correct, the ones with causes and the altruistic. They come to Jesus with His name on their lips. "Didn't we do all those good things for You?" they query. "Sure, we did. We saw all the things that needed to be done and we did them. We are *good* people, God."

With chilling regard, Jesus says, "No, I never knew you." How is that possible? How can it be that we could heal and preach and do all kinds of humanitarian works and *not* get into the kingdom? The answer is startlingly clear. "You did great things, but they were not what God asked you to do." Jesus suggests that it is not *what* you do but rather *why* you do it that matters. Give your body to be burned. Send all your money to the poor. Sacrifice yourself for the church. It's all for nothing – unless what you do is *precisely* what God *asks* of you.

This slaps all our programs and posturing in the face. Good counts for nothing! The most important question in the whole universe is this: What does God want me to do? The verb is continuous present. Do what God is asking moment-by-moment. Jesus can say this because He lived it. Every moment in the Father's will: that is the goal of life.

Contrary to human opinion, your life is *not* about results. What you accomplish doesn't make one bit of difference in the eternal scheme of things, if your accomplishments are not in alignment with God's desires for *your* life. We're not talking about the *general plan*. We're talking about God's *specifics*, just for you. And, by the way, your failures, encountered in the process of doing God's will, are more important to the eternal plan than any great, good thing you or anyone else ever did without God's commission.

What is God telling you? If you don't know, you better find out. "Lord, Lord!" is not going to make it.

5.

*So the men of Israel took some of their provisions, and did **not ask** for the counsel of the LORD.* Joshua 9:14

Divine Due Diligence

Not Ask – It seemed like an open and shut case. Here comes a group of men ready to make a deal. They look like the right people. They talk like the right people. There is every advantage to making the deal. So, the men of Israel go ahead. They act on what they see. But they forgot the only thing that matters, for what you see is not always what you get. They forgot to ask God what He wanted in this deal. The results were disastrous, not just for those men who made the deal but for generations to come. You see, the deal that they made bound them to a promise not to get rid of the presence of unbelief in the middle of their land. They were tricked but it was too late. It wasn't the trick that caused the problem. The problem came when they didn't think God had anything to say about such an obviously good thing.

The word is *sha'al*. It is used over and over to describe people who *beseech* or *ask* from God. Obviously, it is also used to describe situations when men do *not* ask. The lesson here is that there is not a single thing that God is not interested in. But just like the men of Israel, we often think that God gives us license to just go ahead with the obvious without checking for divine due diligence. We let our common sense and personal inclinations dictate our actions – and usually we regret it. God's way is the *only* right way. His wisdom is the *only* real wisdom.

That brings up a very interesting question. If we know that God is interested in all that we do, and we know that His opinion is the only one that matters, then why don't we ask Him about everything? The answer reveals something deep about the human heart. Ultimately, we all want to make our own choices. We want God's *advice*, not His *command*. We believe that most of the time we are just fine doing it our way. We even sanctify this idea; claiming that as long as it is in alignment with God's word it is God's will. But underneath it all, we want it our way. So we don't ask, pretending that if we don't *know* what God wants, then we are somehow excused. What this really reveals is the essential *rebellious nature* of our existence. We want forgiveness from sins – behaviors – but we don't really want to relinquish rebellion – strategy and attitude. Just like the men of Israel, we have forgotten that a single, tiny mistake made without consultation with the Most High has long-term disastrous consequences.

Today the question is really very simple: Are you asking?

6.

*Everyone who practices sin also practices **lawlessness**; and sin is **lawlessness**.* 1 John 3:4

Rebellious At Heart

Lawlessness – Sometimes the writers of the New Testament tell us something that is so hard to hear we would rather slide past the subject. That's what is happening with this statement from John. We think we know what sin is. It's breaking the list of rules that God set up for us. It's being a "bad" person by not doing what we know is right. But then John tells us that if we go on sinning, we practice *lawlessness*. Suddenly we're confused. Lots of my sins don't violate any laws. In fact, the laws of the land make perfectly legal many things I cringe to consider doing. So how can sin be *lawlessness*? How can I be breaking the law every time I sin?

The Greek word doesn't seem to help. The word is *anomia*. It is often translated by another English word – iniquity. Jesus' statement in Matthew 7:23 uses this word to describe wicked people. Paul uses it (Romans 6:19) to describe what happens to us when we pursue our own desires. Now I'm even more confused. I don't think I'm a wicked person. I actually *want* to serve God. Does this verse mean that when I sin, I am filled with iniquity and terribly wicked?

Years ago Watchman Nee wrote something that clears the air. It also hits us like a sledgehammer. "Sin is a matter of conduct; it is easy to be forgiven of sin. But rebellion is a matter of principle; it is not so easy to be forgiven of rebellion." Suddenly I see. John is not talking about my individual *sins*. He is speaking about my *rebellion*: that deep-seated passion within me that fights against the holiness of God, asserting my *independence* and *self-sufficiency*. It is not the particular *laws* that I either keep or break that matter here. It is my basic core attitude. The opposite of lawlessness is not rule-keeping. It is *submission*. That's what is so difficult. I would much rather be the rich young ruler who in all sincerity said that he kept the *specific* rules. I don't want Jesus to expose my basic core rebellion – my desire to keep the control. I don't want to submit. Why? Because *I* don't want to, that's why! And that is what is at stake here. When I operate from a principle of rebellion, I hate God. Even if I conform to all the rules, even if I practice all the religious requirements, I can still be in rebellion. I can still *wish* that life were going according to my plan.

Submission is the most difficult human choice anyone can ever make. Our very nature cries out against it. We will do *anything* but submit. And that is why submission is at the very center of God's grace. Without submission, there is only iniquity – no matter what you call it. Until you settle the rebellion issue, you live under the principle of lawlessness.

7.

Is this not the **carpenter**, *the son of Mary, and the brother of James, and Joses, and Judas, and Simon?* Mark 6:3

Who Am I?

Carpenter – Are you saddled with a history? Jesus was. It is quite common among human beings to refuse to believe any claim that stretches our past experience. This is particularly true when it comes to people. Once a felon, always a criminal. Once a bigot, always prejudiced.

In ancient near-eastern civilizations, a murderer was punished by strapping the dead body of his victim to his back. He had to carry the rotting corpse until it fully disintegrated. Needless to say, the punishment was very effective. That's a good picture of most of us. We are strapped with this old man on our backs. We pass through life carrying a rotting corpse - the person we used to be. What the world sees is not the reborn believer but the old dead corpse. So the world does not believe. After all, those people you knew before your life in Christ still regard you as the person you once were. You were the joker, the jock, the princess, the prude, the nerd, the never-do-well, the prig or the pig. "Isn't this the carpenter?" they proclaimed. Why should we listen to Him. We know all about Him. They didn't believe Jesus and they won't believe you. Until the resurrection.

The Greek word translated "carpenter" is broader than a man with a saw and hammer. *Tekton* is someone who is a craftsman, skilled in producing works of art from other materials. The same word is used for an artisan, a builder and an iron-worker. In this context, we discover another human identification assumption – you are what you do. How many times have you been identified with your work, as though that is all that really matters about you? Jesus knows what that feels like too. Once you have been pigeon-holed, it's unlikely that anyone will think of you differently, especially if the difference is radical and redemptive.

In Nazareth the crowd was convinced that Jesus was nothing more than that boy they used to see around the wood shop. Even His brothers and His mother (who should have known better) succumbed to this assumption. The people of your home town will have the same difficulties seeing the truth. They will want to keep you in their place, neatly labeled for convenient use. Only one thing will change their minds – resurrection.

Death is expected. Resurrection is not. A man reborn is overwhelming evidence of change. They didn't believe Jesus until they saw Him on the other side of the grave. Keep that in mind when you are faced with skepticism. Dying to self is the necessary prerequisite to a change in identification – for you and for them.

8.

*If you will **fear** the LORD and **serve** Him, and listen to His voice and not rebel against the command of he LORD, then both you and also the king who reigns over you will follow the LORD your God.* 1 Samuel 12:14

Audio Inputs

Fear and Serve - Biblical themes are consistent. The prophets proclaimed them. Jesus acknowledged them. Paul based his teaching on them. One of these uniform exhortations is the theme of "fear and serve." The words are important because they help us understand just how comprehensive these two ideas really are. Fear (*yare*) and serve (*avad*) cover the mental, emotional and volitional aspects of life. No part of living stands outside these actions.

Yare is the verb used in the familiar phrase, "fear of the Lord." It is more than reverence. I can revere a great hero but that does not mean he has a direct influence on my daily activities. Reverence must be combined with awe and alarm if I am to appreciate the full range of *yare*. God is not someone to trifle with. Our contemporary imagery of the kindly grandfather is heresy. Let's put it this way: If you were truly *afraid* of God, would your behaviors change?

Avad is the Hebrew verb for work. This word covers all your labor in living but when it is used to describe serving God, it does not include the connotation of toil. Serving God is a joyous fulfillment of life as it was intended to be. Because each one of us was designed to find true satisfaction when we are productive within God's perfect design, *avad* captures that activity of life that liberates us to be who we were meant to be. Yes, *avad* is about obedience, but it is not about compulsory oppression. It is about exuberant, voluntary submission to my God-given destiny under His direction. Let's put it this way: If you are truly serving the Lord, you discover that what you do is the most natural, exhilarating, liberating thing that you could ever imagine doing.

Fear and serve are the prerequisites to listen. You cannot hear the voice of the One Who made you to fulfill His purposes until you reverence Who He is, recognize your insignificance before His majesty and offer yourself to His perfect design. The shout in the thunderstorm, the whisper in the bubbling brook, the cry of the crashing waves, the murmur in the leaves – all these, and His words and deeds, become the audio inputs of God's direction. The world is filled with the voice of the Lord if you have ears to hear it.

9.

*But if you will not listen to the voice of the LORD and you **rebel** against the mouth of the LORD, then the hand of the LORD shall be against you and against your fathers.* I Samuel 12:15

No Revolution

Rebel – In 2007, I traveled to Cuba. It was a stark reality check for those who believe in socialism or the essential goodness of Man. In spite of ubiquitous political placards proclaiming the glory of the revolution, the cities are crumbling, the economy is nothing more than the personal bank account of Fidel and the people express their situation as being in "prison." Fifty years of despotism under the banner of civil liberty has done nothing but remove hope from a once-vibrant island. But we should not be surprised. Long ago the prophet Samuel proclaimed God's inviolable law of government. Rebellion guarantees destruction.

The Hebrew word *marah* has two contexts – political and theological. When it comes to God's governance of the world, these two are mixed. This verb describes "the attempt of the subordinate to escape from a dependent relationship." We might be tempted to cheer such bravery. After all, we abhor slavery in any form. But what is at stake here is not liberty but sanity. My relationship to God is not a two-way street. He is not ruler because I have chosen Him to be so. He didn't take over with a coup. He is the absolute one and only Creator God who rules by divine right. To attempt to free myself from my innate and essential dependency on Him is sheer insanity. Such rebellion can lead to only one thing – death. In fact, God has so ordered the universe that those who rebel against Him are ultimately guaranteed to experience His unbridled wrath. What Creator would act otherwise? It is unconscionable to think that the perfect Creator can abide His own perfectly designed creatures to secede from union with His created order. Yet that is precisely the objective of rebellion.

Rebellion is, unfortunately, deeply embedded in the hearts of men. Under the sugar coating of rights and religion, it is often found in you and me. Humans are infected with a mental disease called self-centered liberty. It is lethal but appears harmless. That's why we need a prophet – one who brings us the warning from El Shaddai. If you want to see what rebellion looks like after 50 years, come with me to Cuba. If you want to see what it looks like after 50 *centuries*, open your Bible. The attitude is the same. So are the consequences.

In God's world, you cannot secede and succeed.

10.

And do not turn aside to go after **worthless** *things which do not profit and do not deliver, for they are worthless.* I Samuel 12:21

Lethal Nothings

Worthless – Let's consider one of the strangest and most difficult words in the Hebrew Scriptures. You might think you are quite familiar with this word. After all, it is found in one of the Bible's most famous passages. It occurs in Genesis 1:2 – "and the earth was without form and void." In Hebrew, this is *tohu wabohu*. *Tohu* occurs only 39 more times in Scripture. To this day, scholars are unable to clearly identify its etymology or exactly specify its meaning. But this much is clear. *Tohu* is antithetical to any living thing.

Tohu generally describes five related conditions. These are: trackless wasteland, desolation, lifelessness, futility and

122

worthlessness. The common thread behind *tohu* seems to be a sphere that is alien to all life. It is an ominous, chaotic, desolate, dark, destructive opposition to created order. Consequently, it is filled with peril, menace and foreboding. It is the *negation* of God and His creation. If there were ever a word that described a place where life is sucked out of you, then *tohu* is that word.

Are you frightened? Don't dismiss this horror as ancient, near-eastern mythology. There is something else about *tohu* that should send a shiver up your spine. In the Bible, *tohu* is contagious. Spend enough time around *tohu* and you will become infected with the very essence of life-denying terror. Touch it often and you will feel its effect, sucking vitality out of you. Chase after its seductive ploys and you will find, perhaps too late, that you are among the walking dead. That's Samuel's point. Once you turn away from God, you turn away from life – no matter how attractive the prospects *seem* to be, the end is always *tohu* – waste, futility, desolation and death.

The opposite of *tohu* is not peace, prosperity, happiness or health. The opposite of *tohu* is God, for God is order, fulfillment, satisfaction, well-being and life itself. So, do a little *tohu* checkup. Are you turning aside to the things that do not profit and do not deliver? Are your days directed at accumulating those things that have no future over the horizon of your life? Are you living the "spend it now" plan? *Tohu* awaits all who serve short-sighted ends. If your dreams and desires can be achieved this side of the grave, you might be infected already.

11.

Solomon also made a house for Pharaoh's daughter whom he had **taken**. 1 Kings 7:8

In the Grip

Taken – In the middle of several chapters that describe the opulence of Solomon's building project comes this one sentence comment. We might be tempted to skim over it. After all, it's not as appealing as the vivid imagery of this enormous palace with all of its artistic construction. But this after-thought is really the focal point of disaster. Yes, it is surrounded by visible signs of blessing and success. From the outside the house appears sound. Everyone would wish to live in this king's palace. But there is a problem on the inside – a problem all the more visible if we recognize the Hebrew word that describes Solomon's relationship to Pharaoh's daughter.

The verb is *laqah*. It means, "to get or take." Since it has a wide range of applications, the exact meaning must be determined from the context. But a look at its other occurrences shows us something we need to understand here. Genesis 12:5 uses this verb to describe seizing an animal. In 1 Samuel, it is used for capturing. In Proverbs, it has the nuance of buying and acquiring. In Isaiah (with a special object), it describes taking vengeance. In Job, it describes the heart being swept away. Now think about Solomon. Pharaoh's daughter is not simply a marriage of political convenience. This relationship has a lot of possible elements that appear much more aggressive and hostile than we would like to see between a husband and wife. Perhaps Solomon discovers that he cannot resist the temptation to have her. Perhaps his addiction to women is beginning to grow. Certainly he has long forgotten God's command for household purity. She comes to him, or he *takes* her, with all her foreign idolatry. Perhaps there is an element to this arrangement that is found in the use of *laqah* in Ezekiel where the word describes the flashing of a lightning bolt. Solomon is mesmerized. He must have her regardless of the cost. In the midst of God's bounty, he *takes* something for himself. It is a terrible mistake.

Solomon never recovered from his addiction. It grew and grew until its insatiable lust destroyed him. But it started with *taking* something God did not give.

All good things come from the Father above. That means we are the recipients of His gifts. **We are not required to pry them out of His hands.** He provides all we need without restraint. But sometimes we find ourselves tempted to *take*. We decide that we should have what we want. Instead of waiting for the gift, we usurp God's generosity. It is always a mistake.

Take care – and take an inventory of your own possessions. What has God given? What have you taken? Addiction lies under the surface of those things taken.

12.

But He Himself would often slip away to the **wilderness** *and pray.* Luke 5:16

The Heart of Darkness

Wilderness – It's likely that you have a marginal note in your Bible about this word. It literally means "lonely places." The Greek is *tais eremois.* It's plural – more than one place. The verb here literally means "withdrawing." Jesus had a very different reaction to fame. Today the great religious leader gives interviews on Good Morning America, has a mega-church, a personal website and a long string of publishing credentials; but not Jesus. When His fame spread through the countryside, He deliberately retreated to the lonely places. He avoided the crowds. He stepped away from the limelight. Why would He do this? Couldn't He have accomplished more for the Kingdom by accepting the recognition?

There is a powerful – and difficult – lesson in leadership found in this word, *eremois.* It's all about the heart of darkness. Jesus knew that reputation and fame among men was the center of a great temptation. We all want recognition and when it is offered to us *for good reasons*, it seems quite natural to accept the accolades. After all, Jesus was healing and preaching. He was famous for *good* works.

But Jesus knew that only One person could grant approval that truly mattered. All the rest was potential distraction and disaster. All the rest was laced with hubris. So Jesus withdrew – to the heart of darkness where the Father offered counsel. He went to the lonely places – the places that were empty except for God.

If you're like me, you will do just about anything to avoid the lonely places. In fact, those places – inside and outside – scare me. I don't like the feelings I find in those places. I walk a little faster to get away from them, or I find a comfortable distraction to push them aside. I'm a product of a culture that hates lonely places. That's why we stuff our environment with non-stop noise and entertainment. We just don't want to be close to the holes in our lives.

But Jesus went there on purpose. He realized that human emptiness is God-space. If I want to be with the Father, I have to go toward the holes. If I want to be a leader who knows the Father's will, I will have to seek Him rather than the kudos of my devoted followers. The leader after God's own heart is the leader who spends more time in the heart of darkness than on the stage. Why? Because God is in the empty places.

Don't tell me you're exempt because you're not a leader. You are called to be like Jesus. That means you are called to the wilderness. Embrace your emptiness. God lives there.

13.

*and what things you learned and received and heard and saw **in me**, practice these things,* Philippians 4:9

The Gospel We Read

In Me – The truth is that the combination of these two tiny words (*en emoi* – "in me") scares me to death. I simply can't imagine telling someone to look at me, listen to me, study from me and discover God's peace! But that's exactly what Paul says. How is this possible? Is Paul such a saint that I can never step into his shoes – let alone the shoes of Jesus? Am I hopelessly condemned to a standard I will never achieve?

I don't think so.

I remember that Paul is also Saul, the man who terrorized the church and who was feared by followers of the Way. I remember that it was Paul who wrote those agonizing words of Romans 7 – "who will deliver me from this body of death?" I remember that this same Paul cried out to God three times to be rescued from a continuous "messenger from Satan" (2 Corinthians 12:7). Perhaps he is not so different after all. What makes Paul a man who can tell others to look at him and see that the peace of God is not in his saintliness? It is his total acceptance of God's surpassing grace in the life of a sinful man. I see the peace of God in Paul because I see *through* Paul into the face of Jesus. It's not Paul who is on display. It's the Christ who rescued that sinner Paul, a man just like me. And if the people in his presence could see Jesus through the struggle, disobedience, heartache, trials and victories of Paul, then I guess they might be able to see Jesus through all of my frustrations as well.

It was never about me. It could never have been about me. I am just a sinner saved by grace. Just like you. Just like Paul.

Read the gospel in my life – and see what God can do with someone so unworthy. That's the *only* reason to look at me. You will discover God's peace because if God can do something with the mess of my life, then He can certainly do something in your life too. *Through* the glass darkly – that's the only way you can see Jesus in me.

14.

*"But you have this, that you hate the work of the **Nicolaitans**, which I also hate."* Revelation 2:6

Satanic Order

Nicolaitans – There aren't many expression where the Alpha and Omega, the Lamb of God, says that He *hates* certain people, so when we read these words, we better pay attention. Most of us will see nothing more here than an obscure reference to some first century sect. We'll dismiss the bold remark as a lost bit of apocalyptic literature. We need to be much more careful.

127

The Greek word *nikolaiton* comes from two other words, *nike* and *laos*. Literally, it means those who have victory over the people. Now the words start to become ominous. Which category of human beings has victory over the people? We usually call them "leaders." Suddenly this verse carries a very contemporary judgment. Is Yeshua saying that He hates leaders? Hardly! But there is a kind of leadership that ranks high on the list of detestable things. It is the leadership that inserts human authority between the believer and God. In other words, Yeshua is saying that wherever we find human beings asserting that their authority stands between God and His children, we are looking at the Satanic order.

It's possible that we just might find Nicolaitans in the middle of the church or in our homes. How can we say this? Because the priesthood of all believers, asserted by God Himself in the designation of Israel, boldly proclaims that you and I have *direct access to God*. We are not required to go through the elders, the deacons, the pastor, the bishop or any other figure in the religious hierarchy. In fact, although God loves order and certain *functions* within the Body are performed at His calling and direction, no human being has authority to act as your mediator before God. Yeshua, the Messiah, fills that role – and only He can do it. Other members of the Body may be able to offer you advice and counsel, but God expects you to come to Him for life instruction. That's why He was so careful (and gracious) to tell us how to live.

This applies to the home as well. Everyone in the household has direct access to God. There is no hierarchy that requires a wife to access God *through* her husband. Order is not the same as intimacy. There is one head of the church and since the church is the assembly of all believers, there is only one head for each believer in that community – and it isn't the man of the house. Whenever husbands begin to act as though they are the spiritual access point for everyone the family, they are walking the path of the Nicolaitans. Be very careful.

We might agree with all this *theoretical* discussion but that is not the purpose of adopting a biblical worldview. The purpose is to change our behavior. It is to align ourselves with God and become transparent transporters of God's design. So, it's time to ask how you're doing? Are you yielding to a Nicolaitan in disguise? Are you acting as though some human being has spiritual authority between you and God? Or perhaps you are tending to be a Nicolaitan. Perhaps you've asserted that you are the one the people need to consult before they can know the will of God. Satan loves to tweak the original design just enough to detour us. Don't become part of his order or participate in any community that follows his influence. Jesus *hates* those who try to replace Him.

15.

Do not rejoice *when your enemy falls, and do not let your heart be glad when he stumbles, or the LORD will see it and be displeased, and turn His anger away from him.* Proverbs 24:17-18

He Got What He Deserved

Do Not Rejoice – How common it is for us to exult in the defeat of an enemy! There is that little bit of human revenge that surfaces when we see disaster befall someone who has opposed us. We feel perfectly justified. After all, he got what he deserved. Even God would agree. Sin requires punishment.

This proverb shocks us. It stands in opposition to all our sense of fairness. But unless we understand its deeper meaning, we will simply pass over its command as unrealistic or unnecessary. How can God really expect us *not* to feel good about just punishment?

The Hebrew root is *samach* (to be glad, to be joyful, to gloat). Here the phrase is *al tis-mach* - "do *not* be glad or gloat." Why? Because gloating over the fall of an enemy misunderstands the heart of God. God punishes but His punishment is always accompanied by tears of sorrow. God weeps justice. Every punishment is intended to bring the wicked back into relationship with Him. The very fact that punishment is needed only underlines the injury and despair that sin has introduced into those who bear His image. God is not only crucified, He goes to the cross with tears of sorrow.

Verse 18 explains just how deeply compassionate God really is. His mercy is so much a part of His character that He will not promote further injustice by rejoicing over the defeat of His enemies nor will He encourage any circumstances that promote callousness or cynicism. In fact, the sin of gloating over deserved punishment is so great that God will turn His anger away from those who are under His wrath in order to prevent callous disregard for the terrible state of the wicked.

Our human inclination is a despicable misrepresentation of the true heart of the Savior. His compassion had the taste of tears, not just for those who experienced injustice at the hands of the wicked, but for the inevitable punishment that the wicked would inherit. No wonder Jesus exhorted us to love our enemies. The heart of the Father was broken over their disobedience. Is yours?

16.

*All that my eyes desired I did not refuse them. I did not withhold my heart from any pleasure, for my heart was pleased because of all of my labor and this was my **reward** for all my labor.* Ecclesiastes 2:10

Christian Capitalism

Reward – What is your reward for your effort? Are you working to accumulate whatever your eyes desire or whatever your heart longs to have? If you're like most modern capitalists, you are in pursuit of something, exchanging your labor for some possession, wondering all the while how you will ever be free from the vicious cycle of consumption. The Bible has an answer but before we can hear it, we need to remember the words of Solomon.

It looks as though Solomon says that the "reward" of his labor was the good life. But the Hebrew word is *heleq*. It means, "a portion, a share, a part." This is not quite what we expected. What Solomon is really saying is that he received his *share* as a result of his efforts. That implies that his portion is only a part of the whole. He is not out to gain the world. He is not trying to take what belongs to another.

He only wants his piece of the pie. Tragically, he discovers that the piece that he desired leaves him empty. After he has eaten his portion, his appetite is still unsatisfied.

Solomon knew about rewards for labor. He took full advantage of his power and position, denying himself nothing. He thought that he could discover happiness in accumulation, but he learned one of life's hardest lessons. In the end, all that we have acquired is left behind. In the end the poorest and the richest rot together under the ground.

Capitalism requires community to make it work. There must be buyers and sellers. I need others if I am going to turn my labor into possessions. God blesses this process, and He has done so since long before Solomon. But what God intended for good, men often twist just a bit. The result is perversion of something holy. The perversion of capitalism is believing that once I have used the community for my own purposes (wealth), then I don't need to care what happens to others. Once I have achieved my own goals (what my eyes desired, what my heart longed to have), I have no further need of the community that I used to achieve my goals. I replace capitalism for divine purposes with capitalism for self-sufficiency.

God wants me to be successful *for the purpose of distribution* to the community. God grants me my share *for the purpose of using it to benefit others.* God is about community. He provides and equips us to act as He would act in this world – and in this world God gives.

If you are feeling like Solomon today, wondering what it will take to bring satisfaction to your empty world of accumulation, try God's way: give your share to someone else. You might discover that life is not vanity after all.

17.

*Whoever would draw near to God must believe that he exists and that he **rewards** those who seek him* Hebrews 11:6 (RSV)

New Testament Rewards

Rewards - Do you want to be closer to God? Then this verse is for you. Just make sure that you know what it says. It's not about rewards. It's about the One Who provides the reward.

If I want to be closer to God, I must first acknowledge His existence. That's a lot more than simply stating that there is a god. The demons acknowledge that God exists but they aren't any closer to Him. Believing that God exists is the equivalent of acknowledging, honoring and submitting to His sovereignty. If I say, "I believe God exists," I imply that I am not God, that God is worthy of worship and that my spiritual duty and desire is to serve Him. Without this, my claim to believe in God is no more significant than the statement of the demons. Unless God is Lord over me, what I claim about His existence means nothing.

There is one other requirement. You must believe that He wants your intimacy. The Greek text actually says, "that He becomes a rewarder to those." Notice that the emphasis in the Greek is not on the reward, but rather on the *rewarder*. God *becomes the rewarder* of those who earnestly seek to draw near while fully submitting to His authority. The word in Greek is *misthapodotes*. It is derived from two words; one that means "wages or reward" and the other that means "to render, to give from." God renders appropriate wages to those who seek Him. God is the perfect paymaster giving exactly what is due based on the effort expended.

Paul said the same thing. Just as the wages of sin is death, so the wages of intimacy with God is life. Oh, you thought that Paul said eternal life is a *gift*, not a reward. You are right, of course. It is not *your* wages. You didn't earn it. Jesus did. Jesus earned life for you. You receive *His* wages because Jesus practices God's version of capitalism – He gives away His share.

What does this mean for you? If you are going to model Jesus, then you will need to do the same thing. What you earn in the presence of the Father must be given away to someone who has *not* earned it.

Take that joy, peace, fulfillment, reconciliation, forgiveness and purpose – take God, the true reward – and give it away. What you try to hold for yourself will be lost. What you freely give will be found.

New Testament rewards are upside-down. They come through emptying. What did you expect? A bigger bank account?

18.

*And just as it happened in the **days of Noah**, so it shall be also in the days of the Son of Man* Luke 17:26

The End – Part One

Days of Noah – In the days of Noah, people assumed life would continue as usual. They were unprepared for the shock of God's verdict. Jesus tells us that they ate, drank and married. Their lives consisted in propagating of the species. Focused on their physical needs, they didn't see the end coming. *Tais hemerais tou Noe* seemed quite ordinary – until the Flood.

Jesus says that the days of Noah are like the days of the Son of Man. That should give us pause. The Son of Man has come – and He will come again. If we aren't aware of our circumstances, we will be caught off guard just as all those citizens of Noah's world were. So, we must ask, "What were the characteristics of the days of Noah and do they look like my days?"

Every day involves eating and drinking if you want to survive. There is nothing new or unusual about this. It is part of the human condition. Jesus did not mean to imply that the reason these people were taken by surprise is that they were not *fasting*. He meant that they were eating and drinking without regard to the true reality of life. They took care of themselves without considering Who was taking care of what they ate and drank. Paul understood their mistake. He proclaimed that those who ignored God's sovereignty and refused to be thankful received what they deserved (Romans 1:21). They should have known better.

133

In the days of Noah, men married and women were given in marriage. They concentrated on the delights of intimacy. Their goals in life peaked in human relationships. This does not mean that they were sexually immoral. They simply forgot that God is also the God of sex. They did not acknowledge that God owns our bodies. They are not ours to do with as we please.

Jesus says that in the days of the Son of Man, things will be pretty much as usual. Men and women will be caught up in the process of daily living. They will seek sustenance for the body in food, drink and sex. None of these are wrong but all of them are inadequate. Unless we live under the lordship of the sovereign God, all our efforts to maintain ourselves are nothing more than dangerous diversions. Unless we are constantly aware of the presence of the Son, we will eat, drink and procreate while we step into the grave.

Today life is very much like the days of Noah. Jesus calls us to see more than a world of food, drink and relationship. There is something else happening here. Do you know what it is? Is it changing your thinking *today*?

19.

*It was the same as happened in **the days of Lot**; they were eating, they were drinking, they were buying, they were selling, they were planting, they were building;* Luke 17:28

The End – Part Two

The Days of Lot – Did you notice what changed in the days of Lot? Life shifted from preoccupation with basic needs to preoccupation with commerce. Now men were buying, selling, planting and building. Economic enterprise took center stage.

Tais hemerais Lot were not days filled with debauchery. Sodom was not destroyed solely for its immorality. Ezekiel clarifies our thinking (Ezekiel 16:49). Sodom was condemned because God's blessing of abundance became a source of affluent indifference and arrogance. Sodom refused to share God's goodness with the poor. Its moral failure was far deeper than sex. It was a failure of vision. Sodom forgot that God is a God of compassion.

Civilization graduated from Noah to Lot. It moved from physical needs to commercial endeavors. But its spiritual appetite did not improve. Human development does not equal progress in God's book. Unless there is a deeper experience of the character of God in human actions, the result is always the same – destruction.

In the days of Noah, human sustenance was no savior. In the days of Lot, human enterprise meant nothing. There is only one Rescuer in this world and He is also the Judge. We can walk without Him for awhile, but the end is inevitable. Life is intended to reflect the character of the Creator. Anything less is simply destruction in abeyance.

Today men are consumed with the Lot syndrome. Money trumps everything. Economic gain overwhelms all human dignity, compassion and mercy. In this world, a man's destiny is determined by his bank account. That is, unfortunately, too often true in both directions. The world lauds the rich while God holds them responsible for His intentions. The fact that the world's wealthiest 250 have more assets than the world's poorest 2.5 billion is only one symptom of this cancer. If I can keep a man's entire family alive for a day on what I spend on a drink at McDonald's, don't you think God will ask me why I had to have that super-sized meal? What will I say that could possibly excuse such selfishness?

Jesus reminds us that in the days of Lot, men thought the economic engine was their salvation. But death came anyway. Life and death are never in the hands of Man. **When we forget that our abundance has heavenly purposes, we live in Sodom even if we claim to be moral.**

Take that to the bank.

20.

*But the Lord became furious with me **because of you** and he did not listen to me.* Deuteronomy 3:26

135

The Tie That Binds

Because Of You – Do you aspire to leadership? Watch out! Leadership carries with it enormous consequences for your personal spiritual experience. Moses discovered that he had to pay a price for those who rebelled against the Lord under his leadership *even though he was innocent.*

We are tempted to think that Moses did not enter the promised land because of some personal sin. But Moses himself says otherwise. God refused to allow Moses to enter the land because the people under his care rebelled against the Lord. In other words, Moses was held accountable for the *corporate* response of all those who were committed to his leadership. Moses paid for another's sin.

What a devastating reminder this is to us! In a day when we aspire to the status and prestige of leadership, we fail to recognize the terrible responsibility that comes with such a gift. How do you feel knowing that God holds you accountable for those He has put under your care? Are you ready to answer for your children, your Bible study group, your church, your employees? Do you see that their acceptance or rejection of God's purposes has *direct consequences for you*? How many leaders have never experienced the fullness of God's ultimate intention because they had followers who fell away from the truth? Suddenly we see that the context of God's plan is always within the *community*. We might stand before Him individually in terms of guilt and forgiveness, but we do not stand before Him individually in terms of the exercise of His purposes. When the Lord asks about our leadership, He will not focus on our personal purity. He will ask about the faith and commitment of those who followed us.

If this doesn't send a chill up your spine, then you do not understand how immense such responsibility is. Moses knew. His entire mission was to bring the people into the land of milk and honey. Everything he did was devoted to accomplishing that goal. But he was denied completion. He ended a life spent in progress unfulfilled – and all because some under his authority chose to disobey. In our Greek world, we think in terms of individual responsibility. But God is not Greek! He thinks in terms of corporate responsibility. You and I better change our point of view.

Is the completion of God's purpose in your life going to be frustrated because someone under your authority chooses to disobey? Does that possibility grieve you? What are you going to do about it now?

21.

*Now I Paul myself urge you by the meekness and **gentleness** of Christ*
2 Corinthians 10:1

Material Distinctions

Gentleness – Did you think that Paul was simply being redundant? Did you think that "meekness" and "gentleness" were really pretty much the same? Not so! There is a material difference between these two Greek words – a difference that is critical if we are to understand and exhibit that true form of meekness found in the Beatitudes (Matthew 5:5 – terribly mistranslated in the NASB as "gentleness").

"Meekness" is the Greek word *praotees*. "Gentleness" is the word *epieikeia*. The problem is that there is no exact equivalent in English for *epieikeia*. It is not about the same thing as *praotees*. *Praotees* we can translate. It means power domesticated. It is about an inner spirit of control that is exhibited in calm assurance. It is *not* about wallflower withdrawal. It is about a deep and abiding sense of inner freedom knowing that what could be done need not be done. **Meekness is deserving your rights and deliberately choosing to forego them.**

Not so with gentleness (*epieikeia*). This word *always* contains the nuance of condescension. It is about someone superior giving something over to an inferior. This word actually implies that the person holds a superior place which is exhibited in outward acts. Therefore, a *gentle* person may act with humility but he knows himself to be superior. A *meek* person knows that he is nothing apart from God and acts accordingly.

Clearly, those who are *meek* are blessed by God. Those who are *gentle* are often hiding self-superiority. They have their own reward.

What do we do with Paul's statement that Jesus is both meek and gentle? Certainly we can see Jesus as *praotees* (meek) but how is Jesus *epieikeia* (gentle) if this second word contains the concept of superiority? The answer is easy. Jesus does not have *false* superiority as do so many of us who claim to be gentle. Jesus is, in fact, the only completely legitimate example of *epieikeia*. He is the superior – of all. Therefore, His outward exhibition of granting blessing and favor is not laced with false pride. He has the right and the authority to act as the superior because God has lifted Him to the place of honor.

For us, *epieikeia* is always dangerous. It is so easy to slip into self-importance, especially when we are giving out benevolence. Concentrate on meekness – your rights placed aside for the sake of others. God will take care of gentleness when He sees fit.

22.

Therefore whoever **wishes** *to be a friend of the world makes himself an enemy of God.* James 4:4

Thought Control

Wishes – "But, I'm not a friend of the world!" you complain. "This scripture isn't about me. I believe in Jesus." Well, maybe we need to carefully examine the Greek here. The translation "wishes" doesn't exactly capture what James has in mind. The word is *boulethe*. It has some unusual connotations that are vitally important. It is distinguished from another Greek word, *thelo*, in the following way: *boulomai* (the root of our word) is about the *passive propensity or willingness* to enter into an arrangement with the world whereas *thelo* expresses the *active engagement* with the things of the world. You see, James is not saying that I must be actively pursuing the world's measurement standards. All I have to do is be predisposed in that direction. All I have to do is *wish* they would apply.

"I wish things would turn out better for me. I don't understand why God has to make it so hard." Passive denial of sovereignty and divine correction.

"Of course God wants me to be a winner. Then I can serve Him even better." Passive willingness to use prosperity as God's measure of acceptability.

"If they would just leave me alone, I know I could be true to Jesus." Passive denial of God's choice of circumstances and use of affliction for His purposes.

"As soon as I have this under control, I'll give more money to charity." Passive acceptance of the world's priority scale.

"But I don't have time to deal with this right now. I have a schedule to keep." Passive denial of God's arrangement of life's interruptions.

Go ahead. Add some to the list. James points out that all we have to do is fawn over worldly fame, fan the flames of celebrity desires, want to "be like Mike" and dozens of other ways that we *wish* we could make our dreams come true. **If your dreams are not saturated with the desires of Jesus, then you are predisposed to adopt another standard.** The devil met you in the wilderness and you were overcome. Bodily needs, community recognition or earthly power seduced you. You made yourself God's enemy.

Now what will you do?

If you really want to visit St. Peter, go to the prison or the hospital. I'm quite sure you will find him there. He never cared a lot about marble. Silver and gold are not on his priority list.

23.

Instead, you ought to say, "If the Lord wills, we shall live and also do this or that." James 4:15

Presumptive Arrogance

Instead – What difference does it really make? We can go through the motions of saying "If the Lord wills," a common expression in the last century, but does it really matter? After all, we still have to do the planning and the executing, right? Who cares if we add this little "religious" phrase?

This is the sort of thinking that James wants to attack. Thinking like this is presumptive arrogance. It assumes that my agenda will happen simply because I decide to make it happen. It is the final result of the *"carpe diem"* philosophy. It is the power of positive thinking made manifest. I rule my universe and I can achieve whatever I want if I just work hard enough at it. How many times have you heard something similar? Go for the gusto. It's all up to you.

James introduces the divine correction to this heresy with the Greek word *anti*. James provides the anti-arrogance pill. Don't you get it? You are *not* in charge of the world – not even your tiny world. You are not in charge of anything, not even your breathing. God is the author and sustainer of life itself. What you are able to do only occurs because He allows it. To think otherwise is to misunderstand the basic structure of the universe. *Carpe diem* only works *after* you have received directions from the Boss. If you go to the planning table without an expectation of God's intervention, you are a fool.

James wants us to re-consider our *ordinary* lives. If Jesus is God, then He is the smartest person who ever walked the planet. Furthermore, He never lies. Wouldn't you want that kind of advice when you start thinking about tomorrow? Then why are you considering agendas without His input? Do you think that Jesus is ignorant about marketing, managing or manufacturing? When He said, "You can do nothing without Me," He meant it. How much of your ordinary planning for tomorrow includes a deliberate pause to allow Jesus to speak His mind on the matter? How many "to do" lists and schedules and arrangements are made without a second thought toward the Author of everything?

James is not trying to overwhelm you with philosophical concepts. He is trying to get your orientation correctly aligned.   God is in charge. Period. Make allowances for that. Don't think you run your life. Let Him direct your every step. That's what He wants to do – and He is quite capable of doing it if you are willing to set aside your presumptive arrogance and wake up to the truth.

"If the Lord wills" should be on the lips of every Christian every day. It is the proper motto of a godly life. Is it your motto today?

24.

*for now I **know** that you fear God, since you have not withheld your son, your only son, from Me.* Genesis 22: 12

A Man Of Principle (1)

Know – God provides us with a very practical definition of what it means to *fear* Him. That definition is found in the story of Isaac's sacrifice. What we learn about proper reverence and attitude before God is so important that we must reflect on it for at least a decade or two. This verse brings it all into focus and in the clarity it provides, we confront several life-altering implications.

First, we have to ask, "Didn't God already *know* that Abraham was His faithful servant?" Why does the verse say that *now* God knows?

To answer this question, we must deeply consider the meaning of the fear of God. Wolff comments that the fear of God is "obedience which does not hold back even what is most precious, when God demands it, and commits to God even that future which he himself has promised." Did you get that? It is not merely releasing what we hold most dear. It is releasing what is most dear even if doing so will apparently alter our future forever. In other words, to fear God is to commit to Him whatever He asks in sacred trust that His purposes are served no matter what the future may portend. It is to ruthlessly trust that God's promise is as solid as rock *no matter how shaky the ground is under my feet*.

Do you think this is easy? I beg to differ. Are you ready to commit your emotional stability, your hopes and dreams, your sense of well-being to the altar *only* on the basis that God asks? Are you ready to let go of all those plans, all that emotional investment in yourself, *confident* that God will make of you what He wishes? Are you able to sacrifice that one special relationship here on earth, the one that keeps you sane, that brings you joy and desire and love, the one you are fully invested in? Do you really believe that God can take care of your future? Or are you afraid that you will finally be like Job, rewarded with a new family but visiting the graves of lost children?

The Hebrew verb *yada* (to know) covers a very wide range of meanings. What it points to in this verse is the startling implication that the fear of God brings a true intimacy found only in a relationship of utter devotion. In other words, Abraham has been faithful as a matter of *principle*. He is obedient as one would be obedient to a king or commander. He follows orders. But this is not what God really wants. God wants *intimate devotion* and devotion is manifested in ways that are strikingly different than compliance (just ask your spouse). Christianity is ultimately not a religion of principle. When relationship is reduced to rules, love is converted to legalism. What God wants, what God must know, is this: "Are you *devoted* to Me?" God does not want you to play by the rules. He wants you to *love* Him.

Is your faith based on *principle*, or is it an expression of *intimate devotion*? How do you know?

25.

*for now I know that you fear God, since you have not withheld your son, your **only** son, from Me.* Genesis 22: 12

A Man Of Principle (2)

Only – Do you have a collection? Maybe baseball cards, souvenirs, stamps, dolls? Then you know the value of a "one-of-a-kind" item. Sometimes such things are literally priceless. What is the value of the Hope diamond or a signed Picasso? In the ancient world, these kinds of collections carried far less value than "arrows in the quiver" – children. The value of an *only* child was priceless. All the legacy, all the name and all the inheritance depended on the life of that one child. When Abraham went up the mountain in devotion to the God that he served, he took with him a *priceless* offering.

This demonstration of the concept of the fear of the Lord rests on the Hebrew word *yachiydh* (only). Bring your offering to God. If it is the first fruits of your labor, the first profit from your business, the first receipt from your earnings, there will be more later. But let God ask for the one-of-a-kind offering and suddenly the act of obedience must be based on something far deeper. Then the test is one of devotion.

Serving God is always subject to *principle* sabotage. Because serving God is such a fragile thing, based as it is in the inner workings of a heart relationship, I am always tempted to convert my obedience to the letter of the law. In fact, I find this quite easy to do when it comes to everything but the one-of-a-kind situation. Why? Because I know that replacements are possible. As a matter of principle, I can offer something from multiple items because there are more to come. But what happens when there is only one? What happens when, in my whole lifetime, there is only *one* like this one? Principle cannot sustain me because principle is ultimately based upon self-interest. I live according to principle because I believe that the principle I accept is for my own well-being. That is why God must break through my principled life. A sacrifice based on devotion is required precisely because it is *not* in my best interests. It is in the best interests of the one I am devoted to.

I love my wife. Doing all the things I am supposed to do as a husband is one of the principles of a good marriage. Doing these serves my best interests. Happy wife – happy life. That's a principle. But how would I behave toward her if I had nothing to gain, if my actions would never result in reciprocity? That would be a test of devotion. In fact, what my wife really wants is devotion. Maintaining the principles is no substitute for true devotion any more than rule-keeping makes a genuine relationship. Devotion is demonstrated when there is nothing in it for me.

The story of Abraham's obedience challenges each of us to take what is most precious, our personal one-of-a-kind treasure, and allow God to test our devotion through this "sacred" possession. Principles will fail in a trial like this. But that's the point. **If you truly fear God, your life must move beyond the principle of obedience.** There are no rules when it comes to devotion. Engage your heart completely and experience freedom on another plane. That's why it says *love* Him with all your heart, not *serve* Him with all your heart.

26.

*"Woe to the rebellious children," declares the LORD, "who execute a **plan**, but not Mine' and who make an alliance, but not of My Spirit"* Isaiah 30:1

Life As It Is

Plan – We are big on planning. We plan for business success, career advancement, income investment and retirement. We plan for our safety. We even plan our children. We congratulate ourselves because we have so much under control. But I wonder if we haven't incited God's anger with all our planning. If Isaiah offers any insight, it is this: my plans lead only to sinful arrogance if I am not executing His plan.

The problem with planning is that our plans usually assume that there is some mysterious force in control of life that we have to tame or master in order to get what we want. We operate under the "life as it is" assumption. We think that it's really up to us to get a handle on living. I am beginning to see that God has a different point of view.

It's not that God doesn't like plans. The implication in this declaration of woe is clear. God has a plan that we can, *and should*, know. Our job is to execute *His* plan, not to execute our plans. There is still a plan. The question is who is the author. God expects me not to take life as it comes but rather to engage in life *as I allow it*. That means that I have to have a personal, involved intimacy with the One Who engineers my life. Life doesn't show up in a tangled mess. Life is carefully crafted so that I have exactly the opportunities I need in order to put *His* plan into action. My faithfulness is determined by my willingness to execute *His* plan, not by my capacity to create my plan. Once again, I am dependent on His instruction. The first step is always the same: listen.

The Hebrew word here is *'etsah*. You will find it in Judges 20:7, Job 12:13 and Proverbs 12:15 where it is translated "counsel" or "advice." That sheds more light on the issue. What if this verse read, "who took advice, but not Mine." That might cause some panic among us. How many times have we sought advice from those who have no alignment with the Kingdom? Financial advice, business advice, legal advice, parental advice – all coming from perspectives that disregard God's point of view. And we call it "planning." It is nothing but sinful foolishness. Certainly it cannot be planning since plans without God are doomed to fail. This kind of advice is the worst kind you could get. It leads directly to destruction no matter how well thought of it is in the world's systems. Now you know a bit more about what Paul meant when he told us not to be conformed to the patterns of this world.

There is a plan. It just isn't mine. Executing my plan is arrogant and foolhardy. Before you decide what you will do next, try a different approach. Listen – hard.

27.

preach the word; be ready in season and out of season; **reprove**, *rebuke, exhort, with great patience and instruction.* 2 Timothy 4:2

Why Reprove?

Reprove – Paul had a Ph.D. is Jewish theology. His source for theological formation is found in the Scriptures of the Old Testament, which he knew very well. So, when it comes to "reprove," Paul does not rely on the larger Greek cultural meanings. Those meanings include concepts like scorn, bring into contempt, expound, investigate, and shame. No, Paul sticks to a very simple application, right from the Old Testament. The Hebrew root, *ykh*, is used in the culture of the ancient near-east for a description of the legal proceeding that takes place at the gate of the city. There the elders sat in judgment of various claims and disputes. The parties presented evidence and the elders *set the matter right*. This is the idea behind the Greek word *elenchos*. Reproof is not just a matter of pointing out someone's guilt or error. Reproof always seeks to set the matter right, to straighten out the situation so the repentance leads to full restoration. Reproof is an essential part of the larger educational plan of God, for each of us will require straightening in the process of becoming His image-bearers. Disciple with reproof never attacks to humiliate. It investigates and proclaims in order to redeem.

Proverbs 9:8 shows us that there are two possible reactions to reproof. The fool will scoff at the presentation of sin but the wise man will open his heart to God's word and humbly seek forgiveness. With this in mind, reproof is an essential characteristic of love. You do not love someone if you are unwilling to confront misaligned behaviors and attitudes. Proverbs 3:12 reminds us that God's reproofs are a sign of His abiding love. To bear another's burden is to take upon yourself the risk of rejection in the presentation of wounds that heal. But don't forget that *elenchos* is bi-directional. Those who give reproof must also receive reproof. No one escapes the need to be corrected. And everyone is called to act as the burden-bearer of other brothers and sisters.

Today it is very uncomfortable to reprove someone. Today we focus on feelings rather than truth. What a tragic mistake we make! Reproof is not devoid of pity. It comes with compassion but it does not bend to the wrong priorities. What is at stake is *life!* When I decide to let the sins of another slide, I place that person in mortal jeopardy. I might as well be kicking them while they are down. Proverbs says that the parent who will not reprove signs that child's death warrant. This is very serious business. Yes, feelings might be hurt but what matters most - feelings or setting right the relationship with the King?

A leader cannot escape the obligation to reprove. And a leader cannot escape reproof. Leaders are people in the middle – able and willing to bring God's word to light when another falters, and ready and willing to receive God's word as a pruning shears. Are you a bi-direction leader?

28.

*and saying, "If you are the King of the Jews, **save Yourself**!"* Luke 23:37

Our Way Out

Save Yourself - A friend of mine is about to lose his home. He took a job far away in response to God's call. His house remains unsold. Now foreclosure breathes down his neck. Another one I know has been unemployed for a very long time in spite of every effort to find work. The prospects look worse every day. I know people who struggle with life-threatening health issues, others who can't seem to resolve damaging relationships, some who cry out to God for relief from pain or suffering. The world stands before each of them, sneering, hurling verbal challenges to stop believing and accept reality. The world gives each of them the same advice given to Jesus. *Save yourself!*

That is the world's answer to the silence of God. Save yourself! No one else will. Certainly God won't do it, right? If He were interested in rescue, He would have acted by now. He might be able but He clearly isn't willing.

This is a favorite attack of the enemy. "Save yourself," is an attempt to get you to doubt the character of God. It is just a little ploy to get to you think, "Maybe God doesn't care." It's just enough for you to question God's integrity. This is a very old strategy (see Genesis 3). "Did God *really say* that He would care for you? Did He really mean it? Then, where's the proof? You're being a religious fool. Everyone knows that in this world you have to *save yourself*."

In Greek, *soson seauton*. Quite literally, *rescue from death thy own self*. It's quite a statement. It is a direct denial of God's sovereignty over life. Do you really think that you have the power to save yourself? Jesus did. He said so. But who among the rest of us can claim that we possess the power to lay down our lives and *pick them up again*? Yet, when the world shouts, "Save yourself," that is exactly what we are claiming. We deny God's goodness at the same time that we assert our omnipotence. "Save yourself," is the exclamation of men who want to be gods.

Jesus had the power, even on the cross, to demand rescue. He was innocent. By the way, that is not the same as "not guilty." We might be accounted "not guilty," but we will never be innocent. Jesus had not one single mark of sin upon Him. He deserved justifying rescue. But He did not exercise that power. He left it in the hands of the Father. The cry of the righteous man is not, "Save yourself!" It is "Thy will be done." When we are able to transition from self-protection to self-sacrifice, then we truly know that the enemy lies. God is glorified when I answer, "Your will, Father, is more important then my desire to take care of myself. I leave it in Your hands because I *trust* you, no matter what the world shouts at me."

29.

*When they say unto you, "Consult the mediums and the spiritists who whisper and mutter," should not a people consult their God? Should they consult **the dead** on behalf of the living?* Isaiah 8:19

Useless Advice

The Dead - Planning is arrogance. Before you jump up and say, "But even God plans!" take a moment and think about the wider umbrella of what we imply by planning. Years ago I started a toy company. Being a Type A person, I meticulously planned every step. The company failed. Why? I could say it was because I forgot to plan for the introduction of an inferior product by a competitor that spoiled the market. But now I realize there was a bigger error. I thought I was in control.

God does plan, but of course, He *is* in control. His planning is legitimate and executable. Our plans are not. James reminds us of our arrogance in that famous line about "if the Lord wills" (James 4:15). When I plan, I assume the position of rational and volitional superiority. I think, therefore I do. But it doesn't work out that way, does it? Isaiah tells us why. We are consulting the dead.

You might object. You don't go to psychics. You don't read horoscopes. You don't consult the stars. But, there are many more dead in this world than just "spiritual" advisors. Jesus made that very clear when He told the would-be followers to let the dead bury the dead. Any man or woman who is not actively being lead by the Spirit of the living God is *dead*. But we still ask them for advice, don't we? We consult dead bankers, dead lawyers, dead doctors, dead investment counselors, dead psychotherapists and dead neighbors. We might even consult dead church members and clergy. We take advice from everyone who has a voice – from the President to the janitor, but we never ask if we are simply listening to the dead.

The Hebrew root is *mut*, a verb that means, "to die, to kill or to put to death." While the Hebrew is a little convoluted here, the contrast is plain enough. Consult the *living* God or the dying advisers. The choice is up to you. Of course, Isaiah suggests that taking advice from the ones who are dying is about as stupid a choice as you can make. But we do it all the time, don't we?

Yes, of course, you will need expert opinion in all sorts of earthly matters. Health, money, legal issues, even things as simple as paying bills and traffic rules require consultation. But remember who really does the planning. Remember that without a divine perspective, all advice is based in the grave. Remember that God has already given you the framework to test the opinions you get. Planning is arrogance. Obeying Him is not. Did you ask *His* advice about your *plans* today?

30.

*You shall have no **other gods** besides Me.* Deuteronomy 5:7

Your Best Life Now

Other Gods – An axiom of human resource management applies here. People almost always do what they believe to be in their best interest. When you aren't getting the behavior you desire from others, use this axiom to discover why they think behaving as they do is serving them better than what you want them to do. You just might discover what has to change to alter their thinking.

God certainly knows all about this axiom. When He sees how many of us act in opposition to His will, He must shake His head in dismay, for what this means is that most people do not believe that acting according to God's rules will really be in their best interest. They think that rules inhibit their freedom. They want what they want when they want it. But, of course, God knows just how foolish all of this is. The interest they serve is really a damning curse. They just don't see it.

Why isn't God willing to let us have just a few other masters? Why is He so insistent that we serve and worship only Him? Well, it's not because He is greedy for our attention or because He is simply a demanding tyrant. God wants us to make Him our exclusive sovereign because *it is in our best interest to do so.* If you want your best life now, then make Him the *only* Lord you serve.

Oswald Chambers once said that the enemy of the best is the good. That is exactly what matters here. God wants you to have your *best* life now. Most of us settle for the *good* life instead. Why? It's not because we are perverse or contentious. It's because we actually think we know what is better for us without God's input. We think we are perfectly capable of effectively managing our lives. God just shakes His head at our foolishness - the blind leading the blind. What a tragedy! Just let time pass and then ask yourself, "How's that working out for you?" If we are honest, we will soon admit that things didn't turn out quite as we had hoped, no matter how successful we are. Life is bent, my friend. It is bent on purpose because it is designed to point out our infirmity, dependence and incapacity. We ignore this curvature of existence at our peril.

But here's the good news. God knows. God is capable of bringing about your best life now. That is, in fact, His intended purpose. Oh, it might not be the kind of life that you thought was *good*, but it will be the life that *best* prepares you to serve and worship Him. We reject other gods (*elohiym akherim*) because we want the best. We serve the King because we want what He offers *more than* what others offer. This is a act of supreme self-interest that also happens to be in perfect alignment with God's will. Isn't that awesome?

31.

*This is the word of Yahweh to Zerubbabel, saying, "**Not by might**, nor by power, but by My Spirit, says Yahweh of hosts."* Zechariah 4:6

Lesson Number 1

Not By Might – You can make it happen! That's the unstated mantra of leadership training today. Just go to this class, or read this book, or listen to these disks, or attend this conference and, "presto chango", you will be empowered to make it happen. You will take control of your circumstances and become leadership material. Since most of us stand on a Greek, post-modern foundation, we feel the inner self resonating with the desire for control and we buy the mythology. We forget that God's way is nothing like our way.

"Not by might," says the Lord. The Hebrew is *lo vekhayil* (combining the negative *lo* with the preposition *be* and the noun *hayil*). Of course, we think that this means "not by strength." But *hayil* covers a broader spectrum than the size of our muscles. It's not the same word that we find in Deuteronomy 6:5 ("with all your strength" – January 22). It's a word that covers the concepts of valor, wealth, influence, virtue as well as physical and numerical power. God rejects it all! If you thought that God accomplishes His purposes through *your* valor or wealth or influence or virtue or physical prowess, think again. Over and over, the stories of God's interactions with men demonstrate His refusal to use the methods and tactics that men can commonly employ. God does not do what human beings can do without Him. He does what no man is able to do so that no man can take the glory for the result.

There is a vital principle of biblical leadership in this fact. Too often - far too often - we look to the world's measures of leadership to determine our direction and our commitment. We fall in line behind those who exercise valor, influence, wealth, virtue and prowess. Why do we do this when it is so clear that God goes another way? Because the natural inclination for control is such a dominate force in our lives. We want to control our risk and make things happen. How else can our goals ever be accomplished? It just seems so obvious.

But God is not obvious. He does not do things the commonsense way. He does not take the human approach. The simple truth is that we are *unwilling to trust Him*. It's a form of decision-making insanity. We know that God is completely sovereign. We know that He loves His children and seeks only what is in our best interests. And we still try desperately to do it our way. We still think it's up to us. We still drink from the "I can make it happen" fountain. We refuse to *wait* on Him.

Every day for forty years God provided sustenance for the children of Jacob. Every day He reiterated His reliable commitment to them. And after forty years of daily trustworthiness, they were still afraid to enter the Promised Land. Here we are on the banks of the Jordan. We have had *centuries* of evidence of God's faithfulness. And we are still trying to build a bridge to get across.

32.

And when we had heard this, we as well as the local residents **began begging** *him not to go up to Jerusalem.* Acts 21:12

What Does God Require?

Began Begging – Leadership doesn't always mean that others will follow. In fact, in some cases, the leader must blaze a trail alone, even when all the good advice suggests retreat. How does the leader know when to go forward and when to listen to wise counsel? Well, that's a matter of character and obedience.

Paul understood only one thing: Jesus Christ and Him crucified. Paul's purpose was to serve his Lord, no matter what. So, when Paul receives the message to go to Jerusalem, he determines that nothing will stop him. In this brief report, Luke tells us that on more than one occasion, Paul's own friends begged him to reconsider. In fact, they came to Paul out of spiritually-motivated concern for his well-being. Agabus, at the direction of the Holy Spirit, provided a physical portrait of the danger. Luke pleaded with Paul. Everyone around him believed that they were guided by God to prevent Paul from continuing. They were right. God did give them the message to warn Paul. But Paul was required to be obedient in spite of the warnings. He told them that he was already bound to the Lord, in life and in death. So, to Jerusalem he must go.

The Greek verb here is very strong. It's a verb you would recognize as the name for the Holy Spirit – *parakaleo* – to aid, comfort, come along side, encourage, beseech. Can you feel its impact? Paul, beloved friend, rabbi and messenger of God, is undoubtedly headed for terrible times, perhaps even death. Do you remember the circumstances surrounding Jesus' last fellowship? Only Mary understood the significance of the moment and she prepared her Lord for burial. The disciples were still arguing about who would be the greatest. They missed the *kairos* moment entirely. But now things have changed. The followers of the Way are in tune with the Spirit. There is grave danger for one dear to them. Can you feel their concern, their tears, their fears? God moved them to act in this way. Do you understand what that means? They were genuinely moved by the Spirit to ask Paul to change course. They were not wrong or sinful or disobedient. But in their actions, God transported Paul to his own Garden of Gethsemane. "If this cup can pass from me." That's what his closest friends suggest. Paul must choose the way of the cross, even when God motivates others to offer another path.

Paul knows what to do because Paul knows Jesus. This is first a matter of character; not Paul's character, but the character of his Lord. Jesus did not let the cup pass. He could have but He chose the will of the Father instead. From character springs obedience. That's the way God wants it. God is not so much interested in compliance as He is in character. So, God engineers our lives so that there are many moments of character development. **Once character is in place, obedience is the natural by-product.** A leader with a heart for God will obey. It's just who he is.

When you face real trials, remember that God may offer *paraklesis* through others as a *kairos* moment for character development. The advice may be good. It may be truthful. But decisions are made on the basis of the character of our Lord. "What would Jesus do?" is still the right direction, even if no one else will follow.

33.

*"for the task is too heavy for you; you cannot do it **alone**."* Exodus 18:18

Powerless Leadership

Alone – Moses is acknowledged as Israel's greatest leader, but the way that he led the people flies in the face of a lot of today's leadership advice. The encounter with Jethro is a prime example of powerless leadership – the only kind of leadership that God seems to endorse.

If you read the whole story here, you see that Moses takes the typical leadership posture – at the top of the hierarchy. His motivation is good. He wants the people to get answers to their questions. He wants to bring them God's decisions. He cares for their welfare. But he falls prey to the top-dog syndrome, even though his heart is in the right place. As a result, everyone waits. The people spend their time uselessly because Moses is the single source of wisdom. What Moses forgot is that God is the God of distributive community. Only one person stands as the head of God's entire family, and that Man doesn't come on the scene for another five thousand years. Even after Yeshua arrives, distributive community is still the operating procedure. God does not endorse hierarchical organization, but He does endorse multiple assignments. Everyone has an *equally important* role to play in the kingdom of priests.

Jethro confronts Moses. "What are you doing? This isn't right." He tells Moses that God's plan requires the delegation of authority, not the accumulation of power. "You cannot do this *le va dekha* (by yourself)." The root word *badad* (the *b* sounds like *v*) is used to describe isolation. It's applied to lepers who are to live apart from all others. What a powerful image! Jethro tells Moses that the top-dog syndrome is *leadership leprosy*. Isolated, alone at the top of the pile, the leader clutches power in order to retain control while all the time his isolation fuels the fear that drives him toward more control. He defeats himself. The leprosy eats him alive.

God has another way. God's leaders give away their power (deliberately) by delegating authority to others. This must be intentional because the distribution of authority cannot happen by accident. A godly leader knows that there is no safety and no victory in power. God is the God of weakness. So, in order to combat the natural, human propensity for hierarchy, and honor the God of weakness, a godly leader deliberately gives up authority – and the power that goes along with it. Why? Because a godly leader knows that all authority is a gift, not a reward. God *grants* authority. I do not earn it. Therefore, when I pass God's authority on to others, I lose nothing. It wasn't mine in the first place. Distributing authority glorifies the Giver by serving the community in the distribution. The act of distributing authority honors the God Who gives liberally and abundantly to *all* His children in order for them to be the kingdom of priests.

Of course, there are requirements for receiving this authority. Jethro spells out some of them, but that's another group of words. Today, we see that powerless leadership is God's way. Is that your objective? Are you deliberately creating a kingdom without hierarchy? Or are you infected with leadership leprosy - alone, at the top?

34.

*For God **has not given** us a spirit of timidity, but of power and love and discipline.* 2 Timothy 1:7

What We Don't Need

Has Not Given – Are you a road warrior? Are you a follower of Yeshua and the Way who sometimes finds the journey excruciating? Do you see discipleship blisters on your feet? Then Paul has something important for you. It's a verse from his own life experience, and it's just right for all of us who know that following the Master really does mean joyful struggle.

Paul starts by telling us what God *doesn't* provide. He calls it "a spirit of timidity," but it might also be translated "cowardice" or "fearfulness." It's the same idea that you will find in Psalm 55:4 (the terror of death) and Leviticus 26:36 (weakness of heart). God *does not give* such anxious concern. The Greek helps us see how important this opening thought really is. It begins with the powerful "not!" (*Ou*). God is never the author of fear and anxiety. The verb is just as crucial. It is *didomi* which means to give of one's own will and with good intent. Here's the best part. The verb is in the aorist tense. That means that Paul considers this a *completed action in the past*. God never gave, and has never given, a sprit of fearfulness. If that's what you're feeling when you see those blisters on your discipleship feet, you can be absolutely certain that it didn't come from God!

Why does this matter so much? Quite frankly, it matters because fearfulness and anxious concern are at the heart of reticence to obey. We know that God says that love casts out fear, but those words don't always seem to translate into actions in our lives. We hold back from complete abandonment to Him because we are afraid. There's no other way to put it. We are fearful of what might happen. We project our terrors into the future. We think about the possible impact on our families. God might not give us a spirit of cowardice, but it's there nonetheless.

If you're facing the call to abandon everything to God, then you know exactly what I am talking about. It's scary. It shouldn't be. After all, God is sovereign. He's in control. He loves us and He will never do anything that is not for our best within His purposes. He is gracious. His compassion outweighs His wrath. All of that should make abandonment obvious. But the terrible truth is that I am weak and afraid. I am a coward. As much as I know about God, I still stumble over total trust. I still falter when I imagine all the things that *might* happen if I give up everything. Jesus knew about this kind of weakness only too well. "The spirit is willing," He said. You know the rest.

You and I need to hear Paul's opening declaration. Our fears do not come from God. Yes, we have them, but God never gave them to us. Obedience is acting *in spite of my fear*. My fear is real, but it does not replace God's goodness. God calls me to *choose* anyway. And with His help, I can.

"Father, rescue me. I believe, help my unbelief."

35.

*For God has not given us a spirit of timidity, but of **power** and love and discipline.* 2 Timothy 1:7

What God Gives

Power - God is not the author of my fearfulness. Quite the opposite, God gives power. That's truly what I need. My anxious concern makes me weak. I find that I am willing but unable. God gives me exactly what I need to move forward into total trust. He gives me *dynamis.* And what does "power" mean to me? It means ability, capacity, vigor, strength and will. All the things I need to trust Him (remember, "trust" is a verb – an action – not a feeling). When I am faced with the impossibility of anxious projection of dread, God gives me the power I need to overcome those mythical fears.

Notice that it is God Who provides what I need. It's His gift to me. I didn't earn it. I didn't run out to the bookstore and stock up on self-help solutions. I didn't work harder, pray harder or give more. God *gave* it, freely, simply because God intends good for me. When I was chasing the answer to my fears, I was grasping for rainbows. But when I stopped running scared, God gave me what I needed. Oswald Chambers puts it so eloquently. He says that as soon as I make the choice to trust, God supplies all the power necessary to do so. I have to turn from my fear and return to Him, but at the moment I reverse direction, He floods me with the strength I could never find on my own.

Fear paralyzes me. It is a straight-jacket on my soul. The only thing I can do to remove those restraints is *look* to Jesus. Everything else is tied down by my dread. But, all it takes is that look. The power I need is given in His gaze.

Remember the Greek verb, *didomi*? That verb also governs this phrase. God *gives* power. He gives it *freely with good intentions in mind*. I don't have to convince God to help me. I don't have to worry that He won't help me. I don't have to offer appeasement in order to gain His help. God *gives* it. As soon as I commit to Him, He rushes in to rescue.

This is what I need to hear today. I don't have to do it on my own. I have lived long enough to know that I can't do it on my own. None of it! No matter how hard I try, I just can't manage life. It always gets the better of me. But, I don't have to be afraid. My *weakness* is exactly what is required to experience God's *strength*. Paul reminds us that when we are weak, then we are strong, but the reverse is true too. When I am strong in my own effort, then I am entirely vulnerable and weak. God does *not* help those who help themselves. Why should He? They think that they are in charge.

The best lesson I can learn from my own fears is that I am weak. That is the purpose of fear; not to paralyze me, but to emphasize my inability. Fear teaches me that God's gift is the only solution. Have you reached that conclusion? Then, what are you waiting for? *Look to Him!*

36.

*For God has not given us a spirit of timidity, but of **power** and love and discipline.* 2 Timothy 1:7

The Second Gift

Power – Mike Yaconelli calls it "happy terror." He suggests that when we follow Jesus, it is thrilling and terrifying at the same time. His comment is insightful. Did you think that God's gift of power (*dynamis*) *removes* your fear? Nope! Life is still terrifying. Bad things can still happen. You are still not in control. God's power does not change the structure of consequences in the fallen world. Power does not *replace* fear. Power *overcomes* fear. The fearfulness that resides in my soul is simply part of the human condition. As long as I am in this world, I will experience fear. But, as Jesus said, "Be of good cheer for I have overcome the world."

My Twelve-Step friends remind me that fear is **F**alse **E**vidence **A**ppearing **R**eal. That's what I need to know. The feeling of fear is real, but the evidence that supports the fear is false. I really *feel* it, but it has no substantial reality to it. Why? Because God loves me. Therefore, He gives me the power to *overcome* my fear. The thrill is knowing that God always arrives on time. The terror is in not knowing how He will arrive. Life with God is blessed uncertainty.

When I abandon my life to Jesus, I opt for unanticipated surprises. Oh, that doesn't mean that my life will always be in the eggbeater. Life still has its general orderliness as a result of God's common grace. God still sends the rain on the just and the unjust. The sun still comes up in the morning. But abandonment to Jesus means that I let go of my *expectation* of orderliness. I am not surprised when the eggbeater takes over. In fact, because God promises power to overcome, I look forward to the moments of blessed chaos as opportunities to see what God will do next. Now you know why James can say, "Count it joy when . . ." We couldn't possibly count trials and tribulations as joyful unless we knew God's power is peeking around the corner.

Think of it from a Hebrew perspective. Genesis tells me God loves His creation. Exodus tells me God is in control of history. Leviticus tells me God provides for my guilt. Numbers tells me God guides my choices. Deuteronomy tells me God rewards my obedience. All the rest tells me that I can't manage on my own and that following Him is the only sane thing to do. Then Jesus comes to tell me that He will never leave me, that He has overcome my enemy and that I can join Him to fulfill God's mission. What else is there to worry about?

False evidence confuses my perception of reality. That's why I can't trust myself. When God says that He gives me His power to overcome my cowardice and apprehension, it's the truth. But it's not *my* power. It's God's gift. It arrives with His blessing bearing the hallmarks of His character. It's *dynamite* in the hands of the follower of the Way, able to clear all kinds of barricades and obstacles. But it only works according to His character, as the next two words will show.

Life in the eggbeater is the perfect place to light a fuse.

37.

For God has not given us a spirit of timidity, but of power and love and **discipline**. 2 Timothy 1:7

A Sound Mind

Discipline – What makes a sound mind? Did you think it was education, logical thinking or encyclopedic knowledge? If you grew up with a Western world mentality, then you most likely view a sound mind as self-disciplined, astute and logically correct. That's why the King James translates this verse as "love and of a sound mind." "Discipline" is closer to the real thought here, but not quite close enough. Discipline can still mean a lot of mental gymnastics for us. That may not be what Paul is thinking when he uses the word *sophronismos*. Knowing exactly what Paul means from a Hebrew perspective is going to be difficult because this is the only place in the entire Bible that *sophronismos* is used. So, what can we do? Well, first we can see how the Greek word is constructed. It comes from *soos* (sound) and *phren* (understanding). Suddenly, we get a clue. *Phren* is literally the diaphragm; but figuratively in the Greek world, it is the seat of mental and emotional activity. Did you notice that the Greeks connected steady breathing with self-control? Emotions and thoughts which are outwardly exhibited by calm breathing are considered disciplined. So, it's not just about the mind, is it? It's about stabilizing my whole inner world.

Now we know where to look in Hebrew. Proverbs tells us that wisdom, understanding and instruction all go together to bring us into alignment with the character of God. But it's not simply mental activity. Wisdom (*hokma*) is about right action. Understanding (*bine*) is about distinguishing good from evil (and making the right choices) and instruction (*musar*) is about correction and chastisement when necessary. All of these ideas are present in the Hebrew view of a sound mind. None of them are primarily about thinking.

When Paul says that God has given us a spirit of discipline, he does not mean that God enables us to study better or to eat less or to exercise more. Paul is speaking as a Hebrew. God gives us a spirit that reveals right behavior, correct moral discernment and necessary chastisement. God shapes *how* we live and *what* we do, not just what we think. God's gift is behavioral alignment and correction. A sound mind is seen in the hands and feet of obedience.

Why do I need this spirit-empowered "discipline"? Because without it, I'm a coward. I might know what the right thing is, but I shrink back from doing it. Knowledge is not my problem. Acting is my problem. So many times we know exactly what we *should* do. We just don't do it. God gifts us with *sophronismos* so that we will be able to execute obedience. He gives us a revelation of the correct action, the discernment to know the difference between obedience and disobedience and, when necessary, a kick in the butt to get moving. God will not abide cowards. He expects unsung heroes and heroines. And He gives us everything we need to become just that!

The next time you find yourself shrinking back from doing the right thing, remember who gave you the opportunity to become heroic.

38.

*"I **regret** that I have made Saul king, for he has turned back from following Me and has not carried out My commands."* 1 Samuel 15:11

Who Would Be King?

Regret – It was a triumph of self-determination, and a tragedy of spiritual disintegration. The man who would be king decided that his interpretation of God's command was good enough. That decision precipitated his downfall and the kingdom was removed from him.

God instructed Samuel to anoint Saul king. But Saul made one mistake, a mistake that seemed insignificant at the time but had disastrous consequences. God sent Saul to eradicate the Amalekites. God's command was terrifying clear. "Kill them *all*." Saul, however, determined that a few were good enough to spare. So, the best of the sheep, the best of the cattle and the best of the people were spared. Why did Saul decide that God really didn't mean what He said? Saul believed that he understood economics. Why waste the best? Why destroy something that had real, immediate value? After all, God has plenty. What does it really matter if a few of the very best are retained for future use? Saul even rationalizes his action by claiming that he preserved the best "for sacrifice to God." Doesn't that make it all right? After all, it's for a religious purpose.

Saul didn't understand the enormity of his disobedience. It looked like such a small thing. But he was king, and God expects those whom He anoints to act in absolute obedience. God says that He regrets making Saul king. The word is *naham*. The word has a wide umbrella of meanings: comfort, pity, avenge, regret, console, revenge and grieve all come from this root. All of these meanings are tied to a deep emotional distress that results in outward action. God's grief over Saul's failure resulted in immediate consequences. In the same way, *naham* expresses God's immediate, comforting response to the distress of His people (Psalm 119:82). Saul experienced one side of *naham*. Hopefully, we will experience the other side.

There is a terrifying lesson in this historical event. God appoints with the expectation of obedience. Those who do not fulfill His commands are *removed* from the appointed office. Sometimes, there is no second chance. Proverbs tells us that there is a way that appears right in the eyes of a man, but the end of it is destruction. That's Saul's life in a nutshell. He was king. He was in command. What he did *appeared* right to him. In fact, he even argues that he has fulfilled God's command. It never crosses his mind that he only did some of what God instructed because, for Saul, some was good enough.

Has God appointed you? Are you called to a particular task or role or office in the Body? Has God given you an assignment to carry out? Then you are in the place of Saul, for you are the one who would be king. This is very dangerous ground, not because fulfilling God's orders is confusing or difficult. It is dangerous ground because it is so easy to think that *our interpretation* of what God says is good enough. It is dangerous ground because we are likely to see something "good" in what we are to utterly destroy, and keep it for our own purposes. Have you really taken God seriously? Have you put *all* of His command into action, without hesitation? Or would you rather be king in your own eyes?

39.

*"In **repentance and rest** you will be saved, in quietness and trust is your strength." But you were not willing.* Isaiah 30:15

Counter-intuitive

Repentance and Rest – "But I gotta' do *something*!" That's the approach we naturally take when it comes to crisis. We want *action*! Something's got to happen. After all, if we just sit around, nothing will change. What we have ignored is the sovereignty of God. What folly!

God tells us that rescue (salvation) does not come through our frantic efforts. Reinforcements arrive through repentance and rest. It just seems so ridiculous. Everyone knows that doing nothing doesn't change a thing. We can't stand waiting. We want to see movement. So, we push ahead – and side step God.

This verse is Hebrew parallelism. That means that the second part of the verse clarifies and explains the first part of the verse. So, the Hebrew phrase *beshuva vanakhat* ("in returning and rest") is explained in the parallel "in quietness and trust." Think about that for a moment.   When I work against my natural tendency by allowing God to act, I *must* put my trust in Him. As soon as I jump to take care of my crisis, I yank the authority out of God's hands. In the process, I prevent Him from showing His grace, mercy and power. Notice that my rest begins with my repentance. Actually, the word is *shuv*, a word that is used hundreds of times in the Old Testament for the idea of returning to God. Repentance is not simply confession. Repentance is returning to right relationship. It is coming back to obedience. It is remembering the former days when God's power brought me out of captivity. It is recalling Who God is. I can rest (*nekhath*) only because I have returned.

Now that we see the parts of the first phrase, we can understand the explanation and clarification of the second phrase. Repentance (returning) is the same as tranquility (*shehket*). It is calm in the face of the storm. And it is coupled with trust (*betach*), the tangible sense of security and well-being that results from absolute confidence in God. Now we see that returning to God results in tranquility and resting in God results in confidence. It's just the opposite of what we would expect. We think that we will achieve peace and security through our effort. We are fools. Isaiah has only this to say about our stubborn resistance to the truth: "You were not willing." We were not willing to give up our myth of control. We were not willing to come back to Him. We were not willing to let Him take charge. We were not willing to submit to His authority.

My friends, God does *not* help those who help themselves. How can He? They are doing exactly the opposite of what allows Him to provide for them.

40.

*You **made him rule** over the works of Your hands* Psalm 8:6

Be A Man

Made Him Rule – David asks the question. "What is Man that You should be mindful of him?" David gives the answer. It's a surprising answer; one that should make us uncomfortable. Man is defined in the same terms that define everything else in God's creation – according to purpose.

What is Man? Man is the one God made to rule. What is Man's purpose? To rule in God's place.

That sounds pretty good, doesn't it? Nothing better than being at the top of the food chain. But hold on. There is a subtle implication buried in the Hebrew text that radically alters our egocentric evaluation. The verb for "made him rule" is *mashal*. It means "to rule, to reign, to have dominion over." David echoes Genesis 1:28, but not with the same verb. We don't see the difference in English, but it's there in Hebrew. In Genesis, God commands Man to exercise *authority* (*radah*). In this psalm, God causes Man to act as His *representative*. The critical difference is in the tense of the verb. In

164

Genesis, the verb is an *qal imperative*. That means it is a normal present tense command, like "Do this!" In Genesis, God assigns a task to Man and expects him to carry it out. But in this psalm, the verb is a *hiphil imperfect*. Once you see the difference, everything changes. First, the imperfect means that it is an incomplete or fluid action; something that goes on and on. So, the first part of the answer to the question, "What is Man?" contains the idea of a continuous, incomplete (as yet) purpose. In other words, you and I are not defined by what we have done, but by what we still have to do.

But that's not all. The verb stem is a *hiphil*. That means it is a *causative* verb. David tells us that God *causes* Man to rule over God's creation. Did you get that? It is *not* voluntary. I didn't choose the assignment. God didn't create me to be His regent and then ask if I wanted the job. God *caused* me to rule. It was divine appointment. Before the Fall, God assigned Man the task of ruling. Now, David tells us that God places that task on us and makes us rule. This verse does not read, "You created me in such a way that I am able to rule." This verse reads, "You caused me to rule, regardless of my desire."

What does this mean for you and me? It means that we are *responsible* for the way that we handle God's creation *even if we don't acknowledge God*. What is Man? He is the steward of God's assets whether he likes it or not. Man was made for the purpose of ruling and God *causes* Man to rule. So, you and I are held accountable for what we do with God's creation. Here's the definition of what we are – we are accountable to Him.

God owns it all. You and I are accountable to Him for everything we act on, with or through. He makes us rule in order to fulfill our purpose. And He expects us to exercise authority in the same way that He would. You have been given the King's signet ring. You can't take it off. He will ask for an accounting of all that your hand touches. So, how are you doing?

Chapter 4

Relationships: Ownership and Responsibility

Community. Nothing is more difficult. Nothing is more rewarding. In spite of our propensity to move toward independent, self-reliance, God created us for community. Without it, we drift toward an existence that verges on insanity and lends itself to destructive behaviors. We were meant to work out our being in the context of others.

In the Hebrew worldview, ultimate value is found in the person of the holy God. Since God is personal, He expresses Himself in relationship. He has a relationship with His creation that sets the foundation for all other interactions. In particular, He has a relationship with men and women. In fact, He created us in His image, an image that includes the priority of personality and relationships.

As a result, the Hebrew worldview considers relationships more important than tasks. It views honor, gratitude, joy, holiness and character as more important than success, influence, happiness, accumulation and power. Ultimately, the Hebrew orientation is about a right relationship with God. This is called righteousness.

The Greek world has a different orientation. The ultimate object of the Greek metaphysics is fully enlightened humanity. The Greeks considered Man the measure of all things, principally because Man employed reason to overcome the resistance of the universe. For the Greeks, relationships were necessary for the establishment of civil community, but in the end, Man stood alone in the universe. He was the captain of his own destiny, forcing the world to conform to his wishes, pursuing the Good, the True and the Beautiful as the highest goal of reasoned existence.

In the Greek world, we are islands in the stream. Born into a fickle universe, we must put away the mythology of the collective and strike out on our own, becoming the heroes or heroines we were meant to be.

166

This vantage point is impossible for a Hebrew. God is the God of community. My identity is intimately connected to those who came before me and those who will come after me. I am part of a line of obedience, not the end product of an evolving consciousness. I seek alignment with the will of God, not independence from my struggling fellow travelers. The two great commandments are fundamentally about the same thing – relationship – with God and with my neighbor. One is empty without the other.

By examining the Scriptural perspective on relationships, we will discover a different way of looking at life's involvements.

1.

*"It is not good for the man to be **alone**"* Genesis 2:18

Dangerous Isolation

Alone – If you could unzip the psychological skin that surrounds your soul, what would be revealed? Would you find an inner harmony of community? Would you discover a multitude of healthy relationships between God, others and yourself? Or would you expose something terrifying – an emptiness where you sit alone, separated from human and divine involvement? Today, we might prefer not to engage in any serious introspection. We might prefer to relax, celebrate or vegetate. But tomorrow the world will wake up with its demanding schedules and exhausting intensity. We will be thrust back into the machinery of capitalist isolation where every one seeks his advantage. So, today is the perfect time to ask: Are you alone?

The Hebrew word translated "alone" is *badh*, an accidental pun in English. Being alone is *badh*. God recognized that being alone was not good. This is quite an amazing statement since our original parents had the fellowship of God Himself. Nevertheless, the Man needed someone else to bring about the community and harmony that God intended in our created state. He needed an *'ezer*, a helpmate who would provide protection against isolation. Do you have someone in your life who overcomes your isolation?

The Hebrew point of view is very different than our Greek inheritance. In the Greek world, all of us are essentially alone. The Greek ideal is individual autonomy. Man is the measure of all things, including his own worth. In the Greek world, the more I show myself capable of independence, the more I am valued and emulated. Our cultural heroes are the supermen, the ones who don't need anyone else to accomplish great feats. We worship the self-made man.

But the Hebrews knew better. In the desert, independence meant death. Isolation, from God and from others, was a terrifying, dangerous and ultimately fatal existence. It is no accident that the Hebrew Scriptures often associated this word with the waste places, the desert and destitution. In the Hebrew world, men and women survive only because they are connected. When I am alone, it is always dangerous. God's answer to the unnatural danger of isolation is the creation of human community. My weakness is overcome in relationship with another, not in brute force individualism.

Who is connected to you? Who knows your unzipped soul? Who brings you out of the desert of isolation?

2.

*that they may be one, as You are **in** Me, Father, and I **in** You, that they maybe one **in** us, that the world may believe that You sent Me.* John 17:21

Intimacy Among Us

In – The tiny Greek preposition *en* can't quite be captured in English. Yes, *en* is translated "in", but it also has nuances of "in the sphere of, in connection with, within, inside, by, on, near, among and with." In this famous passage, this little preposition contains an incredible opportunity and a damning indictment. As part of Jesus' prayer, it's something we need to study very seriously.

Did you know that the general reaction of the Jewish community to the fractured denominations of Christianity is shocked disgust? Do you think that pagans feel any differently? Just consider all of our spiritual bickering, theological "disputes" and general lack of love for our own brothers and sisters who don't share our version of God's revelation. Do you think Jesus had this in mind when He asked the Father for unity?

Don't for a second think that this is about the ecumenical movement. This is not about "agreements" between rival denominations – or even between Catholics and Protestants. Jesus is pleading for a unity of intimacy and of spirit, that results in belief in His deity. Jesus is asking us to *live* as He lives, throwing aside the arguments of the contemporary Pharisees, bringing the good news of transformation to fragmented lives. This is not about my "head" knowledge. This is about my heart connected to your heart in the pursuit of a love for God that overshadows all our human differences.

Does it really matter if I am Methodist or Presbyterian or Pentecostal or Catholic when I stand in the midst of a refugee camp with thousands of starving people? Do I really care if you believe in baptism by immersion or sprinkling or symbol when I confront genocide? Don't you and I just want God's love to flow through us to a world that is diseased, lost and hopeless? Would you withhold your helping hand in an orphanage because the one next to you wasn't from your church?

It might be worth taking the time to imagine exactly *how* the Father is *in* Jesus and Jesus is *in* the Father. It certainly means a clarity of purpose, a daily intimacy, a willingness for self-sacrifice and total obedience. Where you find these in the life of a believer, you find the presence of the Spirit. And what would you rather have: doctrinal distinctions or hearts that cry, "*Abba*, Father."

Why not take a minute today to hug someone who isn't part of your flock but is *in* Him. And all God's children said, "Amen!"

3.

Draw near *to God and He will draw near to you. Cleanse your hands, you sinners; and purify your hearts, you doubleminded.* James 4:8

He's Coming

Draw Near – Today we would never imagine that this Greek word was filled with expectant mystery and terrifying holiness for the early Christian church. Today we don't recognize its explosive connection to the Old Testament prophet Isaiah. Today we think this is just another devotionally stimulating exhortation. Get close to God! Come into His presence! Join the praise and worship band in order to excite your spiritual sensitivity! Twenty centuries later we have forgotten what this means.

In the first century, this Greek word, *engidzo*, was a *sacred* word, a harbinger of God's coming eschaton, a word of power and awe and mystery that pointed us toward the horizon, toward the day of judgment. In those days, "to draw near" was not so much about our need for a devotional experience. It was a declaration of the coming of the King! James, the head of the Jewish Christian church in Jerusalem, certainly had this in mind. God is drawing near – whether we like it or not. He is coming to reclaim His world. We have two options: to run expectantly toward His arrival or to flee for our lives. James suggests the first. All the world clamors for the second.

Now that you know that this word is filled with terrifying power, you can appreciate James' context. Cleanse! Purify! Why? Because the end is rushing toward you with inexorable fury. Wake up! Don't you see that God is approaching? How can you be complacent? How can you tolerate the sin in your midst? Don't you know that God comes this time in wrath? What's the matter with you? Have you forgotten that the God who forgives is still the God who is the Judge of all the earth?

Only with this context in mind can we fully appreciate James' command. There was *never any hope* of drawing near to the Judge until our guilt was cast off by His Son. Now this word, brimming with Old Testament fire, can become a word of comfort. Now we can draw near *without fear of the flame*. And the closer we come to the God who is holy, the more we will need to cleanse our hands and purify our hearts. It is a *lifetime* of repentance that leads to salvation in the middle of the furnace.

Are you ready for God to draw near?

4.

*"And this is **eternal life**, that they many know Thee the only true God, and Jesus Christ whom Thou hast sent."* John 17:3

Life Now

Eternal Life – This is such an odd thing for Jesus to say. It won't seem odd to many of us because we have heard it so often as to make it passé. But take a slower look. Jesus tells us that eternal life has nothing to do with endless living. All of today's evangelistic

171

emphasis on getting on the train to glory seems quite misapplied. I don't want to board the train to glory. I need what God has to offer now, not sometime after my body has been put in the ground. I need the life that Jesus experienced here on earth, in the hours and minutes given to human beings. The truth is that I can't hold my breath long enough to get to the end of these troublesome days in hopes of a heavenly reward. If it isn't good today, it isn't what I need.

I think I have every right to expect eternal life to show up today. After all, Jesus is my exemplar. He is my model of the perfect human being. When I look at his relationship with the Father, I clearly see what I want. I want to know what it is like to hear the Father's whispers, feel the Father's smiles, exult in the Father's will and be pleasing to the Father. That's really what I want. I don't care about the bigger house or the better job or another cause to endorse. I want life with God. I am convinced that this will not only fulfill who I truly am but will be the final measure of deepest satisfaction. The rest is consigned to ashes anyway.

Did you notice in your slower review that this *zoen aionion* (life everlasting) is not an *event*? It is a present tense continuing experience with the only true God and with Jesus the Messiah. Not one or the other, but both; certainly not a gate-pass to someplace else. Eternal life is the direct result of continuous, intimate relationship. It comes as the by-product of *knowing*. It should be immediately obvious that this kind of *knowing* has nothing to do with a collection of facts. My wife and I have a marriage because we are intimately intertwined with each other, not because there is some certificate in the county courthouse. So it must be with God and Jesus. There is a purpose behind the choice of marriage as a symbolic representation of spiritual life. Marriage works when two are all tied up together, when there are multiple levels of intersecting bonds, dependencies, commitments and trust. The fact that the culture has confused a piece of paper with entanglement only shows how pitiful our world has become. So, I ask you: Do you have the same sort of intricate entanglement with God and Jesus? Are you so intertwined with them that every part of your life affects the interaction? If I asked you if you are satisfied with your marriage, how would you reply? And what would your answer be if, under the same imagery, I asked you if you are satisfied with your *present* eternal life?

5.

"But I say to you, Love your **enemies***, bless those cursing you, do well to those hating you, and pray for those abusing and persecuting you, so that you may be sons of your Father in heaven."* Matthew 5:43-44

Necessary Conflict

Enemies – Is God sovereign? Does He have His hand on every aspect of your life? If you answered, "Yes," then you might be surprised at one of the implications: God picks your enemies according to your needs.

Did you think that your enemies were just accidental encounters, the result of bad karma or a twist of fate? Not if God is sovereign. Your enemies are *deliberately* placed in the engineering of your life in order that God's glory might be accomplished in the process. That means they are *exactly* what you need to become more like His Son.

Jesus probably used the Hebrew word *'oyev*. In the Greek text, the word is *echthrous*. While the Old Testament usage includes nations, apostates, the wicked and all those opposed to Israel and Israel's God, this New Testament word focuses attention on the *personal* enemy – the one who is hostile to you, to your God and to all things God desires. The ultimate example of the enemy is Satan, who unashamedly hates God.

Do you have enemies? If you are living according to God's point of view, you can't avoid having enemies. Jesus told us that if the world hated Him, it would also hate us. We should expect enemies. They are part of the plan. If you don't have enemies, you might want to question just how committed you are to God's holiness.

The amazing thing is not that you have enemies. Rather, it is that these enemies are hand-picked by your Lord in order that you will have the opportunity to glorify Him. Let that sink in. Then you will know why (and how) you are to pray for your enemies. You can start by *thanking God* for them. They are the sharpening stones of your sanctification. Then you can *bless them*. They are God's creatures, desperately in need of His grace. Then you can *lift them up* before His throne, earnestly interceding on their behalf that they will find the true comfort of their souls. Finally, you can offer yourself as the sacrifice needed to rescue them. Who knows your enemies better than you? Your presence in their lives is no accident. You carry the cross of their reconciliation.

We are all enemies until the Lord redeems us. Those who oppose you today only stand in the shoes you wore yesterday. If God can count you as friend, you who so violently cast Him aside, how can you not embrace the one who stands where you were?

6.

*Look at the birds of the air, that they do not **sow**, neither do they **reap**, nor **gather** into barns; and yet your heavenly Father feeds them.* Matthew 6:26

Bird-brained

Sow, Reap, Gather – The universe has a built-in economic order. It's not quite the one we recognize. Our economic model twists God's design just a tiny bit, but that tiny bit sends us down a dead-end street. Jesus corrects our vision with this metaphor from the birds.

There is nothing particularly special about these three Greek words. You might recognize some of our English derivatives if you knew that "to sow" was the word *speiro* (which is the root of *sperma* – seed – something containing the germ of the new) or "to reap" - *therizo* (to harvest, but also "summer" since the harvest occurred in the *thermal* time) or "to gather" - *sunago* (to assemble together – the basis of the word "synagogue"). It's not the actual words that matter. It's the order and the sub-ordination.

Sowing comes first. Think of this as the foundation stage. This is the preparation, the nurturing, the diligent overseeing. If you want your seeds to grow, you have to pay attention to this part of the process. You can't toss the seeds anywhere and expect to see a harvest. That is just as true for wheat as it is for careers, capital development and children.

Sowing produces harvest – after the nurturing rains provided by the Lord. In ancient Israel, this was the summer job. This was the time to reap the fruit of all your labors. Bread doesn't walk to the table. Neither do long-tended relationships suddenly become joyful melodies. Harvesting takes more work. It is a partnership with the divine Caretaker, but it is still *avodah* (work).

Finally, there is gathering – the process of bringing together, in this case, to store against a rainy day. Not all gathering is for future protection, but any crop left harvested in the field will soon rot. Bring it in.

We think the pattern is almost universal. But Jesus turns it all upside down when He points out that this order is subordinate to the God of heaven. Jesus explains that we are the bird-brained, thinking that the economic order of our lives is under our control. Jesus notices that the birds don't bother with *any* of this order, not because there is no order but because they know something we don't – God is the power behind every order and they can trust Him. The birds demonstrate a spiritual wisdom far deeper than men. They have learned to utterly rely on the Provider of the order. They are in tune with the universe. Life is a soaring song.

We, on the other hand, have yet to learn to fly.

The *first step* in any ordered universe is acknowledgement of the Orderer. Without that step, you are stuck on the ground.

7.

*"**Who are** My mother and My brothers?"* Mark 3:33

The Christian Mafia

Who Are – The mafia did not begin as a criminal organization. It began as a brotherhood of protection. But long before Sicilians banded together to defend themselves against invading Muslims, Jesus brought into existence an organization that should have made the mafia unnecessary. It's called the *ekklesia* – the church. It was supposed to be the place of encouragement, nurturing, protection and community – with one huge difference. Unlike the mafia, the church operates on the principle of self-sacrificing love.

Today, it seems as though Jesus' *ekklesia* is a fractured image of the original. Perhaps we need a new revolution – a reconstitution of the church as the Christian mafia. Of course, we would not embrace the violence and deceit and illegal behavior. But we should welcome the camaraderie, care for those in the community and, above all, protect, defend and serve the family.

Who belongs to this organization that honors its elders, respects its rules and lives by a blood-oath commitment? Jesus asked, and answered, this very question. Who are included? The answer: *everyone* who does the will of My Father. *Everyone*! Not just those who assemble at my building, live in my city or speak my language. Everyone who does the will of My Father is my family. If you belong, I am obligated to protect you, to care for you, to serve you – willingly – because you would do the same for me. This is a *brotherhood* of believers, not a convenient, social association. This is family. Nothing gets in the way of the family. Not politics. Not power. Not poverty – or wealth. Not personal preference. This is family. Period.

I'm afraid that a great deal of those who call themselves Christians are individually associated with the head of the organization, but corporately disconnected from their family. They think that they are part of the family, but the truth is that they only know the Don. They have no commitment to *everyone* who does the will of the Father. They think that their private conversations with Jesus guarantees inclusion in the community. They're mistaken. The mark of the Christian is not his love for Christ. It is his love for the rest of those who honor and serve Christ. Jesus called it "love for one another." The real Christian is intimately intertwined with the family. That's where his love shows itself.

There are brothers and sisters, mothers and fathers in your family who need you. They need protection, encouragement, assistance and hope. They need more than your occasional visits with the Don. They need your blood, sweat and tears. They are dying for it. So, Jesus asks, "Who are you?" Are you family? Or just a visitor?

8.

*How long, O naïve ones, will you love being simple-minded? And scoffers delight themselves in scoffing and **fools** hate knowledge?* Proverbs 1:22

Three For The Money

Fools – The Bible describes three kinds of unbelieving people. They are the simple (*patayim*), the scoffers (*leshim*) and the fools (*kasilim*). They don't behave the same way, but they all receive the same reward. Until we know the difference, we will not understand how to speak to these people (or how *not* to). Worse than that, we might not know just who is whom when it comes to foolish thinking. One of these might even be us.

The simple are those who live outside of God's will because of ignorance. They just don't know better. What they lack is someone to tell them the truth. Surprisingly (to us), they are still held accountable. Ignorance is not an excuse under God's law, probably because no one is truly ignorant (see Romans 1:18-20). But this much is sure: if you don't speak up, these naïve ones are lost. They may be willing to follow the Way; they just have no idea what it is.

The scoffers know the truth. They've had instruction. They just don't do it. They would much rather discard the words of the Lord than reorient their lives to His desires. They are consumed with their plans. These people are not ignorant of the Lord. They just ignore Him. They love their homes, their jobs, their toys, their vacations, their positions or whatever else they desire more than they love God's purposes. Scoffers can be very religious, but their hearts are far from submission.

Then there are the fools in this verse – the *kasilim*. These are people who know the Way, refuse to follow it and encourage others to go astray with them. These people are to be avoided. In fact, the Bible says that you will *waste your efforts* if you attempt to correct them or offer them an alternative. Not only do they not care, they actively encourage disobedience. Only God can deal with these – and when He does, it is not a pretty site. One of the reasons Proverbs is so adamant about the company you keep is that Solomon knows that accompanying *kasilim* is eternally dangerous. This kind of folly rubs off.

For the *patayim*, there is instruction in God's plan and purposes. They need to hear the truth. For the *leshim*, there is only one message: repent. But for the *kasilim*, only those filled with the Spirit and called by God to the task dare to enter into their world.

If you have been frustrated by your ineffective efforts to see someone else come to the truth, perhaps you were treating everyone in the same category. Time for a check-up, and some pleading prayer. Hopefully you did not discover any similarities between these three kinds of fools and your own actions.

9.

*If, however, you are fulfilling the **royal** law, according to the Scripture, "You shall love your neighbor as yourself," you are doing well. But if you show partiality, you are committing sin* James 2:8-9

Insulting the Christ

Royal – There are lots of laws, but very few of them come with this kind of authority. James calls it a *royal* law. Since we don't live under a king, we don't feel the impact that his readers did. On the official decree was the stamp of the king. To disobey meant death. That makes it absolutely imperative that we understand exactly what this law is – not just what we thought it was.

The Greek text uses the word *basilikos*. It is associated with *basileia*, kingdom. But it is not about a place. It is about the reign and rule of a person. Wherever the king's authority presides, that is the realm of the king. Since this law comes from God Himself, it governs *every action in the universe*. It extends to every part of His reign and rule.

So what is this royal law? James quotes Leviticus 19:18. Of course he does. It is the royal law of *Scripture* and, for James, that means the Old Testament. The law of the King never changed. Since we know that God's law is really just an extension of God's character, we might ask, "What does this royal law tell me about God?" The answer is startlingly simple – and it becomes the simplest of guides for this law's true application. What this tells us about God, God Himself made perfectly clear in another passage of the Law (Exodus 34:6). "The LORD, the LORD God, compassionate and gracious, slow to anger and abounding in lovingkindness and truth." God's definition of Himself tells us all we need to know about keeping this royal law. To love my neighbor is to act with compassion and grace, be slow to anger and abound in lovingkindness and truth.

Forget all the contemporary psycho-babble about "you have to love yourself before you can love others." The royal law does not rest on your inner, emotional disposition. The royal law is about *action*. How do we know that? Because God *acted* with compassion, grace, restraint, love and truth toward us – even when He had absolutely no need or reason to do so! If God can love me as His neighbor when I so richly deserve His *wrath*, what excuse can I possibly offer for not reflecting His spirit on those of my own kind?

Failure to act on the basis of the royal law is the equivalent of spitting in the face of the Christ as He hung on the cross! God's ultimate act of compassion was to freely offer up His Son for my sin.

If I withhold any portion of my receipt of that love by failing to act for the benefit of another, then I insult the Savior – and the One Who sent Him.

Who's your neighbor? Does the thought bring some face to mind, someone whom you avoid, disparage, resent, ignore or just don't like? Look closer. Maybe you'll see a glimmer of the King.

9.

*"You shall be **holy**, for I the LORD your God am **holy**."* Leviticus 19:2

Fundamentals

Holy – The bottom line of God's requirements for men is this single word: *qadosh* – holy.

Jesus thought it was so important that he quoted this verse (Matthew 5:48) when He summarized His discussion of the law. If your translation says, "be perfect," it reflects the Greek word, not the Hebrew word. So, if the Father and the Son both agree that *holiness* is the absolute fundamental, what does this mean in action?

Qadosh describes something (a person, place or thing) that is *inherently* sacred or that has been designated sacred by a ceremonial act. It is exactly the opposite of profane; something that is used commonly, without special attribute of quality. For example, profanity is using language that should have a holy, sacred quality in a common, base way. Profanity strips language of its divinity. Likewise, whenever we act in ways that strip divinity from its rightful place in our lives, we become profane.

Step back a bit and reflect on this. Life, all life, is sacred. God brought life into being and life reflects Him. God designated Life sacred, blessed it and put His stamp on it. If you go back to the Genesis account, you will discover that every step of the creative process is saturated with God's holiness. God is holy and all that He does reflects that holiness. Therefore, in obedience to Him and in recognition of the true character of Life, we are asked to deliberately reflect the same holy attribute. That means that every act, every thought, every word of our lives is judged by the fundamental structure of the universe – holiness!

Hold the mirror of holiness up to your life. Is the reflection clear and bright? Is every part of your life a testimony to the holiness inherent in God's creation? Do you live and move and exist in the fabric of the sacred quality of Life? Or are there some things that you allow to be profaned? Are there some things where your actions, thoughts and attitudes are just like the fallen world, filled with reducing the sacred to the common?

If you are going to be a Christian, you must remove the profane from your life. You have been designated *holy* by the Son's ceremonial act on the cross. Now you need to live up to the high calling.

God wants holiness. We want forgiveness. There's a big difference. We *need* forgiveness in order to pursue holiness, but we often *want* forgiveness in order to pursue our own agendas. It's time to return to the fundamentals. Profane nothing God has given. Be holy because He is holy.

11.

*"If you love Me, you will **keep** My commandments."* John 14:15

Jesus and Holiness

Keep - How many of us would be included in the Kingdom if Jesus came back right now and said, "Now I'll take only those who have obeyed my commandments." Would you be able to step forward and say, "Lord, I have obeyed. I'm ready," or would you try to slip to the back of the crowd, remembering some act that profaned your life?

Amazingly, most of us don't really believe Jesus. We imagine that He is just using hyperbole. He can't really intend that only those who keep His commandments love Him. After all, we reason, we have been forgiven. So what's a little mistake among friends? Jesus has it covered, right?

We don't understand that Jesus does not forgive in order for us to go on with our lives. Forgiveness removes (at great cost) our guilt in order that we can go on in *obedience*. We live with a bastardized view of grace. We sell spiritual indulgences with the catch-phrase "once saved, always saved." I can't find anything in the Bible that indicates that obedience has been replaced with forgiveness. Even if the law is set aside with the coming of new covenant grace, Jesus' words are still the final measure of my life. Did I obey? Is my life governed by His holiness? Do I pursue God with a passionate zeal to fulfill His desires and glorify His name? In a word, do I *keep* His commandments?

The word is *tereo*. This is prison and military language. It has the nuance of guarding, watching over, observing and fulfilling a duty. You are to be the warden of His commandments. But that isn't all. This verb is in the future, active tense. This action is going on now and will keep going on into the future. If you love Jesus, your life will be about keeping His commandments, not just today but every day from now on.

Of course, the opposite applies. If you are not keeping His commandments, today and every day, then you clearly do not love Him. Love equals obedience. The two concepts cannot be divorced. There is no such thing as someone who loves Jesus but does not obey Him. I don't know who invented the idea of the *carnal* Christian, but it certainly doesn't apply here.

Jesus calls us to active duty. Get up! Get going! Stand guard over His words. Put them to work in your life. It's a matter of life and love!

Oh, yes. If you have some house cleaning to do before you can bear arms for Him, get to it. Heaven can't wait!

12.

*"But an hour is coming, and now is, when the true worshippers shall worship the Father in spirit and **truth**; for such people the Father seeks to be His worshipers."* John 4:23

The Agony and the Ecstasy

Truth – God delights in those who worship Him in spirit and truth. Of this we can be certain. Unfortunately, we are not so certain about what it means to worship in spirit and truth. But we better do our best to discern the meaning since the delight of the Father depends on it.

The woman at the well suggested that worship had to do with place and ritual. She was wrong. So were those who claimed the same status for the temple in Jerusalem. God is no respecter of place (or of persons). You don't have to enter into a particular building to worship the King of creation. Sometimes it helps, but it only helps you, not Him.

The woman at the well also suggested that worship depended on doctrine. Once again, Jesus corrects her. Having all the right facts and the correct proof texts does not constitute worship. You are not likely to find God in a seminary library – unless, of course, you are there worshipping in spirit and truth.

So, what about this word, *alethia* (truth). The most interesting thing about this word is that it is not principally about facts. It is about relationships, and, in particular, it is about a personal relationship with Jesus. When Jesus said, "I am the truth," He did not mean that He was the summation of all correct facts. He meant that the universe is fundamentally about relationships and that He is fundamental to all relationships. If you are not storing relationships in the treasury of your life, you account will be empty in heaven. If the first entry in your heavenly account is not Jesus, then all the rest is null and void.

OK, we got that! Now what? How do I relate to Jesus in truth? Ah, but it's so simple. You make the words of Jesus your words. You make His way your way. You keep His commandments, think His thoughts, go where He would go, do what He would do. You sit down with a woman whom your culture and ethnic background tells you to hate – and show her God's love. You weep with those who weep and rejoice with those who rejoice. You agonize over the lost and celebrate with the found. You forsake family and home to follow the King. You put your life on the line. You depend utterly on the Father.

This is not about theology. It's about involvement. It's about character, commitment and calling. You make *truth* a personal project.

Want to worship the Father in truth? Then be Jesus today, wherever you are, whatever you are doing. That worship will delight Him.

13.

*Are you so foolish? Having begun by the Spirit, are you now **being perfected** by the flesh?* Galatians 3:3

Finishing Touches

Being Perfected – God does not work according to human plans or purposes. Of course, we all knew that, didn't we? We often find ourselves saying, "God's ways are not our ways," especially when we just can't see why things don't go the way we think they should. But it's quite a bit different to act in ways that would never be considered the results of human planning than it is to accept things that don't happen according to human planning. Acceptance is passive. It's just the way things are. But how many times have we *deliberately* taken a course of action that does *not* fit the ways of the world? Not so many, I'm afraid. We might be good passive citizens of the Kingdom (usually because we don't have any other choice), but we aren't so good at *choosing* the ways of the Spirit at the expense of what seems perfectly reasonable from the human point of view.

When Paul asks the Galatian *Christians* why they are reverting to the world's systems of operation, he is not suggesting that they have suddenly become immoral idolaters. He is pointing out that somewhere along the way they started to think that God's grace got mixed with human effort. They started to believe that a little bit of human wisdom might help the Kingdom along. They began to incorporate great human principles into God's design. Paul is shocked! Did they forget that those who befriend the world make God their enemy? Paul uses the verb *epiteleo*, an intensified form of the verb for being completed or finished. It's like an exclamation point behind the thought. How can you start in the Spirit and think you can *finish(!)* in the flesh? Impossible! Grace is never mixed with human finishing touches.

Now you may be saying, "But I don't try to mix God's grace with my works. I know that salvation comes by faith alone." Well and good. But examine your actions. How many times have you worried over your job, carefully planned your retirement account, crafted a way to get ahead or tried to maneuver a relationship for your gain? How many times have you proceeded, with noble intentions, without first consulting with God's purpose and plan? How many times have you *waited* until God told you to act before you closed the deal? How many times have you assumed that tomorrow will be just like today? How many times have you forgotten to thank Him for your work, your family, your home and your life (did you think you *earned* them)? How many times have you acted as though the assets in your hand are *yours*? How many times did you fall back on doing good as a way to gain God's favor when you needed things to go your way? How many times have you quoted the world's wisdom about a good job, a good education and a good neighborhood but ignored the need for a pure heart and clean hands?

You foolish Galatians, did you think that once you accepted Jesus' forgiveness you could go back to living a *good* life? What begins with the Spirit cannot proceed from any other source.

14.

Judge not and you will not be judged Luke 6:34

Just Bad Theology

Judge – In our politically and socially correct world, we have propagated the mythology of withholding judgment. All correction has deteriorated into personal opinion and personal opinion has been devalued to nothing. If you tell me that I am doing something wrong, so what? That's just your opinion. It doesn't matter.

With this frightening social condemnation of the place of correction, it's no wonder that we often hear this verse used entirely out of context. Christians are not to offer godly correction because even

Jesus said, "Don't judge." But this is just bad theology. If we look at the Greek, we will learn something very important.

The verb for judging is the Greek word *krino*. It has more than one meaning, determined by context. Its primary use describes the action of *discriminating between good and evil*. In the New Testament, *krino* often means forming an opinion that separates what is right and proper godly behavior, from actions that are evil and opposed to God. In this sense, judging is absolutely necessary for Christian living. We call this "discriminating" rather than "judging," but the Greek word is the same. There is no need to shy away from this use of *krino*.

So what about Luke 6:34? Yes, it's the same word, but here the context tells us that the meaning is judicial. Here the verb is about sitting in judgment over another, which is, taking the position of the one who condemns. In Luke 6:34, Jesus is warning us not to act as judge and jury. Condemnation is ultimately in the hand of God. He knows the hearts of men. When we decide that someone else deserves God's punishment *on the basis of our opinion alone*, we usurp God's role as the Judge of all mankind. That is exceedingly bad theology.

Does this mean that we are never to act as judge? No. In fact, God specifically designates men to act as His regents in the execution of punishment. He appoints judges in both the social and spiritual world. But the judgment belongs to Him. We are here to execute His judgment, not make up our own. God has provided in His word all that we need to know in order to determine the proper course of action in human relationship management. Just go read the Law. The principles of proper conduct, pleasing to God, are all there. There is really very little guess work. When I act on the basis of God's revealed law, I do not judge. I execute *His* judgment. But when I put myself in the place of God, I determine the verdict and the punishment. God has no tolerance for that, so Jesus tells us that if we insist on acting like God, we will be held accountable to the same standard we require.

It's time for believers to stop cowering under the accusation, "Don't judge." There are perfectly good grounds for judging. Just make sure that you have no personal agenda (rebuke gently) and that your discernment is based entirely on God's point of view. Deal self out. Make God the center of all your actions. Then *krino* is quite right.

15.

*Those whom I love, I reprove and discipline; be **zealous**, therefore, and repent.* Revelation 3:19

Passionate Commitment

Zealous – Are you zealous for God? "I think so," you might answer, "but I'm not sure what you mean." Yes, it's confusing. We don't use the word *zeal* much in these days of tolerance and universal humanism. When we do, it is almost always pejorative. No one wants to be a zealot today. But God wants you to be zealous. In fact, He is so interested in your ardent commitment to Him that He is willing to reprove and discipline you until you are absolutely on fire for Him.

Of course, God does not have the Greek understanding of zeal in mind. The Greek word, *zeloo*, brings with it the idea of intense human striving to improve personality. It is the muted battle cry of the moral majority. If only we had the qualities necessary for a richer, fuller life. We hear it from the humanists. If only we were nobler, kinder, more enlightened. The educators follow suit. If only we had better self-esteem or better self-worth. All of this Greek-based appeal to enhanced personality is far from God's view of zeal. That's because God's idea comes through the Hebrew mind. There the word is *qana'*. It is quite literally the state of existence that is consumed with exalting God by "maintaining purity of worship and purity of obedience." It is exactly what Jesus had in mind when He suggested that those who love Him will keep His commandments. This is not a condition built on a *feeling*. This is a commitment to thought and action. God's zealots are sold out to His word, honoring its every implication in order to show reverence to their King. They take every opportunity to worship, offering thanksgiving and praise to their Lord. They live to serve Him. Nothing and no one gets in the way.

Why does God want you to be zealous? Why is He willing to take the time and effort to train and discipline you in order to produce this condition of absolute fidelity? The reason God bothers with all this is because God is zealous – and He wants you to be like Him. In fact, *qana'* is used over and over to describe the character of God. God will not tolerate a rival for your affections. He will not admit any competitor. He wants your full endorsement, trust and love. He guards His relationship with you as a jealous husband, anxious to keep any threat to the union far from the door. That zeal is the reason why God takes us back, even after we have slept with the enemy. God's fervor for our affection never falters. We are seduced and we seduce others. We chase the passions of this world, thinking they will offer relief to our burdened souls. In the end, we are nothing but twitching addicts. Without a zeal for God, life deteriorates into an endless series of hopeless fixes.

God knows that we were made for total, sold-out commitment. We don't really experience life as it should be until we find our place in fervent devotion to Him. God invites us, challenges us, commands us to put everything on the line in worship and obedience. It is the only way – and He will not rest until we are chastened enough to accomplish this goal.

Now, are you zealous for God?

16.

Those whom I love, I reprove and discipline; be zealous, therefore, and **repent**. Revelation 3:19

Becoming a Zealot

Repent – Have you determined to be 100% sold-out for God? That's great. He wants you to have a zealous heart like His. But how do you accomplish this? Do you just make another vow to keep every commandment? Do you pray for more faith, bolster up your demoralized spirit and enter the battle once again? No, you don't!

You and I both know that try as we might, we will fail. Sin is an ever-present reality in the lives of believers. It is cunning, sinister and hideous – and it is always waiting for an opportunity to divert your attention from the Lover of your soul. God told Cain that sin was lying at the door, waiting to strike. It's the same for us. And so is the step toward victory. Cain should have read this verse in Revelation. If you want a zeal for the Lord, begin right here – repent!

God does two things to create the opportunity for zeal in our lives. He reproves (rebukes) and He disciplines (chastises). We are asked to do only one thing – repent. The Greek is *metanoeo*. It is literally "to change the place of your mind." It is more than regret and sorrow. Those are both good, and important, but unless there is a real change in mind – and heart – repentance has not occurred. *Repentance* is the negative side of *return*. Both are filled with Hebrew thought patterns. The Hebrew idea behind repentance is the emotional, mental, spiritual and physical distress that accompanies an attempt to influence a situation or person. It is about both the effective and affective sides of decision-making. Most often, repentance is cast in the context of human futility to alter the course of events. Only God can truly change circumstances; therefore, the ultimate object of repentance is God Himself. This means that only God can grant comfort as a result of repentance because, ultimately, no human being has the power to change the circumstances of my need for repentance.

The other side of repentance is *return*. Over and over, God implores us to return to Him. The word is used more than 1000 times in Scripture. It is the act of repentance seen from the hoped-for goal. Return is possible only because God is compassionate. His unfailing desire to forgive lays the foundation for remorse, regret, re-commitment and regeneration. But here is the key to it all: in Hebrew thought, comfort is never a function of words; it is a description of *action*.

To be zealous for God, I must begin where I am – with my sin. I cannot ignore it, excuse it, avoid it or minimize it. It is the bedrock of my human existence. But I can bring it before the throne of the Most High God. I can offer it with absolute change of mind, asking to be removed from this place of profane disobedience. He may actually *drive* me to this kneeling humility. When I arrive, I have taken the first step toward zeal. Now God can do something with me.

Why wait? Did you think God would forget to push?

17.

*according as He **chose** us in Him before the foundations of the world*
Ephesians 1:4

When God Chooses

Chose – There are only a few verses that cause more argument than this one. Once we decide that our theology needs to close all the gaps, we are bound to confront that age-old question of predestination.   But perhaps we need to pay attention to the emphasis rather than the content. Paul is quite anxious for us to see that the divine operation is based on God's *choice*. *When* God makes the choice is not nearly as important as that fact that God does make the choice, for without God's willingness to choose us, nothing of consequence will happen at all.

God chose us. Oh, how enormously significant these words! I did not go on a quest for the divine and, with unrelenting perseverance, force God to divulge Himself to me. No, God came looking. He made His choice to pursue me long before I came on the scene. God has been hunting for each of us since He put His plan into action.

Paul uses the Greek *exelexato*. The root (*eklego*) is about making a choice between things, selecting out some from many. The word suggests that the purpose of choosing is to establish a relationship between the one choosing and the objects chosen. It does not, however, mean that the objects not chosen are rejected. The emphasis is on the relationship, not the quality of the objects chosen. What's more important is that in the New Testament this verb is always found in the middle voice. That implies that there is a special significance for the *actor* in the relationship. Did you get that? The actor is God. His choice has special significance for **Him**! Of course, it also means a lot to us, right? But the emphasis is not on us

190

(amazingly). It is on what all of this means to God! What God is doing is executing His plan of perfect delight to Him. He is absolutely pleased with how this is all working out. God likes what He does – and you and I are included in His good pleasure.

What a joy it is to know that God is perfectly happy with His choices. He loves to elect. It is all unfolding according to His good will. How it all unfolds might be a mystery to you and me, but that does not mean that we are deprived of the opportunity to celebrate how marvelous it all is to Him! So, join me in praise to the God Who knows exactly what He is doing and is perfectly capable of bringing it to pass. That is the emphasis of election.

I can stop worrying about the fate of the universe now. God will be quite pleased if I just pay attention to what He is asking of me today.

18.

*for us to be holy and without blemish **before** Him in love* Ephesians 1:4

Who God Chooses

Before – Verbal imagery from the ancient world is often lost in contemporary language. Here we have a seemingly common preposition, but if we only could see the Greek, we would recognize something quite significant. The word is not the common Greek preposition for "before." It is the rather complicated word *kataenopion* instead of *pro*. Why does Paul choose this particular word? Because he wants to create a picture that will communicate what it means to stand before the Lord of the universe. It is the imagery that matters most because this imagery is about a very important part of the ancient world – granting honor.

In the Old Testament, we often find the phrase, "found favor in the eyes of." This is a description of *ascribed* honor. In other words, someone who already possesses honor grants or ascribes that honor to someone who does not possess it. The king recognizes the subject. The lord grants favor to the servant. Honor is not honor unless it is publicly acknowledged, and one way that this

191

acknowledgement occurs is "in the eyes." This motif was common throughout the ancient world, in both Hebrew and Greek cultures. The source of acknowledged acceptability came from the face (the eyes) of the noble.

Now look at our word. It is made up of many parts. Literally it means "in relationship to the face", but it carries the sense of lowered before the eyes of another. In other words, this word conveys the same thought of prostrating oneself before the eyes of the king. Why does this matter? Because the verse tells us that the purpose of God's electing choice is to give us the status of "holy and blameless" before His eyes. God intends that we be *ascribed* the honor *achieved* by His Son. In His courtroom, we can look up because in His eyes, He sees us holy and blameless.

The purpose of election is not to issue us a ticket to heaven. Heaven is hardly of any interest at all when it comes to God's choice. To think this way is to put the emphasis on the wrong person – me. God chooses in order that He might favor us with the honor of His Son. God chooses because He delights in acknowledging His Son's obedience, and there is no better way to do so than to touch us with the results of that obedience. Election is not about us. It is about Jesus.

How will this change your perspective about *your* salvation? Will you begin to see that all God's choosing in your life is not about you? Will you recognize that your participation is intended to glorify the Son? Will that make a difference in your own choices? Will the honor you receive reflect the honor He achieved?

19.

*predestinating us to adoption through Jesus Christ to Himself, according to the **good pleasure** of His will* Ephesians 1:5

Why God Chooses

Good Pleasure – Why would God choose me? If you have never asked this question, you have never understood the true depravity of your soul. It is a travesty of modern Christianity that we almost see salvation as a right, an entitlement. We have preached the love of God to death. We have portrayed a God Who would never turn away a single soul, no matter what the cost. We have seduced ourselves into believing that we are entitled to God's favor simply because we have "accepted" the plan of salvation. Let Paul's words correct this fatal error. God is under no obligation whatsoever to provide a single one of us with His grace, no matter what process of repentance you might exercise. God does not choose because of us. He chooses because of Him. It's all about His good pleasure.

The word is *eudokia*. Its root comes from two words that mean "to think well of." But it is not just about nice thoughts. This word emphasizes the willingness and resolve to act according to these thoughts. In other words, *eudokia* results in benevolence and grace. The question is why. Why does God have good will toward us? The answer is found in the basis of *eudokia*. That basis resides in the very character of God Himself. God is *good*. That does not mean, as we usually suppose, that God does good things (especially for me). Our T-shirt slogans about God's goodness are way off the mark. The goodness of God is the concentrated energy of active holiness, zealous to promote and produce what is benevolent, just and pure. The goodness of God is not God's life-enhancing acts. It is His very being, a person who is thoroughly and utterly committed to righteousness expressed in action. God is good because goodness is Who He is, not because He simply chooses to act compassionately today. When Paul expresses election as the result of God's good will, he is telling us that the very essence of Who God is will be found in the choices God makes. There is never any discrepancy between what is good and what God does. God's good pleasure is to bring into existence what is righteous, by thought, word and deed.

Why does God choose me? Because it is the righteous thing to do. It has absolutely nothing to do with me. I am not righteous. I stand in opposition to real goodness. But God will not allow my sinfulness to prevent His expression of goodness. So, He chooses me. Nothing stops His choice to act on the basis of goodness. He does everything according to His character.

And that leaves me with a great question. If God chooses me, will I choose Him? God demonstrates His choice in active engagement of goodness on my behalf. I demonstrate my choice in active obedience on His behalf. There is no such thing as passive salvation – from God's side or mine. That's how you show your acceptance of His choice, right?

20.

*to the **praise** of the glory of His grace*   Ephesians 1:6

What God Chooses

Praise – God chooses me. His choice exalts His Son. It reflects His character. It demonstrates His power. But it also has an eschatological purpose – a purpose that goes beyond the edge of this world. God chooses in order that He might be praised.

Does that sound egotistical, even selfish? Of course it does, because we react to these words from our human perspective – and we are, quite frankly, filled with ego and self when it comes to looking for praise. But God is not a man. He can ask for praise and expect it because He is the only One actually totally worthy of praise. God is good, remember? He is not simply doing good. He is good. Therefore, He deserves – He has a right to – praise. To withhold praise from a good God is the height of sin for it denies what is ultimately due Him. So, *epainos* (applause and commendation) belong to God without qualification.

God chooses me, out of His free and good will, in order to honor His Son, so that *I might offer Him the praise He deserves.* What God chooses is to glorify Himself, and He chooses to do this through my redemption.

Now you have come full circle, and not a single part of this predestined election is about you! It has always been, and always will be, about God. Your role is to fall on your face in awe and reverence that God would even imagine to include your participation in any part of this. Your role is to sing with the angelic host, "Glory, glory, glory to the Lord God Almighty."

Can you set aside your ego long enough to recognize that the plan of salvation is not about you? Can you see perhaps for the first time that God redeems for His glory, not your welfare? You are caught up in something cosmic, eternal, almost unimaginable. God is glorifying Himself – and you and I are part of that cosmic choir. Stop thinking that God's world revolves around your rescue. Yes, He is intimately interested in you, but not because you need to be saved. He is interested in you because your salvation glorifies Him. Get the right glasses on your face. This is a much bigger picture than you thought.

Praise is the purpose of man. If your life reflects praise for the Creator, then you have done nothing more than what would be expected of any created being. Even the heavens shout silent praises to Him. Did you imagine that your life could do any less?

It's time to grow up. Rick Warren was right, but not deep enough. It's not about you. It isn't even close.

21.

June 25 *in these last days has spoken to us* **in** *His Son* Hebrews 1:2

Jesus Unplugged

In – Don't you think that this statement is a little odd? We wouldn't say that God spoke to us *in* someone. We would say that God spoke to us *through* someone. Why? Because for us, the emphasis is on the *message*, not the *messenger*. We focus our attention on what is verbally communicated, not on who does the communicating. That's a mistake. The author of Hebrews wants us to understand that God's full revelation finds its paradigm case *in* the Son, not simply *through* the Son. It is Jesus Himself that is the message of God. It's not just what He says, but rather who He is that matters.

In our culture, we rarely pay attention to the messenger. In fact, we have a common saying that shows just how much we divorce the message from the message bearer. "I'm just the messenger," implies that the content has nothing to do with me. It's as if I were simply carrying something along the way; something that is not really part of me. But this is never true of Jesus. Every action, every word, every feeling and every thought of Jesus reveals the Father. Jesus is God in the flesh – and that means we had better pay very close attention to His "flesh" because it is also God's message to us. It matters how Jesus acted and reacted. It matters how He worshipped, prayed, ate, drank, walked, slept (or didn't sleep). Nothing in the life of the Son of God is insignificant. Nothing is merely the messenger.

The author of this verse uses the Greek word *en*. It's really a very simple word, commonly translated by a whole host of English equivalents like "in, at, on or by." But there is something you need to know about this tiny little word. This Greek preposition stands in the middle between two other prepositions, *eis* and *ek*. All of these prepositions are finally about motion. *Eis* means "into." *Ek* mean "out of." And *en* stands right between them. *En* is the place of rest. What it implies here is that the full revelation of God comes to *rest* in Jesus. Nothing more needs to be added. God *rests* in the place of Jesus.

This is an absolutely incredible claim. If it were not backed up by the resurrection, we would have to rationally reject it. How can the God of the universe, the All Mighty, *rest* in a man named Jesus? It is simply not conceivable. Therefore, many reject this claim. They keep looking for other messengers of divinity. They don't see that *Jesus is not a messenger! He is the message* – the truth, the whole truth, and nothing but the truth about who God is.

Go back to your gospels. Read them in a new light. Jesus is God. Yes, of course, you knew that already. But have you really understood? Jesus is not communicating with you about God. Don't put Him in the category of a messenger. Let who He is show you who God is. You might discover something important.

22.

*"to **love** the LORD your God and walk in all His ways and keep His commandments and hold fast to Him and serve Him with all your heart and with all your soul."* Joshua 22:5

Joshua's Theology (1)

196

Love – Joshua uttered those famous words, "As for me and my house, we will serve the Lord." It's a powerful and noble declaration. What it means, however, is not always so obvious. To know *how* Joshua intended to serve God, we must take a look at Joshua's theology, and there is no better place to do that than right here. If you want to be one of those who can stand with Joshua and declare your service to God, you will first have to know what Joshua means by the verbs that precede serving.

Love the Lord your God. The Hebrew is *ahav*. One of three Hebrew words for love, this verb is carefully distinguished from the other two (something we do not see in English). *Ahav* expresses a passionate desire to be fully united with another in every aspect of living, both inwardly and outwardly. Consequently, it has both emotional and behavioral results. In fact, it is so unique that the translators of the Old Testament into Greek could not find a parallel Greek verb in either *eros* or *phileo*. They chose *agape* in order to capture the full meaning of *ahav*. What this means is that *ahav* demands the full use of all of our energy and faculties. It is a verb that is only found in *relationship*, whether between two people or in community. Its direction is always toward another, expressed in real actions, not merely feelings. It is determined benevolence on behalf of another person.

When Joshua exhorts his listeners to love the Lord, he is not encouraging private, inward sentiment. He knows that *ahav* means action – toward God and toward God's people. It is impossible to love God and mistreat His community. To withhold from another follower any action or affection that would be appropriate for service and worship of God is to deny your love of Him. The second great commandment cannot be divorced from the first, even, as Jesus made abundantly clear, when you are faced with an enemy. Jesus did not invent that requirement (compare Proverbs 25:21). He merely drew our attention to the proper venue of *ahav*. We can go so far as to say love and action are two sides of the same coin.

Now what does this mean for you and me? It means that we must **stop** claiming that we love God if we are not exhibiting acts of grace, compassion, benevolence, forgiveness and restitution. We must re-examine our lives for those seeds of hypocrisy; the tiny discrepancies between our *behavior* and our *proclamations*. We must be able to straightforwardly answer the question, "Do I treat him *as God would treat him?*"

Make your list. There will be names on it that require a new way. Apply *ahav*. God will smile even if no one else notices a thing.

23.

*"to love the LORD your God and **walk** in all His ways and keep His commandments and hold fast to Him and serve Him with all your heart and with all your soul."* Joshua 22:5

Joshua's Theology (2)

Walk – How do you walk the pathway of life? If you're like most of us, you soon discover that the majority of your walking hours are determined by *emotions* rather than reason. Oh, we all have our rational world-views (some are a good deal more rational than others), but when it comes down to walking the pathway, we move by feelings. We are not Vulcans (remember Mr. Spock?). As human beings, emotions are our greatest asset and our most terrible curse.

We don't think about our spiritual lives as pathways of emotions. We usually get stuck at the rational rest stop, exercising our minds with theological arguments and doctrinal debates. But that's not how we live, is it? Life comes with fear, joy, grief, sorrow, enchantment, gladness, hope, discouragement, gloom and dozens of other emotional injections. If your walk can't handle these ups and downs, then you are in for some really treacherous times. What we need more than anything is a theology of emotions.

The Hebrew culture considered the word for *walk* (*yalak*) as a metaphor for an approach and attitude toward life. Their view was simple but profound. Start walking. After awhile, when you stop being frustrated by the fact that you can't drive, you will notice life. You will see things that were never in view at 60 miles an hour. You will discover that life slowed down is life with time to digest what is happening – to the world and to you in the world. You will arrive at a pace that allows you to *feel* the world you occupy. All of that hurry to get somewhere just truncated your ability to be somewhere. The theology of emotions probably begins with walking.

Will life really fall apart if you can't do everything on the list today? Will your future be eternally jeopardized if you don't go faster? What would happen to your inner sense of well-being if you took a stroll instead of a sprint? Is living synonymous with pushing?

Ancient people of the desert knew about walking. It took months of walking to go from Syria to Egypt. It took years of walking to cross the Jordan. But what they gained in the walking journey is something we lost when we invented the accelerator.

Don't tell me how your life is today. Tell me how you're walking. I'll know the rest.

24.

*"to love the LORD your God and walk in all His ways and **keep** His commandments and hold fast to Him and serve Him with all your heart and with all your soul."* Joshua 22:5

Joshua's Theology (3): Occupational Therapy

Keep – *Shamar* has a wide umbrella of meanings. They stem from the idea of watching. Why do we need to know this? Because keeping the commandments is not just about *observing* them. Buried in the verb is something much more exquisite.

When *shamar* is involved, the focus is on the *purpose*, not the process. In other words, in order to "keep" the commandments, I must know *why* I am observing them. It is not enough to just follow the rules. The commands of God were never intended to simply prescribe behavior. They were intended to teach us something about God Himself. That's why Paul calls the Law a schoolmaster. The purpose of the Law is not compliance. It is much bigger than that.

Shamar can also be translated "to preserve, to guard, to carefully watch over and to pay regard to." Behind each one of these possible translations is the question, "Why?" I am not inclined to complete the action required by *shamar* unless I am motivated by something stronger than compliance. When it comes to God's commandments, the purpose of *shamar* is fellowship with Him. Jesus said it best: "If you love me, you will keep my commandments."

Did you think that a relationship with God was just about keeping the rules? Did you imagine that God was the Great Policeman, checking up on your behavior? No way! God gave the commandments so that we might discover His point of view – the truth about life. He gave them so that we could know more about Him. He revealed Himself in those requests. Then He offered us fellowship as we walked the road together. "Come along with Me. I know the way and how to walk to get there. It will be the greatest adventure of your life."

Life's occupation is all about *shamar*, but not the kind of misinterpretation we often ascribe to "keeping." *Shamar* is occupational therapy. It is the process of discipleship, learning from the Master at every turn in the road. Just like any other kind of occupational therapy, it takes effort, time, practice, patience and, most of all, purpose.

Have a good time.

25.

*"to love the LORD your God and walk in all His ways and keep His commandments and **hold fast** to Him and serve Him with all your heart and with all your soul."* Joshua 22:5

Joshua's Theology (4): Marriage Glue

Hold Fast – The first time we see this word sets the stage for all the rest of the occurrences. It shows up in Genesis 2:24 – a fairly significant passage for most human beings. It's about glue. "Cling to" your spouse. In particular, husbands are to cling to their wives. I hope you noticed that the focus of attention is on the sticking ability of the *husband*. That should tell you something about male temptations.

Now apply this instructional passage to Joshua's theology. He uses *davaq* to describe the necessary sticking ability between us and God. Once again, I hope you noticed who is the husband in this metaphor (here's a clue – it isn't God). We, those tempted to wander, are the ones who need the glue. God remains faithful throughout.

Of course, there are plenty of passages in the Bible that describe God in the male gender, but I find it fascinating that when it comes to the Old Testament view of the marriage contract, God is often on the wife's side of the metaphor (notwithstanding the New Testament description of the "bride" of Christ). This seems especially appropriate in our contemporary view of serial marriage (one partner after another). Too often the glue is dissolved with an application of male adultery. Of course, the actual dissolution began a long time before the final separation. The glue was watered down though progressive exposure to "thoughtless" control.

God wants glue. He longs for a sticky relationship – one that will cling fast in good times and in bad times, in sickness and in health, in riches and poverty until death doesn't even part. God not only desires such a relationship, He is fully committed to it. He does not waver or falter but remains the faithful partner in spite of all our struggles.

God invented glue. He knows exactly how it works, how it is to be applied, how much pressure it takes to make it set and under what conditions it will maintain its bond. My suggestion is that you read the manufacturer's instructions if you want glue to work for you.

There is a nice bit of self-interest in gluing yourself to God. First, you'll find it quite an adventure. Secondly, it has significant long-term results. And thirdly, there is no better life than the bonded life.

Stick to it.

26.

*"to love the LORD your God and walk in all His ways and keep His commandments and hold fast to Him and **serve** Him with all your heart and with all your soul."* Joshua 22:5

Joshua's Theology (5)

Serve – Finally! Serve. Serve comes *last* on the list. Did you notice that? Serve is *not* the priority in Joshua's theology. It comes after love, walk, keep and cling. Of course, that makes perfect sense. I can't serve if I haven't embraced a unique relationship, can't set the right pace, don't know why and am constantly wandering off. When these things are in order, then I am ready for *avadh*. Oh, yes, and by the way, *avadh* is a word for serve and for work and for *worship*.

Perhaps we need to reconsider our orientation toward serve, work and worship. We tend to think of these as *separate and unrelated* aspects of life. I serve in the church, I work on the job and I worship on Sunday. Three different functions not necessarily connected. But that's not how Joshua sees it. For him, serving is working is worshiping. That's the Hebrew way – everything tied into one bundle under God. Every aspect of life, whether at home, in the marketplace or in the synagogue, is all just an extension of the marriage contract with the Holy One of Israel. I am just as much at worship on Monday as I am on Sunday. My work is my serving (or it's supposed to be), and all of it is an act of worship.

So, how's your *avadh*? Do you find that your work is worship? Do you recognize service to the Lord in the job that you do? Are you honoring Him in the shop, the office, the school or the hospital? Is He your real boss? Can people tell that He is? Do you feel just as much in His presence when you are driving nails, driving trucks or driving golf balls? Do you think that all that paperwork and all those phone calls and all those meetings are *serving* Him?

Or are you one of the millions who hates the job and can't wait to leave? Research tells us that nearly 70% of American workers fall into this group. Do you suppose that they think of work as service and worship? I doubt it. Since most of us haven't taken a serious look at the four parts of Joshua's theology *before* we get to the "serve" clause, we don't live integrated lives of well-being. We are fragmented, frustrated and foolhardy. Before we realize it, most of life has passed us by and we are still thinking about a retirement plan. Here's a clue: If serve is work is worship, there is *no* retirement plan. God's retirement plan begins at six feet under.

Perhaps this is a day to reflect on the bigger picture – the whole of Joshua's theology. If you have all the pieces in order, life should be significantly different. If some are missing, you probably won't know what in the world Joshua means when he says, "But as for me and my household, we will serve the Lord."

27.

"You are my witnesses," declares the Lord, "and My servant whom I have chosen, so that you may **know** *and* **believe** *Me and* **understand** *that I am He. Before Me there was no God formed, and there will be none after Me."* Isaiah 43:10

Three Transformations

Know, Believe, Understand – Consider this part of the verse very carefully. Did you notice that God's choosing comes *before* you know, believe and understand? In other words, the call to be in intimate relationship with God as His witnesses is *prior* to the revelation of Who He is. Furthermore, your knowing, believing and understanding is not going to happen because you go out and search the universe for the "divine essence." Until and unless God decides to choose you, you just don't have a clue.

If you let the truth of this declaration sink in, you will find enormous relief for your soul. The delivery of the vital information and the essential relationship between God and men is *not up to us*! Election precedes information. Relax a bit. God is working to accomplish His purposes in and through those He has chosen. The weight of the universe does not rest on your shoulders – and, by the way, neither does the conversion of that lost soul over there.

The three verbs here really cover all we need to be fruitful witnesses. *Yada* (to know) includes the relational and experiential aspects of knowing another person. *Aman* (to believe) is really about providing stability, confidence and support. It is the basis of faithfulness and trustworthiness ("believe" is not about creeds or confessions, is it?).

And *biyn* (to understand) is a verb about discernment, perception and due diligence. God has empowered *all* He has chosen so that they can be intimately acquainted in real-time ways with Him, have confidence in Him and discern His handiwork. What more would you need to be a witness?

God chooses you in order that He might provide for you all three aspects of being a witness. You should expect, and look for, *yada*, *aman* and *biyn* in your walk with Him. You should find a deeper and deeper personal relationship, a growing confidence and an improving discernment. That's been the strategy for a long time. God has decided that all He chooses will experience a transformation that shows up in these three verbs. And all of that was determined long before you came on the scene.

Isn't it reassuring to know that God is working all this out in our lives? So many times we start to think that somehow God has forgotten us. The bills pile up. The job doesn't go too well. Someone is sick. The weather doesn't cooperate. Our focus is so easily diverted to what is happening now. That's when we need to think about Isaiah's verse. God has already called you as a witness. Now He is merely equipping you for something that has eternal consequences. Shift your vision to the horizon. Can you see Him over there, beckoning you to keep moving? Knowing, believing and understanding are guaranteed to all who follow.

28.

"You are my witnesses," declares the Lord, "and My servant whom I have chosen, so that you may know and believe Me and understand that I am He. Before Me there was no God formed, and there will be none after Me." Isaiah 43:10

The Divine Summation

I am He – So, you're a witness. A witness to what? Everyone called to be a witness has truthful declarations to make about the *verdict* in the case. You are not called to simply say what's on your mind. God's court is not interested in hearsay. You are subpoenaed because you have reliable evidence that pertains to the outcome. You are a witness to only one critically important thing: that God is!

You are a witness to the verdict, "I am He" (in Hebrew *ki anihu*). What could be more important than this! God is – He is the One and only God. The court declares the verdict. Imagine what this means? No more striving to come to some understanding of what the world is all about – and why you are here. God is – and He knows. No more entertaining hope in one version after another of "fate control". God is – and He is in charge. No more despair over the monotony of life and the inevitability of death. God is – and He redeems. God not only provides the courtroom; He provides the witnesses to His very existence. The summary of the argument is this: God is. What that implies touches every aspect of life, whether you like it or not.

Sure, you can carry the Four Spiritual Laws in your back pocket. That helps. But the witness of your life is a witness, not to God's wonderful plan, but to the very fact that God is the only God. If there is but one God, and this God decides to reveal Himself to Mankind, then *no man* can afford not to seek such a God, especially since this God willingly offers what men need to know.

Do you want to be a witness? Well, actually, you don't have a choice in the matter (remember, God chooses). Once you are conscripted into the witness declaration program, you will be equipped to give faithful testimony to who God is. Supported by the Spirit, endorsed by the Son, guaranteed by the Father, that testimony is enough for anyone to realize that God has a claim on life itself.

Oh yes, by the way, Jesus understood the power of this phrase and all that it implies. It's only unfortunate that we can't see it in our translation of Matthew 14:27 (where the Greek reads, "I AM," not "It is I") and in the numerous occurrences in John ("I am he," "I am the truth," "I am the bread of life," "I am the resurrection.")

We are called by the God Who is. What difference does that make to you today?

29.

*For the choir director, upon **the hind of the morning**. A psalm of David.* Psalm 22:1 (Hebrew text)

Praise and Worship Songs

The Hind of the Morning – If you thought the contemporary passion for praise and worship songs started in this generation, then you haven't read the Psalms. In fact, Moses started the whole genre with his song (Exodus 15), but David is the consummate composer. However, David's praise and worship songs might never make it into our Sunday services. Why? Because they don't always have the upbeat, positive, repetitive outlook that we have come to expect. David's praise and worship songs come from a penetrating experience of life, not from idealized theological answers.

A prime example is Psalm 22. We recognize the psalm by its first English verse ("My God, my God, why have you forsaken me?"), but that is not the first Hebrew verse. The first Hebrew verse is the instruction to the choirmaster to set these words to the music of a tune called, "the deer of dawn." In Hebrew, the phrase is *ayyeleth hashshahar.*

Now, you're probably thinking, "So what?" What does it matter that David wanted this psalm sung to a tune about deer? Ah, but you don't see just how startling this is unless you recognize what David's choice implies. You see, the words *ayyeleth hashshahar* are used in other parts of Scripture (Song 6:10, Proverbs 5:19) as metaphors for a man's beautiful bride. You would have seen the clue if you knew that the word *ayyeleth* is specifically a *female* deer (a hind, not a roe). The tune David chooses might easily have been a wedding song. But for David, the joyful tune of the morning after marriage becomes the vehicle to speak of a terrible loss – the absence of God.

Imagine taking one of the familiar tunes of celebration, like "Here I am to worship", and re-writing the lyrics so that the song is about God's abandonment. Now you have some idea of the marked contrast that David wants to employ. David takes a wedding tune (possibly) and turns it into a funeral dirge.

Why would David create such a jarring juxtaposition? Perhaps David wanted the music itself to underscore the traumatic content of these words. "My God, where are you? Why have you left me? I am lost and hurting. I know Who You are, but I don't see You acting appropriately. What's the matter?" The lyrics are shocking, even more so when they are set to a tune of joyful exuberance. Now the music and the lyrics thrust us into the confusion of these thoughts. We expected a God of grace – and we got a God of silence. We wanted joy in the morning – but we got an empty bed.

Praise and worship? Yes, the Bible does not allow us to escape into the world of make-believe "everything is perfect" repetition. Praise and worship begins here – in disparity between what should be and what is, in desperate cries and emptiness. Praise and worship starts with the absence of the lover of my soul – but it doesn't end here, as we shall see.

30.

*My God, my God, why have You **forsaken** me?* Psalm 22:1 (English)

Divine Divorce

Forsaken – If you want to understand the depth of David's cry, you must know something about the verb he chooses. *'Azav* has a special history; a history that colors this opening line in lampblack.

The first time we see *'azav* in Scripture is in Genesis 2:24, a verse that is at polar opposites from David's cry. "For this reason, a man shall leave," is really the verb "forsake." A man shall forsake, abandon, separate from his parents in order to cling, attach and join with his wife. There is a price to pay to enter into a new union, but this "forsaking" is well worth it.

Marriage is the human symbol of God's intended intimacy for our divine relationship. David certainly must have had this joyful union in mind when he used the same verb to express a forsaking that leaves us empty. The equation is not balanced. Instead of *forsake* resulting in *cling*, we are left at the altar. The intended spouse does not arrive. At the last moment, God seems to have chosen divorce rather than marriage. There will be no celebration, no "deer of the dawn" because the wedding has been called off. What should have been a marriage made in heaven has become a separation straight from hell.

Ingmar Bergman's film *Cries and Whispers* chronicles the life of a minister who no longer experiences God's presence. Asked to pray for a dying woman, he offers his plea but confides that his prayer hits a lead ceiling. There is no answer. God has forsaken men. As Leonardo DiCaprio said in *Blood Diamond*, "God left Africa a long time ago." There are certainly days when we find ourselves in the dark corners of the universe, wondering where the God of grace has gone. This is a time for a genuine theology of emotions. Intellectual propositions cannot touch the despair of feeling that our deepest desire for intimate union remains unquenched. Something is wrong with the world, and we are powerless to fix it. Unless God arrives in all His *emotional* glory, our lives are as unfulfilled as the one left standing at the altar. When love fails, the world falls. This is the message of Ecclesiastes.

A theology of emotions must begin with pain, the universal language of all human beings. If your version of praise and worship skirts the real cries of shattered souls, then you live an anemic Christianity. You faith will not stand up to the deepest questions. If God is to be my really intimate partner, the lover of my soul, then He must come to me when I am overwhelmed with grief, desperate and alone. I need a God Who feels what I feel; a divine spouse Who knows the darkness that wants to drown me. I need the equation balanced. *Forsake must become cling.*

31.

*O my God, I cry by day, but You **do not answer**; and by night, but I have no rest.* Psalm 22:2

The Sign of the Afflicted

Do Not Answer – If you had to boil all of life's heartaches down to a single characteristic, what would you choose? David provides the Biblical perspective in this Hebrew phrase, *lo* (not) *'anah* (answer).

'anah is also the quintessential description of the afflicted. Yes, that's right. The phonetics of the two words are the same, although they obviously have quite different meanings. But more than phonetics is involved here, as we shall see.

The Biblical view of life is saturated with God. The Bible is not a book about Man's relationship with God. It is a book about God's self-revelation to men. It comes with God's perspective on every aspect of living. One of the dominant themes of Scripture is God's total dominion over life. Let that sink in for a moment. According to the Bible, God is fully in charge of everything. Therefore, it follows that if I am afflicted in life, God is somehow, somewhere behind this. God is *never* dealt out of the hand. When I experience affliction, I am experiencing life *without* God's response. The absolute essence of heartache is to live without a word from the Lord. All sorrow, all pain, all tragedy – all of the major and minor heartaches of life – all of them could be resolved with a word from God. And all of them are that much more deeply felt when God is silent.

The central, critical issue of life is really simple – will God speak? Will He speak to me? Life without His word, His personal word to me, is ultimately empty and fruitless. How can I know what I am to do in life's circumstances if I do not have the insight of the Master? How am I to understand my role in the grand scheme of things if I do not hear His answer? There are many, many trials and tribulations in this world, but none of them cuts as deeply nor wounds as fatally as the silence of God. Affliction is, finally, life without His answer. Do you really want to know affliction? Live with silence.

Human beings have learned to cope with a lot. We are constantly surrounded by our mortality (in spite of the contemporary socially correct effort to hide it). We face crisis after crisis. But without an answer from God, we are like fish with lungs (Jean Paul Sartre), purposeless and meaningless creatures in a universe of blind chance. The Bible responds to this charge. The universe has meaning because God has purposes and none of His plans can be thwarted. Now the critical question belongs to me – will God speak to me? Can I know what He has in mind for me?

Quite frankly, if you do not have His answer, what do you think you are doing? Playing guessing games with the universe?

32.

*Yet You are **holy**, O You are enthroned upon the praises of Israel.*
Psalm 22:3

The Answer

Holy – Perhaps this is the wrong word for our inquiry. Perhaps we should have looked at the conjunctive "waw" (a single Hebrew letter attached to the word). It can be translated in a dozen different ways, usually "and," "but," "yet," etc. That's why this verse is sometimes written, "But You are holy." No matter what the translation, the intention is clear. This Hebrew letter *connects* what comes before with what follows. What comes before is David's cry of dereliction. What comes before is the crushing reality of God's silence. And now, we are connected to the answer. It is all that we need, but it is not what we expected.

The answer to the affliction of silence is God's holiness. This is a bit tricky. Go slowly. The holiness of God (in Hebrew *qadosh*) is the most important fact of all creation. It is more important than His compassion, His mercy and His grace. Holiness is the guarantee that whatever God does, He does with absolute moral perfection, without any trace of second agendas or any hint of compromise. Kaiser calls holiness "the central organizing feature of the Old Testament." It is not simply an attribute of God. It is the expression of God's essential character. **Because God is holy, He is utterly trustworthy and totality reliable. Holiness extends to everything that God does.** From an ethical perspective, God's holiness sets the final standard for everything else, and that means that holiness is the reason God can lay claim to all that is, including every aspect of your life and mine.

Now we can see why David's answer to silence is the acknowledgement of God's holiness. The Bible never raises a question that it does not answer (although sometimes the answers are not what we want to hear). The answer to the question, "Why have you forsaken me?" is this: *If I feel as though God has forsaken me, I am the one who needs correction, not God.* God never does anything that does not issue from, support and confirm His holiness. **Since God is utterly reliable and trustworthy, my experience of His absence *cannot mean* that He has gone. It can only mean that either I am not listening or His felt absence is essential to the purposes of holiness**.

One more time. Holiness guarantees that God will never fail to be Who He is. God is the God Who reveals Himself. He will never fail to do so. In those moments when my hands are clean and my heart is pure – and I still feel His absence – my answer resides in Who God is. Because He is holy, He will never do anything perverse, evil or tempting. Therefore, I am assured that He is with me, even when I do not or cannot feel Him. My faith must move from what God does to Who God is. My faith must reside in God's character, not in His acts toward me.

This answer may not be the one I wanted. I wanted God to fix things. But my faith says that I can trust *who* He is. I do not place my faith in what He *does*. There will be many times when I will not understand what He does, but there will never be a moment when I cannot count on who He is. If He is silent, He is still holy.

33.

And those who know Your name will put their **trust** *in You, for you, O LORD, have not forsaken those who seek You.* Psalm 9:10

The Marriage Vow

Trust – "I promise to love, honor and obey . . until death do us part." Recognize those words? Of course, if you look on the Internet for "traditional" wedding vows, you will find a slight (politically correct) variation. Now it says, "love, honor, comfort and keep." Obedience is no longer requirement. Nevertheless, our study of Psalm 22 shows that even the traditional wedding vows have a glaring omission. What God is most interested in as a symbolic representation of our intimacy with Him isn't even mentioned. What's missing is *trust*. *Batach* is the essential character of union with the Spirit. It is the

211

one Hebrew verb that shows up in both relationships between God and man and husband and wife (see Proverbs 31:11). Without *trust*, what good is the rest? Love (but don't trust), honor (but carry suspicion), comfort (without security), keep (unreliably)?   No, without trust, there is no marriage. So, why do we leave it out?

And when it comes to God, without trust, there is no relationship.

Does that seem harsh? Is it too rigid? Maybe we should modify it to make it religiously correct? Maybe all it takes is the proper moral attitude, or a walk down the aisle, or membership? Maybe Jesus was only interested in making sure we were forgiven or got a ticket to heaven? But I doubt it! Trust is the flip-side of holiness. If God is holy, then I am duty bound to trust Him. If I do not trust Him, then I have impugned His holiness. I have suggested that God lies about His absolute moral perfection, and therefore, I can't rely on Him. Do you see the connection? There is no escaping it. Either I trust God because I know Who He is, or my relationship with Him is a shame even if I pledge love, honor and obedience. If you don't believe this, go ask your spouse! Where there is no trust, there is no relationship – there is only accommodation. And God is *not* interested in accommodation. He does not want to live together. He wants to be married.

David, who knew the necessity of trust as any adulterer does, tells us that the reason we can put our trust in God (notice that this is an *active* decision of the will) is simply because we *know* God's name. This verse is chocked full of marriage language. Trust, know, forsake are all words that belong in the marriage covenant. To know (*yada*) even covers the sexual content of marriage. We trust because we *know* His name. But what can that mean? That I know how to spell G-O-D? Of course not! To know His name is the idiom for knowing the essential character of the person. Why do you think so many Hebrew names have meanings that reflect who the person is? Because a name is a shorthand code for the essence of the person. To know God's name (which is not *GOD*, by the way) is to know His essential character. I can trust Who He is only when I know Who He is.

How do I *know* Who He is? Oh, the answer is really simple. *Seek!*

So, I ask you, are you married to the Lord of hosts? Or did you forget the word *trust* when you took the vow?

34.

*But He said to him, "Allow **the dead** to bury their own dead; but as for you, go and proclaim everywhere the Kingdom of God. "* Luke 9:60

When Life Begins

The Dead – When we you born? Wait! Don't give me your "birth" date. That's only the day that you entered into the kingdom of the dead. In order to answer the question from the biblical point of view, you must understand one of "life's" greatest deceptions. You were born DOA. Life is found *only* in the Son. If you haven't been conceived from above, you aren't really alive. The problem is that your physical body just hasn't caught up with its real condition. When it does, your true state will be revealed. Then those who are dead will bury their own dead.

The idea that eternal life begins when we reach heaven is a terrible mistake. That influences us to think that somehow we can go on living here, making the best of it, waiting for the day when we will enter into eternity. But this is not Jesus' point of view. Jesus sees the world as God sees the world. Until you have an intimate, personal, continual relationship with Him, you're dead. Life begins when Jesus arrives to claim you as His own. Before that, you're just waiting for the truth to become evident. In the upside-down reality of the Kingdom, living is dying.

You can stop worrying about cancer, heart attacks, accidents and all the other "life" threatening possibilities. There is only one really important fact about life. You're dead! Those fear inducing eventualities only confirm what was true all the time.

But it's not bad news. Once I recognize my true state, DOA at birth, then I am called to do something about it. And just as the true state of my "living" is backwards, so is the answer to my problem. The only way I can live is to die now. I must take the dead "life" that I have and place it on God's altar, consigning it to destruction. In other words, I must act according to the real state of my existence, stop pretending that I am somehow alive apart from Jesus, and give it up. Let the dead bury the dead. Then I can live.

If life is found in the Son, then I won't live until I am found in the Son. I live when I participate in His life, not before. So, my choice is obvious. By the way, it should not be a difficult choice, should it? How much value does a dead person have? How much can a dead person own or hold on to or strive to achieve?

Now, when were you born? What day did you leave the kingdom of *tous nekrous* (the dead) and step out of the grave into life?

35.

*Jesus said, "Truly I say to you, there is no one who has left house or brothers or sisters or mother or father or children or farms, for My sake and for the gospel's sake but that he will receive a hundred times as much **now in the present age**, houses and brothers and sisters and mothers and children and farms, along with persecutions, and in the age to come, eternal life."* Mark 10:29-30

The Reward

Now In The Present Age – There is hardly a more difficult verse to understand in this materialistic age than Jesus' comment recorded here. You see, I believe that Jesus speaks the truth. When He says that those who leave *everything* behind for His sake and for the sake of the good news will receive *here and now* one hundred times more, I don't doubt Him. The problem is that I don't see it. I don't see more houses and more farms and all the rest. In fact, what I see more of is found in that little addition, "along with persecutions." This verse puts my faith in God's benevolence to the test. I know Jesus doesn't lie, but the evidence seems to be against Him – until I notice what's *missing* from the increase.

Read the verse again. The list of one hundred-fold increases leaves out one critical category. Do you see it? You leave behind "father," but you don't get "fathers." Why do you suppose Jesus includes one hundred times everything else but fails to mention "fathers?" This missing piece is the clue to understanding all the rest. When I choose to follow Jesus, I leave behind my earthly father, but I do not gain more earthly fathers. I gain only one Father, the real Father of the faithful. There is only *one* Father. That tells me that all the rest of these hundred-fold gains fall within the one Father's kingdom. And then I see that I do gain houses and farms, brothers and sisters, children and mothers because I am transferred to a *new* kingdom where all that I have and all that every other citizen of this kingdom has is jointly held in the name of the King. My life, here and now, is suddenly filled with hundreds of brothers and sisters and children in the faith. My assets explode as the stewardship of others becomes available to me. I find that I have the love and care of hundreds of mothers, lifting and supporting me as one of God's children. I leave behind a constrained world where I thought that what I owned was mine. I enter a world where all that God provides to His family becomes available to me and to everyone who follows Him. One Father opens His treasury distributed through all His children.

Jesus is right. When I let go of my possessions, I inherit God's provision. I gain God's graciousness, with persecution, for I cannot move from the world of "I, me, mine" to the world of God's distributed treasury without encountering the attacks of the enemy. Wherever God's benevolence supports a community of wealth distributed, the enemy will attempt to reinstate personal accumulation. God gives. The enemy hordes.

I won't find an extra million in my bank account. I won't get land deeds in the mail. I won't discover a long-lost relative. But I will find hundreds who share their lives with mine, who stand up for me, comfort me, stick closer than brothers and sisters, and can't wait to help when I am in need. I will be rich beyond measure – one hundred-fold – because all that the Father has will be mine to use for Him, *nun en to kairo touto* (now, in this opportune time).

36.

*And Jesus said to him, "**Friend,** do what you have come for."* Matthew 26:50

The Kiss

Friend – Is the spirit of Judas a part of each of us? Oh, I know that we are quick to deny this. We don't want to see the spirit of Judas lurking in the corners of our souls. We can't believe that we would sell the Savior for a little material reward – until we see how vulnerable we are to self-sufficiency, self-protection and self-glorification. It doesn't take much for us to think that we have to take care of ourselves, make our agendas happen and control our own destinies.

And it is all accomplished in the greatest of ironies – by giving the Lord a kiss.

In the New Testament, we do not find Hollywood's version of the kiss. There are no erotic encounters. The kiss in the gospels is a kiss that indicates fidelity, loyalty, acknowledged honor and, most importantly, forgiveness. So, when Judas uses a kiss to betray Jesus, his act is much more than a simple indication. It is a symbolic denial of all that Jesus stands for, including Jesus' divinity. This kiss is the biggest lie the world has ever known.

Perhaps that's why scholars have so much trouble translating Jesus' response to Judas' act. This verse in Greek could be translated in many different ways. It might be, "Friend, why have you come?" But it seems quite unlikely that Jesus did not know Judas' intention. It could be, "Friend, have you come for this?" But, again, the question seems inappropriate. It could be, "Friend, for this then you have come!" But Jesus' attitude toward Judas does not seem to be hostile. It could be "Friend, do what you have come for." This version captures the idea that Jesus knows what is really happening. But behind all of these possibilities is the first word, *hetairos*. You should be immediately surprised that Jesus does *not* use the word *philos* (friend, brother – a faithful companion). That is the word He commonly uses for His disciples. But here He says, "*Hetaire.*" This is someone who associates himself with a leader for the purpose of gaining advantage for himself. This is partner, a pupil, a colleague who acts as a friend but really has a personal agenda. This is the one who plays the role in order to take advantage of the relationship. This is the spirit of Judas – one who attaches himself to the Master to see what he can gain for himself. This is no true friend!

Look deeply into your relationship with the Lord. Is there a *hetairos* hidden under all that appropriate religious language? Jesus would know. A kiss cannot disguise the real motivation of the heart. Where you attach yourself to the King in order to get what you desire, you should hear the sound of thirty pieces of silver dropped in your pocket.

My dearest brothers and sisters, it is not about us! It is not about our desires, our agendas, our dreams or our needs. We follow the King for His glory, not ours. At the end of the day, the *hetarios* says, "But what's in it for me?" while the true servant says, "I only did what was expected."

37.

There is therefore now **no condemnation** *for those who are in Christ Jesus* Romans 8:1

The Antidote

No Condemnation – It seems as though all of my life I have been reminded that I am not good enough. Leftover childhood trauma made me an overachiever, but every overachiever knows that under the skin is a fragile human being trying desperately to prove to someone who matters that we are good enough to be loved. You might not be that overachiever, but you will certainly know someone who is. It's a terrible mental and spiritual disorder because, no matter what you do, it is never quite good enough. Even if the entire world applauds, you still know that it could have been better.

Unfortunately, it is more often the case that the world does not applaud. What usually happens is that the world (and those significant others in it) reinforces your already dim view of your self-worth by pointing out your flaws, or at least mentioning how you have disappointed them. The longer you are subject to this spiritual illness, the less is required to recall all the past failures. Those of us who know only too well the plight of the "not good enough" evaluation are subject to either fight or flight. Neither one actually helps. Both are probably sin. Both make us even more convinced that we are simply not good enough.

That's why we *must* hear what Paul says in Romans 8. We *must* understand that our self-worth is absolutely not a function of our performance plus the evaluation of others. Anytime we let those old messages begin to play, we will be trapped in another bout of self-deprecation and rejection. What Paul tells us is *not* the power of positive thinking. It is *not* a strong dose of self-esteem. What Paul tells us is that God has *decided, entirely on the basis of Jesus' sacrifice*, to remove condemnation from us. God validates us. I won't find my real worth in the opinion of others, no matter who they are. If God is for me, who can be against me?

There are two critical words here. The first is *ouden*. It is much stronger than the English "no." It is literally, "not in the least, not a single time." Once God decides to credit Jesus' worth to me, there is never a moment's hesitation or even the slightest reconsideration about my worth. I count. I matter. I am good enough to be chosen by God.

The second word is *katakrima*. It comes from the word for judging. It's focused on the whole scope of verdict and execution of a sentence. God has set aside all of it. I am not held guilty and I am not subject to the punishment my guilt would incur. Jesus paid the whole price. I am released. In combination, these two words tell me that when I am in Christ, there is not even the tiniest particle of divine guilt and punishment attributed to me. I am truly washed whiter than snow.

Now, if God says that about me, why do I listen to those old messages that constantly reinforce my past unworthiness? I listen out of habit – a habit that has no place in God's divine economy. I need to soak in

His word, not the words of others. Then I will be who He says I am –
worthy to be called His.

38.

But if any of you lacks **wisdom**, *let him ask of God, who gives to all men*
generously and without reproach, and it will be given to him. James
1:5

Theory and Practice

Wisdom – James isn't Greek. That should tell you that when the text
uses the word *sophia* in this letter, James does *not* have the Greek
definition of the word in mind. What he wants to communicate is the
Hebrew concept *hokmah*. Why does this matter? Because the Greek
view is radically different than the Hebrew view. If we confuse the
two, we will end up frustrated and disappointed.

We live in a culture based on the Greek way of thinking. For us,
wisdom (*sophia*) is the accumulation of correct theoretical
knowledge. It is based in the intellect. Wisdom is all about getting
the right information (facts) in the right order so that we will have
insight into the true nature of things. If that sounds too esoteric, just
take a look around you. Our educational system is based on Greek
models. We train the *mind.* Our concept of success is based on the
Greek idea of wisdom. We think we can *plan* our way to prosperity.
Our view of social obligations, politics and ethics is based on
intellectual acumen. We think we can *reason* our way to peace and
proper action. Everywhere you look, the Greek idea of *rational*
perfection stands behind our behaviors.

The Hebrew view is very different. First, wisdom is a *gift from God.*
It is not the result of educational training or mental development.
Wisdom is not centered in the mind. It is centered in the *will.*
Second, wisdom is ultimately *practical.* It is not displayed in a great
storehouse of information. It is displayed in correct *action.* The wise
man or woman *acts* as God would act. Someone who knows what to
do but does not do it is (as James reminds us) a *sinner.* Finally,
wisdom's ultimate goal is to see the world from God's perspective
and to act accordingly in practical, everyday matters. The wise

person lives a life based in fear and respect for a holy God. Conduct is determined not by my reason but by God's revelation.

Now you know why James says that God gives *wisdom* (*hokmah*) to *anyone* who asks. It has nothing to do with *mental ability*. God gives instruction in righteousness. God tells you how to live, how to think, how to act and how to love your neighbor. If you don't know what God would have you do in any particular situation, ask Him! He will tell you what the proper *action* is that will delight Him and keep the covenant.

Stop being Greek! God is not going to give you better brain cells. He is not going to supplement your mental capacity or rational processes. God supplies *instruction in holiness*, not better planning techniques. Wisdom is not about "rising to new levels of success and freedom" by "overcoming the obstacles that prevent you from living to your full potential with 7 simple steps." God's wisdom is not a collection of strategies that "enable you to become a better you." God's wisdom is given so that you might be holy as He is holy. That does not mean all your troubles will fade away. That means you will experience life from God's perspective – and be subject to the same resistance that His Son faced. But the end is glorious. The Father is hallowed, and we are welcomed. Wisdom is practice for living in heaven.

39.

Bear *one another's burdens, and thus fulfill the law of Christ.* Galatians 6:2

Cultural Clash

Bear – How long will it take before we truly understand that when some of the New Testament authors wrote in Greek, they were thinking in Hebrew? Let me tell you how long. It will take as much time as it takes to realize that the Greek world that underlies our culture seduces us into behaviors that not only do not work but are opposed to God's point of view. No better example of this tragedy can be found than what happens when we expect this command to work in most churches.

Paul was as Hebrew as they come. As a student of one of the world's greatest rabbis, he was considered a successor to the position of a teacher of the Torah. In addition, Paul was zealous for the faith. God took those admirable characteristics and used them for His purposes. But that does not mean that Paul lost his Jewish perspective. When Paul tells the newly-formed churches to bear one another's burdens, he means something very Jewish. Faith is not to be found in my private, inward experience of God. It is to be found in the outward *actions* that demonstrate that I see the world with God's eyes. In particular, faith is to be demonstrated by my *care for my neighbor*. I need to step up, to take the load from his shoulders. How else can I fulfill the law of the Messiah – to love one another?

You've heard all this, I'm sure. But have you thought about what it implies? If I am going to lift the burden off your shoulders, and so fulfill the law of Christ, I must *know what burdens you carry*. This implies that you and I *share* our deepest struggles, concerns, hurts and worries. I cannot fulfill the law of Christ if I don't know what kind of load you carry. I cannot lift you up (Greek *bastazo*) and support you if I don't know the real you.

Suddenly, our Greek world is threatened. The Greek world emphasizes *private* religious experience. It is the world *in my heart*. It applauds the *independent, self-reliant* person. It mounts a façade that masks my struggling self. No wonder the very thought of telling you *precisely the burdens that weigh me down* is so frightening. I don't want you to think that I am weak. I don't want you to know that I struggle with secret sins, that I sometimes doubt God's grace, or that I worry about my life. I want to look like I am in control. I want to be Greek.

The Hebrew view of the world is very different. In the Hebrew view, the struggles of life are *part of the process of God's grace in me*. I am weak because *all men are weak*. I falter because *every human heart falters*. If I were the perfect person that I pretend to be, I would not need God and I would not need you. When Paul tells us to *bear each other's burdens*, he is advocating a view of life as it is, filled with faults and frustrations.

Will it be easy to switch? Of course not. I will always be tempted to protect my ego. But it is essential to change my thinking. Without opening myself so that you see who I really am, I prevent you from fulfilling the law of Christ. Do you think God will forgive me when my ego got in the way of His plan to bring both of us into conformity with His Son? Are you ready to strip off the Greek mask and become Jewish? Start now. Who *really* knows you?

40.

***Comfort**, O **comfort** my people, says your God. Speak lovingly to the heart of Jerusalem, yes, cry to her that her warfare is done, that her iniquity is pardoned; for she has taken from the hand of the LORD double for all her sins.* Isaiah 40:1-2

The God of Agony

Comfort – *Nacham* is one of the most important words in the Hebrew language. Without it, we would stand pleading under a leaden sky to an unfeeling God. With it, we have hope, no matter what our circumstances, for *nacham* contains within it the agony of God over our situation and the offer to help.

Read this verse again. Ask yourself, "Who is feeling this pain?" The answer is "God." God identifies with the pain of His people. He is the One Who sends a message of comfort because He acknowledges the dire straits of those He loves. He does not stand aloof, demanding appeasement. He is moved with compassion and comes to comfort. This is a message every man and woman longs to hear and needs to know. God speaks loving words in the midst of our pain because He knows how we feel.

Nacham has another umbrella of meanings that are just as important. *Nacham* is also the word for "repent." *Nacham* captures not only the emotional trauma and agony of human pain, it also opens the door toward restoration. It is the *healing* word. It tells me that God knows my suffering and He offers a solution. *Nacham* combines emotion and decision. It speaks to my heart and to my mind. God comes to me in my pain, demonstrates His care and asks me to come back to Him for renewed life. My emotions open the door for my decision. In Hebrew thought, feelings and choices are interwoven and inseparable.

When Isaiah heard these words from the Lord, he must have rejoiced. The long days of punishment were about to end. Even more importantly, Isaiah saw that the character of God had not changed. God was still the compassionate one. The sin of Israel had not changed the mind and purposes of God. Yes, sin brought calamity. That is what sin does. Yes, God used calamity to correct His people. That is what God does. But sin did not invalidate God's choice. It did not remove God's love. Covenant commitment remained. All that was needed was *nacham*.

You and I stand under the Hebrew umbrella of *nacham*. Yes, the message was addressed to Jerusalem after the days of terrible suffering. But God has not changed. We experience His hand of correction. Sometimes, we are taught the consequences of sin in traumatic ways. But *nacham* is still at the heart of God. He comes to comfort us, to restore us and to rejoice in our return to Him. He is the God Who shares the agony of broken relationships – and Who longs to have those relationships healed.

Do you find terrible pain when you open the secret places in your heart? God's hand rests on your shoulder. He will help you bear it because it is the way back to Him.

41.

*But when Simon Peter saw that, he fell down at Jesus' feet, saying, "**Go away** from me Lord, for I am a sinful man, O Lord!"* Luke 5:8

Chasing Rainbows

Go Away – Simon understood at least this much. The man before him had powers that only God could grant. It scared him. All Jesus did was cause Simon's boat to be swamped with a huge catch of fish. Jesus didn't heal anyone, feed thousands or raise someone from the dead. That was yet to come. But Simon knew that his man, Jesus, had some kind of special connection to God – and that was enough to convict him of his separation from God. So, Simon says, "Depart from me." Don't come close. Why? Because the closer you come, the more I feel the anguish of my sinfulness.

If you read the gospels from Simon's point of view, you will soon discover that he spends the rest of his relationship with Jesus trying to draw closer – and every time he takes a step toward Jesus, he is confronted with a wider and wider gap between himself and his Master.

The Greek text uses the verb *exerchomai*. Literally, it means "to come out, to go out – to exit from." But Simon spoke the verb *yatsa'*, a Hebrew word that means, "to leave an area." It's quite interesting that the idiom, *yatsa' lev* (literally, "the heart goes out") means "to be worried, anxious or distressed." That is precisely what happened to Simon. His heart went out, and all he could think about was asking the source of his anxiety to go away.

Something ironic happens when we pursue intimacy with the Lord. The closer we draw to Him, the wider the chasm between us becomes. It's like chasing the rainbow. The faster I pursue the beauty in those droplets, the faster it moves beyond my grasp. As I draw closer and closer to the Lord, I see the depth of my sin more clearly. I realize that I am a sinful man, not worthy to be in His presence. I can only fall to my face and say, "Lord, depart from me. The very fact that you are close only illuminates my ugliness."

Of course, the irony is two-fold. First, it is that our pursuit widens the gap instead of closing it. And second, the divine irony is that no gap is too wide that Jesus cannot cross it. The moment I see the tragic ungodliness deep within me, in that same moment I find Jesus standing right beside me, looking at my unworthiness and embracing it.

If you are going to pursue Jesus, you will come closer and closer to your true self – the one that hates God and loves the dark. That is terrifying. Most of us avoid that place like the plague, because that is just what it is, a lethal disease. But Jesus came to close the gap precisely where it is most hideous. If you haven't let Him embrace you there, then you have never let Him heal the plague that resides in the depths of your heart. You are still chasing rainbows, hoping to catch up to His beauty. Turn the other way. Look into the dark and you will find Him, right where He needs to heal you.

42.

*And the Word **became flesh**, and dwelt among us, and we beheld His glory, the glory as of the Only Begotten from the Father, full of grace and truth.* John 1:14

An Incarnated Life

Became Flesh – In December each year, we celebrate the Incarnation, that moment when Jesus set aside His divinity and took upon Himself the form of a man. The gospel of John uses the Greek words, "became flesh" (*sarx egeneto*). This event changed everything. It is worthy of worldwide rejoicing. But in the midst of honoring the God Who redeems, we may overlook the fact that the Incarnation is not simply an event. It is a way of life, intended to become the operating principle of all of the followers of the King of kings. You and I are supposed to live *incarnated.*

What does it mean to live *incarnated*? It means that the Spirit lives within us. In the simplest of terms, it means to live like Jesus. If He is the perfect image of God indwelling Man, if He is the perfect representation of what it means to be truly human, then living incarnated is living as He would live. "What would Jesus do" is right on target here.

That all sounds nice, but how does it affect the way that we behave? First, we must (it is not optional) shift our way of thinking and being from the post-modern, Greek viewpoint to the Biblical, Hebrew viewpoint. That means that we are oriented toward action, not simply information. We seek the benefit of others (including enemies) rather than pursue self-interest. We view life as a pilgrimage leading to full fellowship with God, not as a path toward self-fulfillment ending in an escape from this world. We see suffering as a *necessary* part of the development of godly character. We don't seek it out, but neither do we live lives that avoid it. We do not weigh our actions according to what best serves my interests. We spend more time in direct participation with others; less in developing plans and programs for others. We believe that discipleship is the mark of a Christian, not verbal recitation of beliefs. We follow leaders of godly character, and we strive to be one of them. We see that evangelism is a function of exhibited transformed living, not a method of attracting "souls" to a building. We embrace transparency, even when it requires serious ego deflation. We do not allow "image" to cloud our judgment. And, we forgive, as we have been forgiven, taking the burden of consequences on ourselves rather than deflecting the punishment to others. We are far less concerned with "correctness" than we are with "benevolence" toward others at cost to ourselves. We serve.

The incarnated life is radical. It is not extreme; it is simply the real Christian life. Jesus called His followers to a different way of behaving; a way that confronted every natural instinct of fallen men and women. Christmas celebrates that incarnated life. It demands attention – and submission.

If this is not the life that you have in Christ, then whom are you following?

43.

*And the Word **became flesh**, and dwelt among us, and we beheld His glory, the glory as of the Only Begotten from the Father, full of grace and truth.* John 1:14

Audio – Visual

Became Flesh – Every teacher and every leader knows that if you want the audience to remember what they learn, you have to present it in as many integrated ways as possible. That means you need words, pictures, personal engagement and repetition. Should we be surprised that God uses the same multimedia approach? In broad brush, the Old Testament is God's audio revelation. The Incarnation is God's visual teaching tool. Jesus arrives in order to *show* us Who God is. And every step of God's self-revelation involves personal engagement and the requirement for repetition. If you are a fully-tuned-in follower, you are open to sound, sight and action.

That is exactly the methodology of the incarnated life. Don't just give me your words. Show me your life – and then, walk this path with me!

Today's Word is one-dimensional teaching. It suffers the limitation of words. Because it has only these feeble letters to work with, it provides just a small glimmer of the greater reality. But come with me to Haiti or Honduras, journey to the orphanage in Zambia or the street mission in Winter Garden, and you will get the rest of the picture. Words aren't enough. They only change your thinking. You need an incarnated image-bearer to change your life.

Jesus taught with words. But it was His life of total obedience that transformed those first century men and women. He was the visual representation of the Father. He was the *ikon*, the exact duplicate, in living flesh. No wonder men stood in awe. Jesus used God's educational plan. Listen – obey – follow me. Is that the plan you use? Are you listening so intently that every word from God is incorporated into your thinking? Are you obedient to every transforming thought? Does your action demonstrate this transformation? God never delivers the next lesson until you have mastered the first one. He is not interested in "fact" gathering. He is interested in wisdom that results in changed behavior.

"God among us" is the banner cry of the incarnated follower. The Spirit empowers men and women who become image-bearers of God among us. And all of God's image-bearing attributes show up in His incarnated children. There is only one begotten Son, but there are plenty of sons and daughters by adoption, and all of them are designed to incarnate the character of the Father. You are God's visual aid to the world. When the people of the world see you, do they see the image-bearer of God, or do they see their own image in a mirror?

44.

"Say to them, 'As I live!' declares the LORD GOD, 'I take no pleasure in the death of the wicked, but rather that the wicked turn from his way and live. Turn back, turn back from your evil ways! Why then will you die, O house of Israel?'" Ezekiel 33:11

The First Law

As I Live – When sin crushes me to the bone, when I feel the weight of the rot on my shoulders and the Second Law exacts its toll from my life, what basis do I have for hope? Ecclesiastes makes it very clear that there is no real hope in work, in progeny, in legacy or society. The Second Law of Thermodynamics applies. It all goes downhill. How can I have hope? God answers:

Chaiani! As I live! I have reason to hope because GOD LIVES! He is not the God of the dead. He is the God of the living. When He comes to rescue, He brings life with Him. Because He is alive, I can trust that He will make me alive. I don't worship some past relic or some ancient memory. I worship the here-and-now, living God!

This Hebrew word (from *hayah*) is an in-your-face, basic, reality word. It's not the word for some eternal, ethereal existence – a transcendent God high above the clouds. It's not the word for spiritual realms and the mystery of Being. It's the basic word for living things. It's the same word that is used for the life of animals and beasts. God shouts, "I am as much alive as that pet at your feet. I am as much alive as the animals in the forest. I am right here and now alive." Of course, we know that God is far more than all this, but in the midst of our decomposing lives, we need to hear the *First* Law, not the Second. And the First Law is this: God lives!

Just as we cannot voice the depth of our inner reality – the despair that goes with the slide into darkness – so we are not able to shout the solution. God voices our true condition – rotting away – and He proclaims our only solution. He lives! Do you realize that because God lives, everything else is possible? Do you not see that all that we are, and all we are meant to be, is based in the *living* God? Put your hope there, and nowhere else. Listen to Him, and nothing else. God announces in the strongest possible terms that He is *not* interested in death – yours or mine. He does *not* want to see the wicked perish. (By the way, the wicked are not those terrible pagans. In this verse, God is speaking to His own chosen ones.) He wants restoration. He wants us to *live*!

What beauty, harmony and glory is there in the disintegration of God's creation? None! He wants what He has created to shine with the splendor of His handiwork. He has set a beacon ablaze in the universe and He desires it to light up the night. So, God exhorts His sin-sick children to *turn back*. That's one of the most important themes in the whole Bible. It's worthy of exploration. But today is a day of hope. Today, God is alive! The First Law reigns supreme.

45.

So then, my beloved, just as you have always **obeyed***, not as in my presence only, but now much more in my absence, work out your salvation with fear and trembling* Philippians 2:12

The Right Stuff

Obeyed – The motivation for obedience is not always the same. Why you obey is sometimes just as important as the fact that you do obey. In Greek, there are words for this distinction – words that we do not have in English. One kind of obedience describes submission. It's the kind of obedience that comes from putting yourself under the authority of another.   Paul uses this word (*hupotasso*) in 1 Corinthians 15:27 ("God will put all things under His feet"). But that is not the word used here, and the difference is important. Here the word is *hupakouo*. This is a word used to describe the obedience of a child to parents. It has direct links to the Hebrew word *shema* because *hupakouo* means "to listen attentively in order to answer." Just as the Hebrew *shema* means both hear and obey, so *hupakouo* means to hear and respond. In fact, it comes from the root word *akouo* which means "to hear." Guess what? Paul is reminding the Philippian Christians about something they already were doing – listening and obeying, just as they did when they responded to the *shema*.

Of course, that doesn't mean that the other word for obey does not apply. We are asked to *volunteer* to submit to the Lord's authority. We do so because it is in our best interest – and He is worthy of our allegiance. But when it comes to working out our salvation, there is another kind of obedience needed – hearing and doing.

Many Christians concentrate on the last part of this well-known verse, namely, "work out your salvation." But do you see now that this is directly connected with hearing and obeying? So, you might want to ask, "Hearing and obeying what?" And for the answer, we have to look at the little word *pantote* ("always"). Paul commends his brethren because they have *always* known the truth of hearing and obeying. They have exercised properly motivated obedience for a long time. Now, what do you suppose they were hearing-obeying? That requires a little research. In Acts 16:11-15, Luke describes the beginning of the assembly in Philippi. Lydia was at the center of this group. She was a devout convert to Judaism. That implies that she was familiar with, and obedient to, the Torah – the Law of Moses. When she becomes familiar with the Messiah, she embraces Him as the fulfillment of God's promise to Abraham. So do the others in Philippi. In spite of the fact that this assembly was not Jewish, these people were already observing God's way through Jewish roots when the news of Jesus arrived. They knew all about the *shema* because it was already part of their lives. It was a very short step from *shema* to *hupakouo*.

We learn something important here. We learn that submission is not at the heart of working out our salvation. Listening and doing is! We learn that listening and doing has been part of God's plan all along – long before Jesus arrived. But now we know that listening and doing are only one aspect of obedience. The other aspect is *submitting*. Both are needed. God is not interested in compliance. He wants voluntary acceptance demonstrated by attentive listening and responding.

46.

So then, my beloved, just as you have always obeyed, not as in my presence only, but now much more in my absence, **work out** *your salvation with fear and trembling* Philippians 2:12

Plowing

Work Out – Paul is never very far from the Hebrew Scriptures. So, when he talks about working out our salvation, he uses a Greek word that recalls a very familiar Old Testament context. It's all about the plow.   If you thought working out your salvation was about preparing your soul, clearing your mind or cleaning up your emotions, then you need a good dose of dirt.   Paul's word takes us right back to Genesis 3 – a world filled with thorns, thistles and sweat.

The Greek word is *katergazesthe*.   It is the combination of an intensive prefix (*kata*) and a verb that is about toil, particularly about laboring in a field.   It is the same word that is used in the Greek Old Testament in Genesis 2:15, when God placed Man in the garden to *cultivate* it.   This kind of work has been in the plan since the creation.   It is the work of stewarding the earth on God's behalf.   Paul adds an exclamation point to this work!   Do you want to know how to *work out* your salvation?   By redeeming God's creation, that's how! As a result of the Fall, that toil is incredibly more difficult.   Now we have to deal with thorns, thistles and sorrow.   Work comes with sweat.   But the plan of working out our salvation *has not changed*. This is exactly the same assignment given to Adam.   God *always* intended that Man should work at stewarding the creation.

In the contemporary religious world of *inner* spirituality, it's easy to overlook God's general assignment.   It's easy to focus on confession, prayer, denial, cross-bearing and religious "feelings."   All of that may be important, but it's not where your salvation is going to be worked out.   If you want to work out your salvation, start plowing!   Exercise stewardship.   Transform the world.   Act as a representative of the God of compassion and mercy.   Love others – and that means to act benevolently toward another *at cost to yourself.*   Yes, you can spend important moments in the study of the Word.   Yes, you can enjoy conversation with the Lord in a quiet place.   Yes, you will need to seek purity and truth.   But if your religious experience ends there, you will not work out your salvation.   You'll stay stuck on the sidelines of the great game of redemption.   If you want to work this out, you will have to get dirty in the world.   There are no ivory tower Christians.

By the way, God does not allow *proxy* Christianity.   You can't assign working out your salvation to someone else.   There are no *professional* Christians.   Yes, your resources and finances must be used to bring transformation and redemption to this world, but you yourself will have to put a hand to the plow sooner or later (hopefully, sooner, since working out your salvation takes a long time). Is it any wonder that Jesus talked about giving drink, food, shelter and encouragement to those in need?

How's your plowing going?

47.

*"Oh, that there were a heart like this in them, to fear Me, and to keep all My commandments all the days, that it might **be well** with them, and with their sons forever."* Deuteronomy 5:29

The End In Mind

Be Well – "All things work together for good." Paul said that. He believed it. Do we?

I'm pretty sure that we sometimes doubt Paul's statement (we'll have to take a closer look at exactly what he says). But Paul is only echoing what God said in Deuteronomy. God desires our best. He is determined to bring about the best for us in and through His good purposes. God always starts what He finishes (better read that again). God's purposes are always based in the eschatological perspective. In other words, unlike us, He actually knows where He's going before He begins. Therefore, He only starts those things which will ultimately bring about the end He desires.

Let's apply this to our lives. From the Hebrew perspective (and Paul was a Hebrew), no man knows the end from the beginning. You and I are not intelligent enough, righteous enough or powerful enough to know how life will turn out. With but a moment's reflection, you can see just how true this is. My guess is that twenty years ago you could never have imagined all the twists and turns your life has taken. The simple fact is that you are not God, so, of course you don't have a clue. Nevertheless (and this is a big one), all of us imagine we are in charge. Therefore, we act according to *our* view of life. That's really the essence of sin – pretending that we know better than God what's good for us, and acting accordingly. God's heart agonizes over such shortsighted arrogance. Why? Because our eschatological blinders prevent the real good from manifesting itself in our lives.

The reason God gives us specific directions about how to live (the *torah*) is not because God wants to put His divine thumb on us and force us to do His will. He gives us directions so that *yatav* may manifest itself in us. *Yatav* is that great Hebrew word that means "to be good, to be well, to be pleasing." God wants you to have a full, glorious, satisfying, wholesome life. Like any parent, He wants His children to have joy and peace and prosperity. So, He is more than willing to tell us how to live in a world that is filled with danger and difficulty. God always starts what He finishes. He invites you to the finish line with Him, and then He tells you where the race starts.

Sin is simply not trusting that God has your best interest in mind. Sin is simply doing it your way. And, of course, sin has its own built-in consequences. When you sin, you can't finish because you didn't start in the right place.

Sometime today the world will present you with the opportunity to take charge of your life. It will whisper to you, "You need to take care of yourself here." It probably won't come in the form of an outright moral conflict. It will be the subtle suggestion that you know what you're doing. That's the moment when you need to recall God's commandments. You don't know what you're doing! You can't see the finish line. Listen to the One Who does. Start what He finishes.

48.

*But we know that all things work together **for good** to those who love God, to those who are called according to His purpose* Romans 8:28

The End in Mind (New Testament Version)

For Good – Paul writes his letters in Greek, but he thinks like a Hebrew. Here he has *yatav* in mind. God wants *yatav* to manifest itself in His children. There is no higher purpose for life on earth*. In Greek, Paul calls this *eis agathon*. But there's a catch. What we think of *yatav* or *eis agathon* is not always what God has in mind.

Remember the Hebrew perspective? I don't know the end of the story. I'm not smart enough, clever enough or powerful enough to see where the road goes. What I think is *yatav* (well-being) or *agathon* (good) is sometimes not what's good for me at all. God is the only One Who knows, and God always starts what He finishes. So, the twists and turns of my life *right now* might not appear as though they are taking me toward *yatav* or *agathon*, but who am I to tell? When Jesus hung on the cross, it certainly didn't *appear* that He was on the road to *yatav*. The crowd jeered at Him. "If you are the Son of God, save yourself!" They couldn't imagine that crucifixion was the road to *agathon* – but it was. God knew. Jesus trusted. End of story.

Paul uses an important preposition here that is disguised in English. It's the preposition *eis*. We translate it as "for" but it usually means "into or toward." You see, most Greek prepositions are descriptions of movement. *Eis* is movement from one place to another. It is movement *into* a place or *toward* a place or thing. Its opposite is *ek*, to go out from. Now read this again, but this time read it as "all things work together *into* or *toward* good." Paul is giving us a Greek view of *yatav*. God causes everything in our lives to move in the direction of good; to go from less than good into good. That doesn't mean that every stop along the way is good. It just means that everything is arranged to lead us *into* good. Every heartache, every trial, every disaster, every joy, every disappointment, every victory, and yes, every *sin* is reconfigured to lead us into good. We are going somewhere. We don't see the pathway that will take us there, but He does. If we want to get to the finish, then we will have to trust Him with the roadway engineering.

Where are we going? Well, that's *agathon*. This word also has a range of meanings, but when it is applied to people, it means what is virtuous, upright, of noble character and quality. In other words, God is taking us on the road to holiness. *Yatav* hasn't changed just because Jesus came into the world. God's finish line is still the same. The goal is holiness – to be like Him. Just remember that on the way *toward* holiness, the road goes through a war zone. The good we pursue, the good that God engineers, is not found in the R&R time-out during the war. And sometimes the way to holiness means hanging on a cross.

The same God. The same goal. No real difference between part one of the Bible and part two. "Be holy, for I am holy," never varies. And God is making sure that we get there.

*Sorry, but the purpose of life on earth is not to evangelize the world. Evangelism is the natural by-product of *yatav* manifested in your life. Without *yatav*, evangelism is shallow and pointless. With *yatav*, evangelism happens automatically because you *are* what the world desperately wants.

49.

*And coming near, his disciples awakened Him, saying, "Lord, save us! We are **perishing**."* Matthew 8:25

In The Boat

Perishing – Do you realize that we are in the boat with Yeshua? If the boat sinks, He sinks with us. That's what Paul had in mind when he said that if the Christ isn't raised from the dead, we are the most miserable of all. If the boat sinks, we all go down.

The disciples didn't see the irony of their situation that day on the sea of Galilee. Of course the waves were crashing. Of course the boat was being tossed back and forth. But Jesus was sleeping on the deck. Doesn't that strike you as a bit odd? If the storm was so bad that the disciples thought they would drown, how can Jesus be sleeping through it? And when they wake Him, don't they perceive that He is in just as much danger as they are? The whole story is strange. Jesus doesn't act like we would act. He is unconcerned by the circumstances. What the disciples failed to grasp is that if they are in the boat *with* Jesus, they are just fine.

These men plead with Jesus. "*Apollumetha!*" (in Greek). It's a verb that means "to destroy, to lose, to perish," but with the added emphasis (*apo*) of emotional terror. We would say, "Lord, we're going to die!" In fact, the same verb is used to talk about eternal death in the gospels. From the disciples' point of view, things are getting worse by the minute. They might have said to themselves, "What's the matter with him? How can he sleep at a time like this? Doesn't he know how serious this is?" That sounds like dozens of times that I have been in the boat on the rough seas with Yeshua. I pled with Him to take a closer look at my situation. "Lord, don't you know how desperate this is? Look at all those dark clouds. Look at that lightning." I grip His arm. "Lord, don't you know we're going to die?"

Pretty funny, isn't it? I mean, here I am in the boat with the God of the universe in human form. I'm riding the waves with the One Who made the sea, the wind, the lightning and the thunder. He's not one bit afraid. I'm standing right next to Him. Do I really think He's going to let the boat sink under us?

The lesson is obvious. Circumstances do *not* dictate the outcome of life. Relationship does. If I am truly in the boat with Jesus, I have *nothing* to fear. We are riding the waves *together*. The only time I need be afraid is when I am *not* in the boat with Him.

Jesus' response to all this terror is so typical of God. He makes a joke. "You little-faiths! Why are you so upset? I'm right here with you. It's no problem."

Every day is a boat ride on the high seas. The only thing that matters is your companion. All the rest is just water off a duck's back.

50.

*Then rising up, He **rebuked** the winds and the sea. And there was a great calm.* Matthew 8:26

Calm Terror

Rebuked – Are you in the boat with Jesus? If you are, the first question that comes up in the midst of a storm is this: "Where's the life preserver?" It's the last question you need to ask, but unless you are a lot more spiritually inclined than most of us, it will still be the first question in your mind. Jesus answers this question, but not in the way we expect.

As a rule of thumb, biblical interpretation should begin with what the text means to the first audience that heard it. So, we have to resist the temptation here to immediately spiritualize this story. We'll try not to do that. Instead, we'll try to stick with what the disciples experienced. But the implications are pretty powerful and we won't try to avoid them. After all, if you're in a sinking boat, you want to know how Jesus will rescue you (remember the Hebrew word *yasha'*?).

The disciples are very concerned. Any one of us would be. It's a long swim to the shore and in this perfect storm, not many will make it. They cry out, "Save us!" There's something ironic about that very cry. Jesus is also in the boat without a life preserver. How is Jesus going to save them? He's in the same predicament. Men in panic often don't think straight, but at least they noticed who wasn't worried. Since Jesus was *sleeping* in the midst of this chaos, they reasoned that He must know something they didn't. He seemed unconcerned. Maybe He had a secret raft.

They were not prepared for Jesus' solution. Jesus rebukes the storm. The Greek verb is *epitimeo*. It means to admonish with emphatic authority. It's the kind of word we find when Jesus casts out demons. Now put yourself in that boat. Has anyone you know ever castigated the wind and the sea and told them to behave? If someone did that, would you consider him sane? When you are about to drown in the violent surf, does reprimanding the ocean sound like a reasonable solution to you? If it does, then you probably need to see a friend of mine who specializes in mental illnesses. No one in his right mind believes such a thing is possible; no one, that is, except Jesus.

Amazingly, the elements obey Him. No wonder these men marveled. In fact, they were more frightened *after* the calm than before. What kind of man commands the earth and the sea? Only a Man who is God. Sitting in the boat next to such a man must have been terrifying indeed.

What is the lesson here, if we might be so bold to ask? First, the lesson is about the sovereignty of our Lord. He rules everything! Then, there is an implication. When I am in the boat with Jesus, I have *nothing* to fear. He rules everything! He is quite capable of doing something that appears insane, and pulling it off. I need to fear *Him* far more than any circumstance in my life.

But there is another lesson. The solution to my problem is never a change in circumstances. The disciples traded the storm for a man who controlled the weather. Were they better off? They would be, if the man in the boat loves them. Fortunately, He does. The solution is not about physical reality. It's about who loves me.

51.

and all these blessings shall come on you and **overtake** *you, if you will listen to the voice of* YHWH *your God.* Deuteronomy 28:2

Capital Gains

Overtake – "God bless you." How often have you heard that? Now, let me ask you, "What does it mean?" Is it just an expression of wishful thinking? Is it just a polite greeting? What if I told you that God has a specific method for blessing your life? Did you know that He wants you to enjoy these blessings? Did you know that *you* are the only one who prevents them from being realized in your life?

Take a look at this verse again. The Hebrew verb here is *nasag*. It means "to reach, to catch up with, to overtake." What do you think that implies? Isn't it obvious? God's blessings are coming at you like a run-away freight train. They are designed to overtake you as you journey along the way. You don't control the speed at which they approach. All you do is get run over, or, step out of the way. That's the problem, isn't it? God designed His blessings to catch up to you and overtake you. He designed them to pour on your life like a fast-moving rainstorm. He planned them to bowl you over. He engineered them to knock you down with goodness. In fact, if you carefully read the section on blessings in this part of Deuteronomy, God says that His children will reap where they *did not* sow and

238

harvest where they *did not* plant. So, who's responsible for all this overwhelming goodness? Not you and me, that's for sure.

Now let me ask you the second question. What happened? If this is what God had in mind, why is life so hard? If God's blessings are aimed at us like a benevolent, spirit-guided missile, how come we aren't exploding in joy? The answer, my friend, is in the *conditional* clause. *"If* you will listen to the voice" is the reason that we don't get knocked down by goodness. Of course, you know that the verb for "listen" is *shama*. It means both "listen" and "obey." You see, God's guided missiles of goodness take aim at the life of the one who obeys His instructions. Disobedience is the sure-fire way to sidestep the blessing because disobedience causes you to step away from the center of God's target. The Hebrew word for "sin" literally means "to miss the mark," like an archer who misses the center of the target. Blessings never miss the mark. God aims them at the center, pulls back the bow and lets them fly right into the bull's-eye. Of course, if you and I aren't standing in the center of the target when God's blessing arrives, we won't experience it, will we? If we are not following God's instructions for living, then we will not be in the center of His target when He arranges the divine blessings of the universe to overtake us.

Seems pretty simple, doesn't it? We follow God's instructions. He aims at the center of the target. We're standing there when the rain arrives. We get dumped on. How cool is that?

So, want a better life? Then go stand in the bull's eye. Become the target of God's aim. (Oh, by the way, being God's target also means that the world will do all it can to get you off-center, but that's the other side of the story.) Of course, that raises a very important question. Are you *really* following God's instructions? I guess the best way to answer that is this: Has God rained on you recently?

52.

*and all these blessings shall come on you and **overtake** you, if you will listen to the voice of YHWH your God.* Deuteronomy 28:2

Rate of Return

Overtake – There is no magic formula. In a world dominated by self-reliance and self-control, realizing that there is no magic formula is critically important. It's so easy to be seduced into thinking that I can manipulate God into delivering His blessings when I want them. That's the problem with the "name it and claim it" crowd. They believe that they control the heavenly rate of return. They don't understand the Hebrew verb *nasag* (to overtake).

Take another look at this verse. It implies that the blessings are *not* under your command. God's blessings are designed to *overtake* you when you are doing something else. In other words, blessings arrive at their own rate when you are being obedient to God's voice in other matters. If you pursue the blessing, you focus on the wrong objective. You don't control the speed of the approaching blessing. Your job is to stand in the path of the coming heavenly cargo. How do you do that? By obeying God's voice in all the trivial things of living.

Does that mean that there is no place for self-interest? Not at all! It is always in my best interest to do God's will. In fact, God wants me to do what is in my own self-interest, because when I do, I am aligned with His interests too. There would be no reason for God to tell me that He intends His blessings to overtake me unless He knew that I would be motivated by the result. Self-interest is perfectly scriptural. Of course, self-interest is not the same as *selfish* interest. The difference is this. Self-interest is being motivated by what is *ultimately* best for me. Since my *ultimate* best is to be in perfect harmony with my Maker, I submit to His instructions about what is the right thing to do. In other words, I can't rely on my own perception of self-interest because I know that my perspective has been tainted with selfish interest, and selfish interest (even though it might appear to be the best way to achieve my goal) always moves me off the center of the target. Consequently, selfish interest causes God's blessings to miss me.

Since I know that I can't trust my own perceptions (remember that Proverb about *not* leaning on your own understanding), I have to rely on God to tell me how to act in my own self-interest. Don't get confused. So often the reason that we rebel and resist is that we think God's instructions are opposed to our self-interest. We hear the "deny yourself" sermons and we assume that God's ways are tough and restrictive. What we fail to realize is that Jesus wants us to deny our *selfish* interest, the things that stand in opposition to God's true instructions about the way to get in the center of the target. Selfish interest keeps me out of the bull's eye. The paradox of selfish interest is that I think I am getting the most out of life when the truth is that I am standing outside the focus of God's blessings.

Do you want your best possible life? Of course you do. Then put aside your own methodology for getting there. You don't know what you're doing anyway. You can't see the biggest picture. Put yourself in the path of God's blessings, not by seeking the blessing itself but by doing what God tells us to do in His instruction book for living. Then watch out! Blessings are likely to sneak up on you out of nowhere and run you down.

Practice: The End Game

$\mathcal{H}$ow are you doing? Have you learned something? Are you putting your discoveries into practice? There is no purpose in merely accumulating more Bible information. Unless you start to use what you know, you will not progress. So, get going!

If you want more, look deeper. The Bible will exhaust you before you exhaust it.

Thanks for accompanying me on the journey. If you want a daily dose, sign up at skipmoen.com

Skip Moen

Index of Scriptural Verses

Old Testament

New Testament

Skip Moen is the author of

Words to Lead By

Jesus Said to Her

God, Time and the Limits of Omniscience

Guardian Angel

and several thousand pages of daily explorations called *Today's Word*

All are available at:

skipmoen.com

Readers of *Today's Word* and members of *At God's Table* offer many blog comments about the Hebrew view of Scripture at this web site.

61154275R00137

Made in the USA
Columbia, SC
20 June 2019